Pet
has
Na
bo
sub

Co
Co
fro
Go

wa
art

de
Ox

se
W
Pa
Pr
the
in
the
M

va
co
G

an
m

This book is dedicated to –

*Leila, with gratitude for her clarity of mind, her
wisdom and encouragement, and much more;*

*the memory of my father, KHB, who taught me the
importance of grounding concepts in reality; and*

*my colleagues of the Human Rights Commission
1981-86, both staff and Commissioners, who for the
first time in Australia systematically explored
human rights aspects of peoples' problems.*

Bringing
Human Rights
to Life

Peter Bailey

THE FEDERATION PRESS

1993

Published in Sydney by

The Federation Press
PO Box 45, Annandale, NSW, 2038.
3/56-72 John St, Leichhardt, NSW, 2040.
Ph (02) 552 2200. Fax (02) 552 1681.

National Library of Australia
Cataloguing-in-Publication entry

Bailey, P. H. (Peter Hamilton)
    Bringing human rights to life.

    Bibliography
    Includes index.
    ISBN 1 86287 103 5.

    1. Human rights. I. Title.

323

Typeset by The Federation Press, Leichhardt, NSW.
    Printed by Australian Print Group, Maryborough, Vic.

Contents

CONTENTS

Acknowledgments

No book can be written without an enormous amount of help from many people. Apart from those who have provided a basis for the stories around which this particular book is centred, many have contributed to it to whom I would like to express my gratitude.

First, for the general ambience, there is the Faculty of Law at the Australian National University. Successive Deans, Professor Don Greig who arranged the study leave during which much of the book was written, and Professor Dennis Pearce who has encouraged me since, have made the whole project possible. I have greatly appreciated the six years during which I have been privileged to be a part of the Faculty as a Visiting Fellow with full time teaching duties.

More specifically, several of my academic colleagues have, through discussion, encouragement and their perspective, been particularly helpful to me. Professor David Hambly for his scholarship, patience, empathy and, simply, friendship; Dr Tim Bonyhady for his enthusiasm, interest and perceptive comments as a now experienced and successful author; and Professor Paul Finn as a kindly critic and source of suggestions when a dead end seemed to have been reached. Many other colleagues in the academic community, and particularly in the Law School, have also helped. I thank them all, though not by name, which I hope they will understand.

Assistance in finding or sourcing stories has come from many places. But I would like to record special thanks to Professor Harry Rigby for suggesting the Brodsky story (Chapter 12), and Rosh Ireland for suggesting follow-up material; to Dr Bill Andreen of the University of Alabama Law School for his wonderful assistance in sending material not available in Australia on Dr Kevorkian (Chapter 5); to Fessehaie Abraham and the Eritrean Relief Association for the material on Awet Josef (Chapter 10); to Dr Ann Kent for her writing, interest and support on the Tiananmen Square incident (Chapter 13); to Professor Jock Brookfield of the Faculty of Law in the University of Auckland, New Zealand, for his most helpful comments and information on the Maori of Orakei (Chapter 1); and, last but not least, to Heather McGregor and Michelle Leslie for their insight into the kinds of problems presented by the case of Patient Vera, and to my friend and former colleague Carolyn Stuart for her perceptive comments (Chapter 11).

I was fortunate to have two excellent research assistants during the preparations for the book. The first, over the summer of 1990-91, was Kay Barralet, who helped particularly with the "life" problems in Part II. The second, Shannon Cuthbertson, was with me much longer – until the spring of 1991. She provided an enormous amount of material, many notes and some highly perceptive and valuable comment, on Parts I

ACKNOWLEDGMENTS

and III, and portions of Parts IV and II. I thank them both, for all the skilful effort they put in, and for their continuing friendship.

The Faculty Library is a wonderful place in and from which to work. I thank all those informed, hard-working and friendly staff who make it so. Especially, I mention Mrs Imme Gray, the Readers' Adviser, who, along with her relief Ruth Booth, has given me so much expert assistance in identifying and locating useful but difficult-to-find material.

All that support helps, but none of it would come together effectively without the devotion of those who make the machinery run. Mrs Sue East has been tireless, patient and accurate in helping me clean up, format and print the text and also in helping me find my way round the obstinacies of my word processor. Terry Polleycutt, our specialist adviser on word processors, has also helped me keep my sanity when even worse things happened, and patiently – and quickly – sorted them out. And our administrative support group: despite an ever-growing workload from an increasing student population (student numbers have more than doubled since 1986, but they are still the same in number), they have managed to continue to give that effective, cheerful and concerned service that is their hallmark. Rita Harding, Bev King, Lou Wilson and Bernice Williams, I salute you!

I thank you all. None of the faults or blemishes in the book are, of course, attributable to anyone but me.

Peter Bailey
23 October 1992.

Introduction

Every day we hear about breaches of human rights. We see pictures of atrocities on television, read stories in the papers and hear radio reports. But what *are* human rights? Do they give any remedies to the people hurt or wronged? Is there a way of getting at those who violate our rights?

These are tough questions. There are not any easy answers. But there are *some* answers. This book suggests that human rights provide one important way of getting justice – a fair go for everyone. It also suggests that human rights can provide a way of getting to agreed solutions to problems while avoiding violence, bloodshed, and abuse (unfair use) of power.

The chapters that follow are all based on one or more stories. Each is a real-life incident from somewhere around the world. It has been chosen to show that people everywhere find their human rights are being infringed. The relevant human rights, and the role law can play, are then analysed and discussed. Suggestions are made about what can be done. For example, Chapter 1 tells three stories about indigenous peoples. It points out that in a surprising number of countries in every continent indigenous peoples are being prevented from living the kind of life they want to live and proposes some new policy directions. Chapter 2 tells of some successes and some failures in the struggle by peoples for the human right to self-determination – to freedom from a foreign yoke – and notes what needs to happen if peoples are to be able to enjoy that right. Chapter 6 tells about the abortion controversy, and analyses the human rights involved. Chapter 7 discusses the environment – something we are all beginning to be worried about – and tells the stories of Chernobyl and of cutting down the rain forests of Brazil. Chapter 8 deals with discrimination on grounds of race. Chapter 9 tells of discrimination on grounds of sex, and shows how in many countries women are beginning to be able to assert their rights as equals with men – though often they still don't succeed.

Some are beginning to say that, with the growth of anti-discrimination and affirmative action legislation, there is too much support for disadvantaged groups. They say the mainstream people should be better looked after, and not be put second to the disadvantaged groups – a live issue discussed in Chapter 9. What happens if the state locks up one of your friends without trial, or keeps her in a psychiatric ward? Chapter 11 considers those issues. Then again, people claim a right to work, but criticise the lack of freedom Eastern European citizens have when the right is enforced. Do you prefer unemployment and the dole, or being forced to do work you don't like or which isn't meaningful? Those issues are discussed in Chapter 12. And what happens if you join others to make a public protest about something and you find the police or the army confronting you with guns and taking you off to gaol? The Tiananmen Square protest, and others, are discussed in Chapter 13, and the right not to be tortured or subjected to cruel or inhuman treatment in Chapter 14.

All these are lively issues. No book can cover all the human rights problems currently being fought through, but the object of this book is to show how human rights can help both in understanding, and in finding solutions to, the underlying problems.

WHAT ARE HUMAN RIGHTS?

Suggesting that human rights can provide solutions leads naturally to the question – what are human rights? Every day one hears people claiming that they have a right to this or that, and one wonders where it will end. Do I have a right to just whatever I want? Clearly, no. Because we share our world with many others, my doing exactly what I want would often result in preventing someone else doing what he or she wants, or even in injuring that person. The same goes for everyone else, so there has to be some understanding of what human rights are all about.

Essentially, human rights are statements of the standards of behaviour we should be able to expect between individuals and groups. Because they are *human* and not *citizens'* rights, they apply to everyone everywhere. Their purpose is to define what rights are essential if all of us are to live lives in a secure and healthy environment that provides maximum opportunities for ourselves and the communities to which we belong, and which operates on principles of justice and equality.

How can we stop the list of human rights from getting so long that being termed a human right loses all significance? In a small community, the most practical way of deciding what rights are basic would be to discuss our desires and needs with other members of the community, and to agree both about what the rights are and how they should be enforced. But when one is talking about *human* rights, one is talking about rights for *everyone* – all people everywhere, not just rights for one's own community or even one's own country. What is needed is some definition of rights that applies equally to all people in the world.

Somewhat miraculously, that is just what the international community has succeeded in doing. Back in 1948, after World War II, the members of the United Nations General Assembly agreed without dissent to the terms of the Universal Declaration of Human Rights. In the 30 Articles (paragraphs) of the Universal Declaration they stated what they believed to be the key rights that all of us, as human beings, should have. The leaders of the world united, for the first time, to declare our rights as human beings, not just as Australians, or Americans, or Chinese, or Germans or Zambians or Brazilians.

The Preamble to the Universal Declaration said in part –

> *Whereas* recognition of the inherent dignity and of the equal and inalienable rights of all members of the human family is the foundation of freedom, justice and peace in the world,
>
> ...
>
> *Whereas* it is essential, if man is not to be compelled to have recourse, as a last resort, to rebellion against tyranny and oppression, that human rights should be protected by the rule of law,
>
> ...
>
> *Now, therefore,*
> *The General Assembly*
> *Proclaims* this Universal Declaration of Human Rights as a common standard of achievement for all peoples and all nations ...

What the international community has done, then, is to provide people everywhere with *standards* of human rights which can be translated into domestic law and against which each of us can measure our own country's performance. In the chapters that follow, the focus is on action that has been taken in local communities, and at national and international levels, to get human rights enforced. The battle is not always successful, and is often costly to the participants, as it was for the Chinese students in Tiananmen Square (Chapter 13) or for the minorities in Belgium and the United States (Chapter 3). But out of the battles often comes encouragement, and decisions at policy and political level not to repeat the violating behaviour. And so the cause inches forward.

GETTING HUMAN RIGHTS OBSERVED

The question facing the international community, when it agreed to the Universal Declaration in 1948, was how the rights declared in 1948 were to be enforced. Eighteen years later, in 1966, the United Nations opened for signature two Covenants – the International Covenant on Civil and Political Rights (ICCPR) and the International Covenant on Economic, Social and Cultural Rights (ICESCR). The Universal Declaration *declared* rights the General Assembly approved, but did not provide ways of enforcing them. The Covenants put *obligations* (in international law) on countries that ratified (agreed to implement) them.

The story since then is of a continuing development. This is giving us new rights – such as the right to a sustainable environment (Chapter 7). It has given us improved recognition of already recognised rights, such as the right not to be subjected to torture or to inhuman or degrading treatment (Chapter 14). And new and more effective remedies are being developed, though there is still a lot to be done, as discussed in Chapter 15.

All the time, there is growing pressure on governments, who are the main enforcers of human rights in the legal order as we know it today. Local opinion, gradually becoming more aware of its rights as agreed at international level, is increasingly putting pressure on governments. International opinion, expressed through the Covenant machinery, through discussions in the United Nations forums and through exposure by international non-government agencies adds its pressure. Although there are setbacks, there are also notable achievements. These are recorded in the chapters that follow. It is the author's view that there is a slowly growing acceptance of the worthwhileness of the standards set by the international community in 1948. There is also growing public expectation that governments and other powerholders will exercise their powers in accordance with those standards, and without unfair discrimination.

It is the message of this book that the human rights cause deserves and needs your support. Each of us in our own ways can promote or set back the enjoyment of rights by all human beings – it is impossible to be neutral. Equally, it is the message of the book that human rights provide a new way of looking at vexed problems and of resolving them in a way that maximises rights all round.

For Further Reading

Books to read on the issues covered in the book are suggested at the end of each chapter.

A useful introduction to the international law of human rights is Sieghart P, *The Lawful Rights of Mankind: An Introduction to the International Legal Code of Human Rights*, Oxford, 1985. Another good introduction is a book edited by Henkin L, *The International Bill of Rights: The Covenant on Civil and Political Rights*, New York, Columbia, 1981, which contains many authoritative contributions on the meaning of the various clauses in the Covenant. Unfortunately, it has not been followed by a book on the Covenant on Economic, Social and Cultural Rights. A more general approach to human rights is given in Vincent R J, *Human Rights and International Relations*, Cambridge, 1986.

A somewhat controversial book on human rights generally is Cranston M, *What Are Human Rights?*, Bodley, 1973. The author has also written a text *Human Rights: Australia in an International Context*, Butterworths (Australia), 1990 which covers the general question of what human rights are and the way they can be used to resolve issues. It contains references to many more texts that take further the issues raised in this chapter.

PART I

Group Rights – Indigenous Peoples, Minorities and Self-Determination

The land is my backbone. I only stand upright, happy, proud and not ashamed about my colour because I still have land. ... I think of land as the history of my nation. It tells us how we came into being and what system we must live. ... The law of history says that we must not take land, fight over land, steal land, give land and so on. ... My land is my foundation. I stand, live and perform as long as I have something firm and hard to stand on. ... Without land, I am nothing.

James Galarrwuy Yunupingu,
"Letter from Black to White",
Land Rights News, *December 1976.*

This Part addresses the rights groups must have if their individual members are themselves to be able to enjoy to the full their own rights. Groups can take many forms. Considered here are the universal plight of indigenous peoples, the precarious hold of minorities on their rights, and the difficulty of becoming a separate nation in today's tough world.

Chapter 1

The Aborigines of Noonkanbah, The Penan of Sarawak and the Maoris of Orakei

The Rights of Indigenous Peoples

I. NOONKANBAH

The Story. About noon on Tuesday 12 August 1980, a convoy of more than 50 trucks drew to a halt on the Aboriginal property at Noonkanbah.[1] The convoy was accompanied by representatives of the Western Australian Government, representatives of the United States multi-national firm Amax and by some seven car-loads of police. Its mission was to search for oil. The proposed four-hectare drilling area was on an Aboriginal sacred site.

On Friday 29 August, after the drilling area had been enclosed by a protective fence, the first of the processes for exploratory drilling began. The Yungngora community had lost its three-year fight to keep out the explorers and, more importantly, to protect one of its sacred places from intrusion.

The Aboriginal community saw the conflict as being between their way of life and beliefs on the one hand and, on the other, the economic thrust of the Australian community. That thrust was epitomised by the desire of the government and the foreign and local corporate giants to exploit the resources of the land. Said the community in response to a letter from the Premier, Sir Charles Court –

---

1   The property runs north from the Fitzroy River and is located some 200km southeast of the port of Derby, in the Kimberley region of northwest Western Australia.

... We have our own Law which we must live by, and we have our own religion which we must protect. By forcing this drilling programme to go ahead you are denying us our right to religious freedom.

We do not trust the State Government or Amax or any mining company as they put money above our Sacred Areas ... . (Letter of 9 June 1980)[2]

In a poignant final comment, after drilling had commenced and their sacred land had been violated, the community expressed its despair and accurately forecast the failure of the exploration –

We will make our peace with the spirits in that place as best we can. ... Let it be known that this is not a surrender or a recognition of the Government's right, but a withdrawal in the face of overwhelming force. ...

... When this business is over and Amax has found nothing, let people remember what sort of a government this is that would get an army in and do all in its power to try to humiliate and destroy us for a dry hole in the ground. (Statement of 10 August 1980)

For its part, the Western Australian Government claimed a significant victory. Within the framework of the (recently amended) mining laws it had asserted the right to development for the international community and the white population of Australia. It had persevered with its decision to use Noonkanbah as a test case, despite the wavering of first Amax and then CSR, a major Australian company with significant mining interests. In the end, it was a dummy company named Omen that gave the order to commence drilling. The company had no paid up capital, but was registered in the names of two Perth solicitors and was apparently formed at the instigation of the government. Later, Amax was to pick up the cost of the drilling and of getting the convoy, most of which was carrying the parts of the oil rig, to the site.

Said Sir Charles Court in a letter to the community on 31 May 1980 –

---

2   This and the following two quotations are taken from Hawke S and Gallagher M, *Noonkanbah: Whose Land, Whose Law*, Fremantle Arts Centre Press, 1989.

I am sure that most members of your Community would agree that the Western Australian Government and myself have shown a genuine desire to consider your representations ...

I am sure your Community would understand that the Government must allow the drilling to proceed. ... The programme and conditions we proposed have full regard for your expressed views. ...

I would be failing in my duty if I did not remind you of the damage your stand on this matter could do to the Aboriginal people ... you make it very difficult if you adopt an uncompromising attitude by demanding what you claim are your rights but refuse to acknowledge that other people might have some needs and rights also.

Discussion. The main issue to emerge from this story, only different from earlier pastoral invasions in the size and formal ordering of the forces arrayed against the Aboriginal community, is the clash between the two laws. Against the law of the indigenous people was marshalled the law of the state, of the dominant white community.

Law reflects the values of a society. The Western Australian Government was able to enforce the provisions of the mining legislation and to overrule the protections conferred by the Aboriginal Heritage Act 1972 of Western Australia. The Aboriginal community, inexperienced in its new ownership role and aware of two centuries of oppression of fellow Aborigines, ultimately submitted with breaking spirits and yet another blow to its traditional beliefs and the force of its law. Little allowance is made in the dominant "white man's law" for the views of Aborigines to be heard, much less given effect. It is true that allowance was made in the Aboriginal Heritage Act for the identification of Aboriginal interests by a special commission. But the Act also provided that its views could be overruled by the government, as they were in this case.

The consequence is a sense of despair in the indigenous people, a sense that the dominant law not only does not protect them, but also may actually be used against their interests. Worse, the dominant law may be used to override their own "law", their own way of looking at the world and orienting their lives. The experience of indigenous peoples round the world has been that the superior force of the majority culture law has

3

overridden their law, and with it their sense of identity and purpose.

Much attention is paid to the need to enforce rights to land for indigenous people. The significance of land, however, is really more in its symbolism than in its economic utility. Western concepts of the ownership of property are not natural to indigenous peoples. It may indeed be truer to say that the land owns the people or that they are a "part of" the land.[3] For the majority culture, it is important to recognise that merely giving land is not enough, if the sequel is, as it was at Noonkanbah, a failure to recognise the deep need for identification with the land in its wholeness. The law of the dominant culture must genuinely recognise and protect the interest the indigenous group has in the land, if it is to achieve its purpose of allowing them to live according to their own laws and customs. That will require careful modification of existing legal rules that has hardly yet been explored, let alone implemented.

II. THE PENAN OF SARAWAK

The Story. Between November 1988 and January 1989 some 128 members of the Penan forest people of Sarawak were arrested and held in remand (without trial) for various periods before being brought, in September, before the court in the (for them) distant town of Marudi. Protests, and gaolings, were still going on in 1991, when it was reported (*Canberra Times*, 11 August 1991) that two European women – one Australian and one English – had been imprisoned for 80 days, and 6 others the previous month. The Penan live in the remote eastern parts of Sarawak, the Malaysian State with the largest area, and are largely nomadic. They rely for their livelihood on fishing, hunting and gathering wild fruits and herbs. Rattan is skilfully woven into baskets and provides their main source of currency. But they are largely subsistence livers, which means that they do not have cash for bail or even for return trips to a court.

The offence with which the detainees were charged under Malaysian law was erecting blockades on some of the forest

---

3   See the quotation from Galarrwuy Yunupingu in the introduction to Part I (page XX).

roads being driven through their customary lands. Logging has become a major industry in Sarawak. During the 1980s the pace gradually intensified, and some estimates are that by the end of the 1990s there will be no substantial remaining reserves. Malnutrition among the children is becoming a serious problem (more than one-quarter being affected by 1988). As one Penan man said –

> Now, if we are lucky, we may find food after walking and searching for two or three days. Our fruits, herbs and medicines, rattan and burial grounds – all are gone.[4]

Matters had been made worse by amendment, in November 1987, of the Malaysian Forests Ordinance. The earlier legislation had proved difficult to enforce in the courts: the offence was wrongfully to restrain access through a public thoroughfare. So the prosecution had to prove that whatever was done by the protesters did actually restrain traffic. The amended offence became to erect any structure on any logging road so as to obstruct its use. All that needed to be shown was that there was a structure in place that *could* obstruct traffic. A LAWASIA mission found many defects in the trial process, largely because of insufficient demonstration of the guilt of the specific individuals charged. It pointed to the dire effects of months of detention on the accused and their families.

Discussion. As in the case of the Yungngora at Noonkanbah, the dominant law was used against the indigenous group without regard for the true cost of the action in terms of social upheaval and economic depredation. For the Penan, the main focus is on the rapid destruction, in the interests of the logging industry (again largely international in structure), of a way of life that had been enjoyed by a substantial group over centuries in an environmentally harmonious way and without destruction of the forest environment. In short, the Penan are being deprived of their livelihood, a right which, as discussed in Chapter 7, is recognised in international law. True, the income from logging is substantial, and funds have been set aside for support of those affected, but they seem never to materialise.

---

4   Quoted in the Observer Mission Report for LAWASIA (The Law Association for Asia and the Pacific), *The Human Cost of Sarawak's Timber Revenue*, Boniface D, April 1990, p 8.

So seriously is the position regarded that in November 1989 the European Parliament passed a resolution noting with concern the felling of timber and the arrest of the protesters. The resolution called on the Sarawak authorities to release those arrested and to initiate genuine negotiations with the indigenous people. It also called on European Community Foreign Ministers to protest to the Malaysian authorities about the situation. It is too early to know what success this international attention will have, but one hopes it may be at least a catalyst in changing for the better the prospects for the Penan and other indigenous people in the Asian region.

III. THE MAORI OF ORAKEI

The Story. Before European settlement came to New Zealand in the first half of the 19th century, Maori tribes had asserted authority (mana) over particular areas of land, which they used partly to cultivate and partly as a base for hunting and fishing. One such tribe was the Ngati Whatua (pronounced Ngati Fatua) of Orakei (Orahkei), which is now part of Auckland, New Zealand's largest city, though not its capital. The Ngati Whatua are one of the ancient peoples of New Zealand. Gradually they wandered south. By about 1740, they consisted of three sub-tribes (hapu), and had established authority (mana) over the whole of the Tamaki (Auckland) Isthmus, which is in the centre of the Auckland area. The extent of their territory was some 500 square kilometres. Included in that narrow part of the North Island was all the land between the two oceans with its twin harbours – Waitemata to the north, opening to the Pacific, and Manukau to the south, opening to the Tasman.

Soon after British settlement began, Maori possession of the land was recognised. Accordingly, treaty negotiations were entered into with more than 30 tribes to cede land to the British Crown in exchange for its protection. The basic treaty text varied a little on each occasion it was used, and the authentic text appears in what is now known as the Treaty of Waitangi. The text was different in the English and the Maori versions, and there has been much argument about the meaning of the differences, as will be mentioned further below. It is sufficient at this stage to note that the Ngati Whatua were signatories of the treaty, and under it were protected in their possession of their lands.

Unfortunately for the Ngati Whatua, the Tamaki Isthmus is a much prized estate. Over the next century, the Ngati Whatua were to see their holding whittled down to a few acres and then ultimately extinguished, by a complex process that it is not necessary to describe. As a culminating disaster, their meeting house (marae) was burned –

> Finally ... [by 1950] the Crown took the last acres of the village (excepting, for no stated reason, the chapel and the cemetery). The necessary proclamations were issued in March ... and the meeting house was burnt down in December. At the time the wells of anguish in the hearts of those who gathered mutely about the cinders of their meeting house seemed likely never to run dry.[5]

Fortunately, the story does not end there. During the 1960s and 1970s an attempt was made to restore the situation by building a new marae, carrying the name of a Ngati Whatua ancestor, for use by the many Maori tribes represented in the city population. However, this did not result in restoration of the Ngati Whatua authority (mana) over the land they had regarded as theirs alone, and left them unsatisfied and dispossessed. Time and again they were misled or cheated by both the Crown authorities, the city and the inexorable demand for private land to meet the growing needs of the area. A further petition by the tribe to the Waitangi Tribunal resulted in the marae being restored to them. But much of what they had sought – land to live on, compensation, and expungement of their debts – was not given. Although full recovery of the community may take decades, processes available under the law have, in this instance, resulted in some reinstatement of the centre of its life.

Discussion. Once again, the pattern emerges of the inadequacy of the protection the dominant (not always European) law affords minority interests. Although, in a long-established

---

5   Extract from Kawharu IH, "Orakei, A Ngati Whatua Community", (1975) 12 *Wellington New Zealand Council for Educational Research* quoted in "Mana and the Crown: A Marae at Orakei" by the same author in *Waitangi – Maori and Pakeha Perspectives of the Treaty of Waitangi*, Kawharu IH (ed), Oxford University Press, Auckland, 1989.

community, it is easy to overlook, the fact is that law embodies and, more importantly, is a vehicle for enforcing, the main values of a particular society. It cuts hard against those who are different. It means, as will be discussed later, that the rights of groups as such, as well as the rights of individuals, have to be given protection if there is to be adequate enjoyment of human rights.

Two aspects of the New Zealand experience are interesting. The first is the amazing persistence of the indigenous people, despite more than a century of disregard and being put down. It is also amazing that, as recently as 1918, the Maori were being called "natives" in official documents; and that in 1950 a Prime Minister (Peter Fraser), thought at the time to be progressive and enlightened, referred publicly to the residual 10 acres of Ngati Whatua land at Orakei as "a blot on the landscape"[6] It was following that statement that the remaining 10 acres of Orakei land were resumed (but never used) by the Public Works Department for housing purposes.

The second interesting aspect of New Zealand experience is that the existence of a treaty, however solemn, is not necessarily effective. The nadir was reached in the 1877 case of *Wi Parata v Bishop of Wellington* 3 NZ Jur (NS) SC 72, when Chief Justice Prendergast stated that the Waitangi Treaty was a nullity. Indeed, it was only a century later, in 1987, that the status of the Treaty was revived with the statement by the President of the Court of Appeal, Sir Robin Cooke, that –

> ... the Treaty signified a partnership between the two races ... [it] creates responsibilities analogous to fiduciary duties ... the duty of the Crown is not merely passive but extends to active protection of Maori people in the use of their land.

This landmark case was *New Zealand Maori Council v Attorney-General* [1987] 1 NZLR 641[7] In it, the court unanimously held that the State-Owned Enterprises Act 1986 (NZ) must be construed to prevent the government's corporatisation policy from in effect extinguishing all Maori land rights by transferring Crown land to state corporate enterprises. It was only, however, because of the provision in section 9 of the

---

6   Kawharu, op cit fn 4, at 222.
7   The quotation is found at p 664.

Act that the "revival" occurred. Because a treaty is not automatically part of the law, it has to be specifically enacted, and this has not happened in many Acts.

Finally, it needs to be noted that the marae, the meeting house, is of key significance to the Maori people. Just as the longhouse is a centre of the Penan community, and the dreaming sites are central to Australian Aborigines. Each indigenous people has, and steadfastly retains, its own set of core concepts and community practices: to survive, the people needs the local law and not just practice or custom, to recognise and accept their culture and its expression. Only as the superficial differences such as dress, food and appearance cease to hold the centre of the stage, and the more basic differences such as different cultures and values are revealed, will it become possible to deal positively, supportively and creatively with the needs of the indigenous peoples.

IV. Overview

The three stories briefly told above have been drawn from the Pacific region. They could equally have been drawn from Europe, Asia, Africa or the Americas. As each year passes, more indigenous peoples are being identified, and the latest count puts them at well over 140. It is a mark of all indigenous peoples that they have an identity separate from the dominant or majority population, have from old-age time[8] inhabited the lands where they live, and have a character, social traditions and language of their own.[9] They also, taken together, can be seen to suffer from similar disadvantages. They all have low levels of education, high unemployment, poor standards of living, short life expectancy, high rates of sickness and infant mortality and high rates of imprisonment, when these indicators are compared with those for the dominant community.

As the stories have shown, steps are being taken by many governments to ameliorate the conditions of their own indigenous people. But the steps are often halting, too often are

---

8   Often, in British law, referred to as "time immemorial".

9   This sentence is adapted from the definition proposed in about 1980 by the World Council of Indigenous Peoples.

misconceived and, even when reasonably suitable, seem to encounter resistance and often only token implementation. In Australia, for example, the former Chief Justice of the High Court, Sir Harry Gibbs, has been reported as saying that an Aboriginal treaty would "imperil our sovereignty and place the very existence of our nation at risk". He suggested that there was already ample legislative power to do all that is necessary, and that no further constitutional or treaty measures were needed![10]

The international community has taken some significant initiatives towards promotion of the status of indigenous peoples. International Labour Organisation Convention (No 107) of 1958 – Concerning Indigenous and Tribal Populations, was assimilationist in thrust.[11] But it paved the way for the much more sympathetic Convention (No 169) of 1989, which has not yet become operative, but which even in its title contains a significant change: it is called the Indigenous and Tribal *Peoples* Convention (italics supplied).

In addition, the Commission on Human Rights has been developing a new Universal Declaration on the Rights of Indigenous Peoples. It is planned for submission to the General Assembly of the United Nations in 1993, the International Year of Indigenous Peoples. If agreed to by the General Assembly, this statement will put on a new plane the rights of those peoples. They will have a right to be granted recognition as distinct peoples and to be protected against genocide; they will be protected against any form of forced assimilation or integration; they will be supported in practising and preserving their own cultures; they will be granted the right to own or reclaim lands and resources they have traditionally occupied or used; and they will be granted special state structures to allow them to consult and to participate on an equal footing with all other citizens in the political, social and economic life of the state.

If the nations of the world can be brought to agree to this Declaration and, more importantly, to implement it, a new era may open for the world's indigenous peoples. One particularly

---

10 "No special rights for blacks", Crispin Hull, *The Canberra Times*, 25 July 1992.
11 Terminology in this area is always changing but, in this context, "assimilationist" means "designed to ensure the absorption of the indigenous group into the majority culture".

important consequence would be to focus much more on the particular needs of minority racial or cultural groups within the nation state. Recently, the trend has been towards greater decentralisation within nation states – that is the essence of "deregulation". If ways can be found of fostering within the general law of the state the very particular and local interests of indigenous peoples, then more liberal provision might also be possible for other minority groups. There should be no real basis here for the "floodgates" argument so often used, as will be seen throughout the book, to block moves for freedom or independence. The "floodgates" argument is to the effect that if there is any compromise in favour of the claimant group – in this case indigenous peoples – then the whole society will suffer great damage. Therefore, so the argument runs, no concession should be made to the claimants.[12]

Equally important, the growing recognition of the rights of indigenous peoples makes necessary a reassessment of the nature of human rights. Traditionally, these have been thought of as the rights of individuals. Indeed, it has been said that a true *human* right can only inhere in an individual and not in a group (or a people). The argument has been that human rights are really the rights of individuals over and against that of the group, the community or the organised state.

In the view of the author, that is to take too narrow a view of what it is to be human, and of what it is to have a "human" right.

The indigenous peoples illustrate an aspect of life that is relevant in greater or lesser degree to everyone: that much of the significance of an individual is derived from being a member of some identifiable and cohesive group. It is an illusion to consider an individual as being only a free-standing, autonomous unit. He or she is also a part of one or more groups or communities – tribal, minority or national. So to be human means to be both an individual and also a member of usually more than one group. Human rights can be threatened if either the group or the individual is threatened, and particularly if the individual is threatened because of his or her membership of the group.

Since individual identity is formed in part by group membership, some process is necessary to allow enforcement of the rights of the group as a means of protecting individual

---

12   Compare the comment of Sir Harry Gibbs, p 10.

identity.[13] There are difficulties for lawyers in seeing how groups can have rights enforced, but these are procedural rather than substantive. What is necessary is to ensure that only properly accredited members of groups – broadly, members appointed by a proper consensual process – can speak for the group and enforce its rights. But groups should be able to enforce their rights. Otherwise, the powerful or majority groups and individuals will simply pick off individual members or families one by one, as in the cases of the Aborigines (through the mining legislation), or the Penan (through prosecutions), or the Ngati Whatua (through purchases of land).

In almost all cases, what is destroying the indigenous group are the voracious demands of Western industrial economies – either immediately, as in the case of the Australian Aborigines and the New Zealand Maori, or indirectly, as in the case of the Penan, where loggers respond to the demands of others. Although in the broad sweep of history an indigenous people may ultimately decide to blend into the majority, its members have a right to time to decide how and when that is to be done. They also have a right, as the draft Universal Declaration points out, to have the state organise itself so that they can be accommodated. Encouraging efforts are being made in many countries round the world to recognise and protect the rights of indigenous peoples and their individual members. Canada has gone further than most in that direction. Indeed, with the decision to make 1993 the International Year of Indigenous Peoples, it may be that the beginnings noted above will lead to gathering momentum as the decade of the 1990s proceeds.

Finally, it still has, in most countries, to be recognised that "the Aborigines" or "the Maori" or "the Penan" are artificial constructs. What in fact we have in each case are numerous small communities or tribes or clans. There really is no short cut. Each community has to be dealt with individually, and a solution worked out for each, and for the individuals within it. The problems are not insoluble. But they need time, effort, dedication from members of the majority community and, in the end, resources.

---

13   The somewhat myopic view that groups cannot have human rights is parallel to the view which holds that economic and social rights are not human rights – a matter discussed further in Chapter 7.

For Further Reading

There are not many books on indigenous peoples as such, but a series of papers in Kawharu IH (ed) *Waitangi: Maori and Pakeha Perspectives of the Treaty of Waitangi*, Oxford UP, Auckland, 1989, although based in New Zealand's problems, gives a very good survey of the main issues. There is also a useful book with more of an international law focus which, as the text above will have indicated, is important: Heinz WS, *Indigenous Populations, Ethnic Minorities and Human Rights*, Quorum Verlag, 1988.

A very readable, and much the best, book on Noonkanbah is Hawke S and Gallagher M, *Noonkanbah: Whose Land, Whose Law*, Fremantle Arts Centre Press, 1989. Two other books, more oriented towards the law, are Hanks P and Keon-Cohen B (eds) *Aborigines and the Law*, Allen & Unwin, Australia, 1984 and Hocking B (ed), *International Law and Aboriginal Human Rights*, Law Book Co, 1988 which contains, despite its title, a quite substantial contribution on Australia.

Little material is available on the Penan of Sarawak but, if available, Hong E, *Natives of Sarawak*, Institut Masyarakat, Malaysia, 1987 is very informative, as is Boniface D, *Observer Mission Report: the Human Cost of Sarawak's Timber Revenue*, Law Association for Asia and the Pacific, 1990.

The position of the Maori people is well analysed in the book referred to above, *Waitangi*, edited by Professor Kawharu. A more personalised account is given in Macdonald R, *The Fifth Wind: New Zealand and the Legacy of a Turbulent Past*, Bloomsbury, 1989. The *Report of the Waitangi Tribunal on the Orakei Claim* (Wai-9), Wellington, New Zealand (Department of Justice), 1987 gives a clear but chilling account of the process by which the Ngati Whatua were gradually divested of their heritage and the means of community life.

Chapter 2

Bangladesh, East Timor and Lithuania – The Struggle for Nationhood

The Right of Peoples to Self-Determination

I. BANGLADESH

The Story. The people of Bengal trace their origin to the pre-Christian era. They have a high degree of ethnic homogeneity. Originally Hindu, many of them changed to Islam in the 12th-15th centuries. For nearly 200 years from 1757 they were under British rule. In 1947, although there was a proposal that they become a separate state, they were divided. The western section, based on Calcutta, stayed with Hindu India while the eastern section, based on the Ganges and Dacca, became a separate part of Pakistan (East Pakistan).[1] Pakistan itself is a name made up of the first letters of Punjab, Afghania (the frontier with Afghanistan, not Afghanistan itself), Kashmir and Sind, and the last four letters of Baluchistan. The name did not, therefore, include Bengal, which was added to Pakistan because of its largely (well over 80 percent) Muslim population.

---

1   In the 1956 Constitution of Pakistan (it took until then to reach an agreed document) the Eastern part of Bengal became East Pakistan (one of the two "wings" of the country) and sent 44 representatives to the 80 member National Assembly.

The union with Pakistan was not a happy one for the Bengalis. The province, although 100 million strong, was treated rather as a colony of West Pakistan than as of equal status. Although the native Bengali language was spoken by almost all residents, it was not made an official language of Pakistan. In the 1970 national elections, the Awami League, initially a language movement and now standing for nationalism, socialism and democracy, was pitted against the Muslim League, which had been formed in 1906 to represent the interests of Muslims. The Awami League, considerably more radical than the ruling Muslim League, swept the polls with the support of 73 percent of the voters, after a campaign in which the national (Western) authorities had attempted suppression of the Awami cause. The election resulted, nevertheless, in the Bengali-based party obtaining an absolute majority of the Eastern wing delegates and a majority in the National Assembly.

The Awami party's six-point program, largely designed to give East Pakistan greater administrative and economic autonomy and to even up equality of representation between the two wings, was rejected. A passive campaign of civil disobedience began. The Western authorities moved in with force. Mass killings by the Army occurred in late March and during April 1971. Independence was declared on 26 March. A provisional government under the leadership of Sheikh Mujibur Rahman (most often called Sheikh Mujib) announced its formation in April, but the attempts to repress the revolt against the central (Western) authorities continued. Several million refugees (probably between 8 and 10 million) poured across the frontier into India during the summer (the middle months of the year). It was estimated that by the end of the summer some 300,000 citizens of East Pakistan had been killed and thousands more maimed, injured, displaced from their homes and imprisoned. There was considerable international activity in support of the new country as the months wore on. In December, India moved its army rapidly into East Pakistan and recognised the government of Bangladesh. By early January 1972, Sheikh Mujib, who had been imprisoned in March 1971, was able to return and begin the difficult task of forming a new regime.

Bangladesh's problems were not to end there. Its economy was in ruins, there was insufficient administrative experience in the local people because of the dominance of Western appointments (one of the grievances in the period before independence), there were several coups and its place in the world was not yet recognised. Nevertheless, under the leadership of two gifted men, Sheikh Mujib and General Ziaur Rahman (General Zia), both of whom were assassinated during their term of office,[2] Bangladesh had by the late 1970s been generally recognised as a new state and as a viable entity. However, successive difficulties since then, including disastrous floods in 1987 and then again in 1988, famine, pestilence, civil unrest and internal security problems among the hill tribes in the Chittagong Hill District, corruption and a period of ruthless dictatorship under President Ershad (1982-91), dogged the new nation during its second decade. It remains to be seen whether the 1990s will see the consolidation and development of a sounder political and economic base for the future. With the election as President in February 1991 of Begum Khaleda Zia, widow of the former President, at least it can be said that there is the chance of an era of less repressive government.

In the Eastern part of Bangladesh, where its territory sweeps round the north-eastern curve of the Bay of Bengal, lies the hill country behind Chittagong. This area, bordering on Burma, contains some 600,000 indigenous tribespeople. They live mainly in the mountain forests, are largely Buddhist or Hindu by religion. They still try to follow their ancient "slash and burn", or shifting method, of land use. During the British Raj they were identified (about 1860) as being in the Chittagong Hill Tracts District and were given some protection from the encroachment of the people on the Bengali plains. However, throughout this century portions of their land have been annexed. With the independence of Pakistan in 1947, the tribal peoples found themselves within a Muslim state. A large dam was built at Kaptai in 1963, with the resulting loss of 20,000 hectares of tribal land and displacement of 100,000 local tribal people. Little compensation was given.

After the establishment of Bangladesh in 1971 the tribespeople sent a delegation to their new ruler Sheikh Mujib, requesting local autonomy and prohibition of non-tribal entry into the area. The requests were ignored by the government and

2   In August 1975 and May 1981 respectively.

there are continuing reports by Amnesty International, and from other sources, of violations of human rights in the Chittagong Hill area. The people are being displaced without adequate compensation in much the same way as the forest dwellers in Brazil (Chapter 7) and the Penan of Sarawak (Chapter 1). As they have no permanent habitat, the "unoccupied" land they are not currently using is all too frequently declared vacant and leased or sold to others, usually from outside the tribal area. Their resources of minerals are being exploited without benefit to them, and troops have been posted to maintain order. The consequence is that violence occurs, with the inevitable but personally tragic cases of rape and murder, as well as of mass killings and destruction of villages.

Bangladesh is a party to ILO Convention 107 on indigenous and tribal populations, and in 1985 the ILO Committee of Experts expressed concern over apparent contraventions of the treaty, particularly in the displacement of peoples from their land. On the other hand, despite continuing reports of human rights violations, the UN Sub-Commission on Prevention of Discrimination and Protection of Minorities reported, late in 1989, some satisfaction with progress made in Bangladesh's treatment of its tribal population.

Discussion. Bangladesh is the first of the "post-colonial" peoples to become a nation. Until 1971, it had been thought by many that the era of self-determination as a right of peoples under an alien government to establish their own nation state had come to an end with the dismantling of the former Western European empires. It had been said by the Secretary-General of the United Nations, U Thant, in January 1970, referring to the claim by the Biafran people to separate from Nigeria, that –

> ... the United Nations has never accepted and does not accept and I do not believe it will ever accept the principle of secession of a part of its Member State [in this case, Nigeria].

The remarkable tenacity of the Bengali people, hardened by the horror of the Pakistani repression, proved this statement wrong and gave hope to other subjugated peoples.

The reason for U Thant's statement is not difficult to identify. It would be subversive of the international order if any disaffected group within a nation were to be able to claim a right to secede. Indeed, if that were to be possible, governments might be forced, confronted with group resistance, to take harsher measures than would otherwise have been necessary to maintain order and national unity. Accordingly, the international law of self-determination, as illuminated by Bangladesh's assertion of independence, in effect requires a number of conditions to be fulfilled before the claim to independence can be accepted. Not unnaturally, the conditions include an emphasis on a peaceful rather than a violent process. But it should not be forgotten – and this stands in sharp contrast to what U Thant said – that the two great human rights Covenants (on civil/political and economic/social/cultural rights) both proclaim a right to self-determination. Article 1 of both Covenants is in identical terms and reads in part –

1. All peoples have the right of self-determination. By virtue of that right they freely determine their political status and freely pursue their economic, social and cultural development.

2. All peoples may, for their own ends, freely dispose of their natural wealth and resources without prejudice to any obligations arising out of international economic co-operation. ... In no case may a people be deprived of its own means of subsistence.

The basic rules are clear. There must be a "people" and it must be able to choose its destiny freely. The people must not be deprived of *their own* means of subsistence. In international law it may be said that for a group to be identified as a "people" to whom the right of self-determination applies, it must be able to comply with five conditions. First, its members must have some sense of identity, some sense of belonging together as a group. Second, this sense needs to be marked by a uniting feature or features. These may be one or more of language, ethnic origin, or cultural or religious affinities. Third, there must be an identifiable territory to which the people can lay claim. Fourth, there must be a degree of viability, involving a capacity for the people to maintain itself both politically and economically. Fifth, the people must clearly express their desire to be separate, preferably by peaceful means and through a free vote of some kind.

The people of Bangladesh complied with all except, arguably, the last of these conditions. They have a long shared history, a common language and religion, and an identifiable and viable territory and governmental system. Although there was no internationally supervised plebiscite, they made their views clear through the 1970 vote and again through the struggles of 1971. The main tragedy is that the suffering of the two decades prior to independence had to be endured rather than there being an opportunity for a free expression of their will back in the late 1940s.

It is also recognised in international law that there is more than one way to express self-determination. In 1970 the General Assembly of the United Nations, when thinking of the obligations of the former colonial powers, resolved that a people could choose one of three courses, any of which would be sufficient to remove any further special obligations of the trustee state. The three courses were full separate nation status; some kind of free association with another (usually the former trustee) state; and integration into an existing state. The people of Bangladesh, after trying unsuccessfully to obtain a degree of autonomy within Pakistan, opted for separation.

II. East Timor

The Story. For the past 20 years there have been claims by the people of East Timor for independence. Initially, the claim was for separation from the imperial power (Portugal) and for acceptance as an independent people as part of the dismantling of the Western European colonial empires. Since 1976, when Indonesia formally annexed East Timor, the claim has been for termination of Indonesian rule. The main protagonist on the side of independence has been FRETILIN[3] Although most of FRETILIN'S leaders are living in exile, there has been continued resistance inside Timor to the control the Indonesian authorities continue to exercise. That control has been stern. At the less violent end of the spectrum, people could not obtain government posts unless they formally accepted Indonesian citizenship, and

---

3   FRETILIN is an acronym based on the title of the independence party Frente Revolucionaria Timor Leste. It was formed in 1970 and has been described as "populist Catholic" in orientation but appears not to be essentially communist, as has sometimes been suggested by its critics.

other obstacles have been put in the path of those who oppose Indonesian rule, including censorship of mail and telephone, and denial of the right to hold an identity card. At the more violent end, there have been repeated reports during the period since the Indonesian annexation in 1975-76 of bombings, murder, burning, torture and other atrocities. Perhaps the best known of these occurred in November 1991, when a military force fired indiscriminately on people attending a funeral in Dili, the capital. Estimates of the number killed in what has appropriately been termed the Dili Massacre range from 50 (Indonesian Government) to over 100 (FRETILIN and others) or even 150.[4] In Canberra, the supporters of independence placed 124 crosses in the ground near the Indonesian Embassy to indicate solidarity, and their maintenance has been the subject of legal action. The reaction of the Indonesian Government has been defensive, that of the Indonesian army unapologetic.[5] Indeed, it seems that the population of East Timor has been reduced from between 600,000 and 700,000 in the mid-1970s to perhaps 500,000 in the early 1990s. Although some of the reduction is due to emigration, much must be attributed to the savage response to the resistance of the people and to the associated shortages of food and other basic necessities.

The island of Timor lies some 1000km east of Java, the main island in the Indonesian archipelago, and about 800km northwest of Darwin. It is about 500km long and mostly less than 100km wide. Inhabited in pre-historic times by fairly numerous tribal groups whose origins appear to be partly Australoid and partly Mongoloid, it was not evangelised by any of the major religions until the European visitations began in the early 16th century. From then on the Portuguese in the east, and from the 17th century the Dutch in the west, have been the effective rulers of Timor, though Portugal did not appoint the first resident governor until 1701.[6] The main interests in the area were the sandalwood forests and the production of coffee. Until 1950, Timor was divided into two parts – a Dutch colony in the south and west, and a Portuguese colony in the north and east.

---

4   In November 1992, the governor of East Timor admitted that possibly 200 people had died in the massacre.
5   "Dili massacre: no regrets says army", Canberra Times, 7 July 1992.
6   Before that, the colony was ruled from Goa.

In 1950, following Indonesian independence in 1949, West Timor was ceded by the Dutch to Indonesia, but Portugal under President Caetano did not relinquish its control of East Timor.

The troubles really began with the collapse in Portugal in April 1974 of the long-ruling dictator Caetano. Immediately, steps were taken to dismantle Portugal's overseas empire. Three political groups were already established in East Timor: UDT, FRETILIN and APODETI. Initially, the Portuguese authorities favoured the UDT,[7] which sought a gradual transition to independence and was less radical than FRETILIN. However, there was an uneasy coalition between the two parties and they appeared to be making progress towards independence. By early 1975 the Indonesian authorities, realising that the other active party, the pro-Indonesian APODETI[8] was without much local support, began to approach UDT. The alliance of UDT with FRETILIN had in the meantime broken down, partly as a result of Indonesian efforts to destroy the coalition. An internal civil war, to which Indonesian forces were later contributed, began. In August 1975, UDT launched a coup because it feared the progressive strengthening of FRETILIN's position and open fighting broke out between the two. By mid-September, FRETILIN forces had the upper hand and were re-establishing control. In November FRETILIN, alarmed by Indonesian incursions and support for UDT and APODETI, declared independence. In early December Indonesia, claiming that it was moving in at the request of the people of East Timor, bombed and invaded the country and assumed control. Indonesia was fortified in this action by knowing that Australia supported its actions, through a statement in August by the then Prime Minister (Mr Whitlam) during a visit to Indonesia, and by the visit to Jakarta, immediately before the invasion, of United States President Ford and Secretary of State Kissinger.

The United Nations General Assembly, on 12 December 1975, and again a year later and for several years thereafter, passed resolutions deploring the Indonesian action and calling on the parties (including Portugal) to bring about independence

---

7   A much smaller party than FRETILIN, named Uniao Democratica Timorense, which was founded in May 1974.

8   APODETI, Associacao Popular Democratica de Timor, sought integration with Indonesia and was formed in May 1974.

for the people of East Timor. The Security Council passed similar resolutions on 22 December 1975 and in April 1976 and November 1977. Despite a series of missions by a Special Representative of the Secretary-General of the United Nations, no further action occurred. Indonesia continues, uneasily and with not infrequent resort to violence, to rule the whole of Timor.

The strongest argument for Indonesia is that, as it already had legitimate control of West Timor, it should now administer the whole island. Once the invasion had occurred, this changed to an argument that to recognise the claim to independence of East Timor would be a destabilising influence. In addition, Indonesia claimed that the invitation from UDT and APODETI amounted to a free expression of popular desire for becoming part of Indonesia. It also has made the point that there are ethnic links with the East Timorese population and that the territory would not be viable as an independent country. On the other hand, FRETILIN claims with justice that it was far more widely representative of the people than UDT and APODETI; that it could have been economically and politically viable with only modest initial support; that there are no clear ethnic connections; and that the linguistic affinities within East Timor are strong (Tetum and Portuguese) and are different from those in West Timor (Indonesian and Timorese).

Discussion. The continued internal and external resistance, heroic in its proportions, and apparently not abating, and the ability of the leaders of FRETILIN, suggest that there is a sense of peoplehood and a capacity for self-government in East Timor that should be recognised. It hardly seems to accord with the principles of human rights to respond that "there does come a time when the reality of an annexation or an absorption of this kind has to be accepted".[9]

It is true that the stability of the international order must not be unduly threatened, as U Thant so clearly put it, by claims for self-determination. This is another example of the "floodgates"

---

9   Response to a Parliamentary question from Senator Vallentine by the Minister for Foreign Affairs, Senator Evans, on 18 December 1990 – see Hansard for that date and *The Monthly Record*, prepared by the Department of Foreign Affairs, December 1990, p 879.

argument referred to on page 11. Here, it is invoked both by U Thant's defence of the sovereignty of nation states, and by the Indonesian argument for no separartion of parts of their territory. The point also needs to be made that the continued struggle by a people for independence is itself a destabilising factor. It seems that in 1974 and 1975 the attitude of the Indonesian government was not altogether settled![10] One is prompted to wonder whether, if Indonesia had had the benefit of foresight in late 1975, the armed invasion would have occurred. In effect, the cost of administering the territory has been enormously high in budgetary terms alone. In human terms it is devastating – the 2000-3000 lives lost in the civil war in 1975 pale into insignificance beside the subsequent loss of 100,000-200,000 lives and the many other human rights violations.

The mood of the people is reflected in the poem by Francisco Borja da Costa, an East Timorese poet killed by Indonesian paratroopers on 7 December 1975 –

> We must shout aloud
> > That the people of Timor
> > That the Maubere people
> > Will never be slaves again.[11]

It is difficult to see how granting this small people their independence could seriously destabilise the Indonesian nation. It is also difficult to see how refusing to grant independence can be reconciled with the Charter of the United Nations, which stipulates in Article 1.2 that the purposes of the UN are "to develop friendly relations among nations based on respect for the principle of equal rights and self-determination of peoples"[12]. As Judge Dillard of the International Court said in 1975 in the *Western Sahara Opinion* (1975) ICJ Reports 3, at 122, "it is for the people to determine the destiny of the territory and not the territory the destiny of the people".

---

10   There are reports of the Foreign Minister and the President stating in 1974 that the independence of East Timor should be respected, but in 1975 there were contradictory statements and actions.

11   Quoted in Kohen A and Taylor J, *An Act of Genocide: Indonesia's Invasion of East Timor*, Tapol (UK) 1979.

12   It may also be recalled that Article 1 of each of the two International Covenants on human rights expressly states and spells out the right. It may well be significant that Indonesia is a party to neither.

It is also appropriate to record that Portugal has given notice of an application to the International Court of Justice in relation to the position of East Timor. It is challenging the validity of the agreement reached by Australia and Indonesia about the search for and use of oil that may be found in the sea lying between the two countries. The sea in question would be off the coast of East Timor, were it to be a separate country. The action has been brought to test the validity of the annexation by Indonesia. Portugal has joined Australia as a party because Indonesia has not accepted the jurisdiction of the International Court, and presumably also because of Australia's support for the Indonesian position.[13]

III. LITHUANIA

The Story. This chapter was originally written in August 1991, as the Baltic peoples of Lithuania, Latvia and Estonia seemed likely to obtain their full national independence once again![14] Their most recent spell of bondage dated back half a century to 1940, when the USSR demanded the appointment of puppet governments as part of the mutual defence pacts hastily prepared between it and the three countries in the face of Nazi invasion. By an ultimatum delivered in May 1940, the existing governments were dismissed and communist puppet governments appointed. Two of the former presidents were carried away to unknown destinations, while Lithuanian President Smetona (who had ruled since 1926) managed to flee. Shortly after the Soviet ultimatums, the republics were overrun by the advancing German armies. They remained under German control between 1941 and 1944, since when they have been part of the USSR.

But the last half-century is only a small part of the centuries-long suffering of the people of Lithuania under foreign yoke. It seems that the three Baltic peoples have a different ethnic origin

---

13 Prime Minister Hawke announced Australian recognition of Indonesia's sovereignty in August 1985.

14 Independence was declared by the newly elected government in Lithuania following the first multi-party elections under Soviet power, on 11 March 1990, but the USSR government refused to take early steps toward separate statehood.

from that of the Russians or the Germans, and the Lithuanian language is both ancient and distinctive. The first known written reference to Lithuania comes from the Roman historian Tacitus in the 2nd century AD, and the name was established in writings in 1009. The first kingdom was established in the 13th century, and the high period of Lithuania was in the 14th century, when parts of the Ukraine and Byelorussia were within its boundaries. However, as the surrounding areas, and particularly the strength of the Russian people developed, continued separate existence became more difficult.

To meet this external challenge, a Commonwealth of Poland and Lithuania was established. It lasted for more than two centuries. When the Commonwealth was partitioned in 1795, Lithuania was annexed by Russia. The Lithuanian spirit was not crushed, however, and is exemplified by a number of contingents which joined Napoleon on his invasion of Russia in 1811.[15] With the defeat of Napoleon, Russia strengthened its grip. The University of Vilnius was closed in 1832 and in 1840 Russian law replaced Lithuanian law. Lithuania remained under Russian rule until 1915, when it was occupied by Germany. It was only after World War I that Lithuania again became free. The right of self-determination contained in the Soviet Constitution was invoked and enforced by the 1920 peace treaty with Russia. But this did not mean an end to deprivations. Later in 1920 Poland invaded from the south, and occupied about one-third of the southern part of the country, including Vilnius. A democratic constitution was adopted in 1922 and the story ends with a military coup in 1926 in which Antanas Smetona became President.

During all these centuries, the Lithuanian language flourished, Lithuanian culture was maintained and a sense of national unity was preserved. Even in the worst days of Stalin, the Lithuanian people maintained their self-awareness and, as matters eased a little in the Kruschev Thaw period (the 1960s), Lithuania excelled in the production of *samidzat* literature (the name denotes that it is non-state-approved). This literature took many forms but, because so much of the Lithuanian culture is

---

15 A century and a half later, in 1944, while under German domination, a Freedom Army was formed, but was disbanded in 1952 because of lack of external support.

centred on the Catholic church (80 percent of Lithuania's 3 million people are Catholic), much of it was concerned with religious matters. It was in ways like this that the people sustained themselves until the ultimate day of freedom in 1991.[16] It is this unremitting and often inventive struggle over long centuries that explains the enormous joy the people are now experiencing, and their dogged determination to achieve independence.

Discussion. The undergirding case for Lithuania, as for both Bangladesh and East Timor, is that a self-aware people has struggled for independence and that time and suffering have not diminished the desire. Lithuania is different from the other two peoples in that it has had long periods in which it has been an independent nation. Its people may have suffered less grossly than those of the Indian and South-East Asian regions (though its population declined sharply between 1939 and 1959 due to Nazi and Soviet genocide), but how can one compare suffering, or presume to measure the extent of the inhumanity all the peoples have endured? Also different about the Lithuanian prospect is that independence was achieved by relatively peaceful means, with the breaking up of the Soviet hegemony, rather than through immediately preceding fighting, as was the case in Bangladesh and may eventually, and regrettably, be necessary in East Timor. That independence is not the end of the road, but only the beginning of a new venture, is aptly illustrated by the political and economic difficulties the people of Lithuania have experienced since 1991. Those difficulties were the main cause of the ousting by overwhelming popular vote in November 1992 of the outspoken independence leader, President Lansbergis. He was replaced by a new leadership drawn from, and relying for its support largely on, former members of the Communist Party, itself now banned. This change must, however, be seen in the context of Lithuania's continuing struggle for independence.

---

16 The UN Security Council voted to approve the admission as members of the UN of the three Baltic republics in September 1991. North Korea, South Korea and the Marshall Islands and Micronesia became members during the same month.

IV. OVERVIEW

The first observation to be made about the three case studies above is that it can no longer be maintained that the international law of self-determination was only applicable to former colonies of Western European nations. The independence of Bangladesh and the now completed independence of the three Baltic States shows that the doctrine can operate in respect both of peoples who are part of a former colonial country and of peoples who have been part of the Soviet system. The case of Yugoslavia suggests that the scope of the "Soviet system" needs to be interpreted broadly as applying beyond the borders of the former USSR.

Thus there must be modification of the implications of statements of many international lawyers, and of U Thant in 1970, that self-determination is not an operative doctrine. True, self-determination does imply erosion of sovereignty, may liberate national minorities and give separate statehood and membership of the UN. But those things have now happened in more than a small number of cases, and the consequence has not in most cases been disaster.[17] The overall consequence has been a liberation of the people involved, removal of a burden from the relinquishing country and an increase in the enjoyment of at least some human rights. Further, the case of Lithuania has opened up the prospect that the separation process can be reasonably sophisticated and humane, which means, *inter alia*, greater recognition of the equality principle contained in Article 1.2 of the UN Charter. However, the future remains difficult for the new countries, and perhaps uncertain.

Third, it can be said that the five marks of a people ready for self-determination – sense of identity, common features such as language, identifiable territory, political and economic viability and a preferably free expression of will – need to be supplemented by at least one more principled, and perhaps one practical, consideration. The principled consideration is that the intent of a people can be identified by their maintaining *over a substantial period of time* their desire for independence. That continued adherence to a common cause should be capable of

---

17   The tragedy of Bosnia-Herzegovina must be set alongside the successes in the other new states.

being regarded as sufficient, without plebiscite or other ad hoc expression, to justify a claim for independence. Indeed, if the desire has been well known for some time, requiring a plebiscite is something of an insult, unless there are large dissenting minorities.

The practical consideration is that the firm support of a great power or of a strong neighbouring state is of enormous advantage. The great power support is clear for the Baltic States; has been sadly lacking for East Timor, which probably for that reason alone failed to gain recognition; and was available for Bangladesh. The strong neighbour was available in the form of Germany for Lithuania; was absent, in the form of Australia or Malaysia (or of the United States as a great power) for East Timor; and was present in the form of India for Bangladesh. The "practical" question may in fact turn out to be a question of principle, if it is noted that what is involved in self-determination is a breaking of the sovereignty of a nation state. The principle involved is that to divide a nation state where there is resistance to the move, at least a powerful neighbour, or a great power, must be supportive. Otherwise, the stress on the international order is too great. Of course, if there is general agreement, as in the case of the Baltic peoples, the difficulties disappear.

One feature of each of the cases examined has been the question of economic viability. The International Covenant provides that peoples have rights to use and dispose freely of their own resources and not to be deprived of their own means of subsistence. How much easier it would have been for all the cases discussed if this right had been respected by the sovereign power *while the people was part of the nation state*. Putting the matter another way, it is possible to see how the nation state is one of the chief enemies of a fair enjoyment of economic (and also social and cultural) rights. The traditional thinkers have observed that it is often the organised power of the state that has deprived people of civil and political rights. Equally, the power of the nation state has deprived peoples within it, and their members, of economic and social rights.

Another aspect of the economic viability criterion is the prospect of ever-increasing numbers of non-viable mini-states. That is a risk which it would be preferable to avoid. However, if a nation state cannot or will not meet in a just way – politically, economically and administratively – the aspirations of one of the peoples within its border, it should be regarded as forfeiting its "right" to govern that people. That people should have the right to separate, even if the consequence is greater economic difficulty, as perhaps has been the case with Bangladesh.

Finally, it needs to be observed that unliberated peoples exist in all parts of the world. Apart from the cases selected here, one need only mention the many indigenous peoples around the world (see Chapter 1), and the situations of Quebec, of the Falkland Islands, of Nigeria, of Cambodia, of the many peoples in the former USSR and of Tibet. There is no absolute right – or need – for a people to become a separate state. Nor, however, is the existing list of UN members and non-member states inviolate. The message of this chapter is that the enjoyment of human rights can be increased in many cases by recognising the right of a people to become independent. It is also that, if a state wishes to preserve for itself territory that is resource-rich or otherwise desirable, it should take care to protect and promote the human rights of its inhabitants, particularly if they can claim to be a "people".

For Further Reading

One of the most informative books about Bangladesh is by CP O'Donnell, *Bangladesh: Biography of a Nation*, Westview, 1984. It surveys the land and its people and culture and gives details of the national struggle and of events to the assassination of President Zia. A closer-in account of the political struggle is contained in Bhuiyan Md AW, *The Emergence of Bangladesh and the Role of the Awami League*, Vikas, New Delhi, 1982. A clear and persuasive account of the post-colonial-era law of self-determination is given by Nanda VP, "Self-Determination in International Law: The Tragic Tale of Two Cities – Islamabad (West Pakistan) and Dacca (East Pakistan)", (1972) 66 *American Journal of International Law*, 321.

The story of East Timor is told with sympathy and documentation by Dunn J, *Timor: A People Betrayed*, Jacaranda, Sydney, 1983. The account by Ramos-Horta J, *Funu: The Unfinished Saga of East Timor*, Red

Sea Press, New Jersey, 1987 is by one of the ablest and best known leaders of FRETILIN. The legal aspects are well covered in Elliott P, "The East Timor Dispute", (1978) 27 *International and Comparative Law Quarterly*, 238. *Timor Past and Present*, by F Hiorth, contains a useful brief history of the independence movement, and analysis of the present situation.

The story of Lithuania is well told, but with an obvious bias, by Vaitiekunas V, *Lithuania*, Vol 5, Assembly of Captive European Nations series, New York, 1965 and a companion account is contained in Vizulis IJ, *Nations Under Duress: The Baltic States*, Associated Faculty Press, Washington, 1985. A broader account, concentrating on the past half century, is contained in Misiunas RJ and Taagepera R, *The Baltic States: Years of Dependence 1940-1989*, Hurst, London, 1983. A more law-related book is *The Rights of Peoples*, James Crawford (ed), Clarendon, Oxford, 1988.

A clear and forward-looking piece on the general question of self-determination as a human right is contained in Cassese A, "The Self-Determination of Peoples" in Henkin (ed), *The International Bill of Rights: The Covenant on Civil and Political Rights*, Columbia, New York, 1981, p 92.

Chapter 3

The Amish of Wisconsin and the
French-Speakers of Belgium

The Rights of Minorities

I. THE AMISH OF WISCONSIN

The Story. In the autumn of 1968, the fathers of three children in
a new Amish settlement in New Glarus, Green County,
Wisconsin, were arrested for not enrolling them in the local high
school. The three arrested were Jonas Yoder and Adin Yutzy of
the Old Order Amish Religion and Wallace Miller of the
Conservative Amish Mennonite Church. Their children, who
were aged 14 and 15, should have been enrolled because in
Wisconsin schooling is compulsory until the age of 16. They did
not make the enrolments because they believed the children
should not be exposed to the "worldly" influences embodied in
the compulsory system of high school education. They saw the
state system as enshrining competitive, secular and individual
success-oriented values. In the discussions that followed, they
refused the compromise the Wisconsin authorities offered, based
on what had been adopted in Pennsylvania in 1955. Under the
Pennsylvania arrangements, it was permissible for Amish
children who had completed their primary schooling and were
of high school age to be trained in the ways of the Amish people
and to work on the farms, while doing three hours a week of
"advanced education" in classes near their homes in an
unregistered Amish school. The Wisconsin authorities, faced
with the refusal, felt the parents should be compelled to enrol
their children according to the law, so that they could be taught
along with other children from the same area.

The three Amish fathers had refused, again in accordance with their beliefs, to pay the fines (of $5 each) levied on them by the authorities and so were arrested. When taken to trial, first in the County and then in the District Court, they had been convicted. The two courts considered the state had a compelling interest in ensuring all children in its territory were exposed to the same educational processes, notwithstanding that this meant overriding their religious belief and practice.

The case went on appeal to the Supreme Court of Wisconsin, and finally to the Supreme Court of the United States. Both courts found in favour of the Amish people. In a unanimous decision on the question of the right of the Amish people to educate their children as they believed, the Supreme Court drew on the First Amendment,[1] which guarantees that no law is to be made "prohibiting the free exercise" of religion[2] In *Wisconsin v Yoder* 406 US 205 (1972), as the case is known, Chief Justice Burger, delivering the opinion of the Supreme Court, said –

> The Amish do not object to elementary education through the first eight grades as a general proposition because they agree that their children must have basic skills in the "three R's" in order to read the Bible, to be good farmers and to be able to deal with non-Amish people when necessary in the course of daily affairs. (p 212)

He noted that the Trial Court, when holding against the Amish, had recognised that compulsory high school attendance would interfere with their freedom to act in accordance with their sincere beliefs. The trial judge had, however, considered that compelling education to age 16 was "reasonable and constitutional". Against this, and reviewing earlier cases, the Chief Justice said –

> We can accept it as settled ... that, however strong the State's interest in universal compulsory education, it is by no means

---

1   The United States Bill of Rights is not contained in a separate part of the Constitution, but consists of the first 10 and the 14th Amendments of the Constitution, made in 1791 and 1868 respectively. So the First Amendment is in effect the first article of the Bill of Rights.

2   Although the First Amendment prevents only the Congress of the United States from making such a law, the Supreme Court has held that the 14th Amendment, which was made after the Civil War, has the effect of applying to the States the First and some other of the first ten Amendments.

absolute to the exclusion of all other interests (p 215) ... to agree that religiously grounded conduct must often be subject to the broad police power of the State is not to deny that there are areas of conduct protected by the Free Exercise Clause of the first Amendment and thus beyond the power of the State to control. (p 213)

But while holding that the Amish could escape from state control in the later years of their children's upbringing, there was a warning. The reason for withdrawing the children had, first, to be based clearly on religious belief. Mere philosophical opinion would not be enough. More than that, although the Chief Justice was not explicit on the matter, it seems that the conduct of the minority may need not to represent a violent threat to the general community –

The Amish alternative to formal secondary education has enabled them to function effectively in their day-to-day life under self-imposed limitations on relations with the world, and to survive and prosper in contemporary society as a separate, sharply identifiable and highly self-sufficient community for more than 200 years in this country. (p 225)

The Amish people have a remarkable history. They link their establishment to the beginning of the Reformed Church in Switzerland. In effect, their origins can be traced to the breakaway of the Reformed Church from the Roman Church, which in Switzerland occurred in 1522 under the leadership of Huldrych Zwingli. Following the example of Luther in Germany in 1517, Zwingli published his own collection of principles in his 67 Theses of 1523. The infant Reformed Church itself had an early split, when in 1526 the Anabaptist group, which among other things denied the validity of infant baptism and insisted on mature age baptism, broke away. Led from 1536 by Menno Simon, formerly a Catholic priest, this group became known as the Mennonites, deriving its name from him. The Mennonites have, despite some dissensions, continued to the present as a loosely related group of churches. It is estimated that there are some 500,000 members of the Mennonite churches in several countries, with the largest concentration being in the USA and Canada. The main migration to North America was in the mid-18th century (about 1720-70).

The focus of our interest is on the Amish people, who in 1693 broke away from the main body of Mennonites. They were led by Jacob Amman, from whom their name is derived. They formed their own group of churches that were stricter than the Mennonite movement generally. Amman appears to have been a dominating, and in many ways extremely rigid, leader. He took the view that former believers who had been expelled because of sinful acts or perverse doctrine should be "shunned", that is, cut off from all contact with the believers. In the end, a number of groups of Amish churches were formed. In Pennsylvania, there were about ten groups, of which the Old Order Amish (to which Yoder and Yutzy belonged) and the Conservative Amish (to which Wallace Miller belonged) are among the most conservative. They all base themselves on a strict and fairly literal understanding of the Bible.[3]

The Amish are conspicuous in the 20 States of the United States in which they live because of their homemade clothes, usually black or dark in colour and dating in style essentially from the 17th century. They are distinguished also by their use of horse-drawn vehicles rather than cars, their refusal to have telephones or electric power joined to their homes, their refusal to use lawnmowers, and their insistence on having no separate meeting places. They speak still a dialect of the German language. Their communication is partly by word of mouth and through using the Bible in a meditative and accepting rather than a critical mode to convey their thoughts. Communication is also partly through the practice of silent discourse – in which silence and a sort of community coming-togetherness are the mode. Their way of life is simple and they avoid, as far as possible, being involved with the rest of the world. They set great store by honesty and hard work – "work makes life sweet" is one of their sayings. Their main means of livelihood – in self-sufficient farming communities – is ideally suited to maintaining these values and their separate existence.

Nonetheless, they do not isolate themselves wholly from the wider community. Rather, they have moderated its influence on

---

3   The members of the Amish communities number perhaps 90,000, spread across 20 States of the United States. The greater proportion of the Amish population – about three quarters of them – is in the central northern States of the United States – Ohio, Pennsylvania and Indiana (all bordering on each other and on the Great Lakes). The Amish communities are loosely related to the other branches of the Mennonite Church.

themselves. They will use pay phones, ride in buses or others' cars, send their children to primary school, and even on occasion vote. But they live very much as self-sufficient communities held together by their faith and their sense of unity in serving God in the way they have adopted. Surprisingly to many, they have not diminished in number as the pace of change quickens. Their population has more than doubled over the past 30 years – to about 90,000 at the end of the 1980s. The Supreme Court's decision has assured them, and other minorities in the United States, a perhaps less threatened life in the future.

Discussion. *Wisconsin v Yoder* shows the United States Supreme Court at its most effective in the protection of minority groups within the American community. It stood foursquare behind the right of the Amish to live their own lives as an intact and protected community within the broader society, and not always according to the requirements of that broader society. Yet there is a possible lingering apprehension left by the words of the Chief Justice quoted above. What, one wonders, would the court have concluded if the state had made much of the rather elementary (but natural) sanitation conditions, and of the other seemingly (to the rest of society) primitive aspects of the life of the Amish people? One hopes the court would have still been robust in the defence of the rights of the religious minority, even if some of the possibly implied conditions contained in such words from the Chief Justice's opinion as "survive" and "prosper" and "highly self-sufficient" had not been complied with. Otherwise, it would be too easy for the court to equate "different" with "unsatisfactory" and thereby to rule out the rights of the minority.

Another aspect of the court's judgment also calls for comment. Justice Douglas entered an opinion that dissented from the majority on one point. He noted that the court was in effect supporting the power of the parents to decide the nature of their children's religious upbringing.[4] He considered the children should have been given by the court "an opportunity to be heard before the State gives the exemption which we honor today". (p 246) He thought the Wisconsin courts should be asked

---

4   As to the notion of the "power", rather than the "right", of parents to
     control their children, see the discussion in Chapter 10.II.

to hear what the children thought before the case was finally decided. He commented that the children may not all have thought the same. To this point, the Chief Justice rather tartly replied (pp 230-1) that it was the parents, not the children, who had been prosecuted, and whose cases were being heard.

In law the Chief Justice was no doubt correct. In substance, it does seem Justice Douglas had put his finger on an important issue –

> Religion is an individual experience. ... Our opinions are full of talk about the power of the parents over the child's education. ... These children are "persons" within the meaning of the Bill of Rights. (p 243)

The enlightened view of the acceptance of minorities that lies behind the judgments in Yoder was well epitomised by Speaker Maurice Baringer of Iowa, a Republican. When debating the question of enacting special legislation to exempt the high school children of the Old Order Amish of Iowa from the general law requiring attendance at state or certified high schools, he said –

> [The] Amish are a people under God, living according to their religious beliefs. We should be willing to bend in order to let these people live.[5]

Governor Hughes of Iowa, in the same dispute, made in his weekly broadcast what might be regarded as a classic (if not altogether grammatical) statement in support of the religious freedom of minorities. In doing so, he referred especially to the religiously based origins of the United States –

> Our country was founded and based on religious freedom and I don't believe our society should ever progress to the point where any small minority by any means is deprived of their rights or their beliefs if it can be determined that it is a belief of conscience in God as they understand it.[6]

The eventual solution for Iowa was an amendment of the education legislation to allow the Iowan State Board of Public Instruction to give an exemption from the school standards to certain schools. Specifically, the exemption was to be available to

---

5   Quoted in Rogers HR, *Community Conflict*, referred to in Further
     Reading, at p 36.
6   Ibid, p 31. The broadcast was made on 18 February 1966.

the representatives of a local congregation of an established and recognised religious denomination that differs substantially from the goals or philosophy of the law setting the standard for the state.

The international community has been very much aware of the importance of protecting the rights of both minorities and individuals to practise their religion unfettered. Two Articles in the ICCPR are relevant: Article 27, dealing with the rights of minorities; and Article 18, dealing with the right to freedom of thought and religion.[7]

Article 27 is somewhat negative in its terms because it only provides that minorities are *not to be denied* the right to practise their religion. Nevertheless, it places a clear limit on what states may do if faced with even disagreeable groups –

> In those States in which ethnic, religious or linguistic minorities exist, persons belonging to such minorities shall not be denied the right, in community with other members of their group, to enjoy their own culture, to profess and practise their own religion, or to use their own language.

The Supreme Court decision in Yoder clearly fulfilled the letter and the spirit of Article 27. It said that the States did not have a "compelling interest" in relation to the education of the children of minority groups,[8] though it might in some other areas, such as in relation to the criminal law, or taxation laws, or the keeping of contracts. It is also compatible with the aspect of the right that flows from protecting the individuals in a group practising their own religion "in community with other members". There is a real sense in which the minority *as a group* is protected, and not just the individuals within it, if they decide on some unacceptable course of action. The action must be done "in community with other members of the group".

The Article is also felicitous in that it refers to individual members of the group *enjoying* their culture, or using their own language. There is a real sense in which the whole human rights

---

7   Ibid, p 35.
8   In United States discussions, a "compelling interest" is one that allows a state, or the United States, to legislate to *prohibit*, as distinct from *regulating*, an activity – see particularly Chapter 6, Section I, where the concept is discussed in relation to abortion.

exercise is about maximising everyone's enjoyment of life. Article 27 effectively captures that.

Article 18 of the ICCPR is also important, and to some extent overlaps Article 27 in the area of religious freedom. It is more positively phrased than Article 27, because it confers a positive rather than a negative right. It reads in part –

> 1. Everyone shall have the right to freedom of thought, conscience and religion. This right shall include freedom to have or adopt a religion or belief of his choice, and freedom, either individually or in community with others, and in public or private, to manifest his religion or belief in worship, observance, practice or teaching.
>
> ...
>
> 4. The States Parties to the present Covenant undertake to have respect for the liberty of parents and, when applicable, legal guardians to ensure the religious and moral education of their children in conformity with their own convictions.

Article 18 contains a classic definition of the right to freedom of religion, and emphasises the right to put it into practice – to "manifest" it. Here again, the Supreme Court comes out with flying colours. And note also the subtle change in balance, compared with Article 27, between the individual and the community to which he or she belongs. There, the emphasis was on the community, here it is on the individual. The Amish of Wisconsin would have complied with either test.

Finally, it is worth noting that paragraph 4 of Article 18 comes down on the side of the "liberty" (or power) of parents to ensure their children are brought up according to the parents' beliefs. That is an excellent statement of the desirable position if the rights of the parents as against the *state* are concerned. It is proper that, against the state and its education authorities, the wishes of the parents should be able to prevail. But, as Justice Douglas mentioned in his partial dissent, the rights of the children against their parents also have to be considered. On this matter, Article 18 is, in the author's view, somewhat deficient. Unfortunately, the Convention on the Rights of the Child is not much better, though it does provide specifically in Article 5 that the autonomy rights of the child are to be respected?[9] This, as is suggested in Chapter 10 on the rights of the child, is an area where that Convention has really not gone far enough in defining the need for very specific formulations of the rights of children in relation to general human rights as defined in the International Bill of Rights.

Finally, and as discussed in Chapter 1, it seems anomalous that a religious minority such as the Amish should have their rights so well protected, while indigenous groups (or peoples) such as the American Indians or the Australian Aborigines do not. Indigenous peoples do not like to be regarded as minorities – they see themselves as "peoples", and thus as having a more fundamental, and ancient, claim to recognition than do minorities. It is not easy to see why they have failed where groups such as the Mennonites have succeeded. Perhaps it is that their very claim is more than the legal system can deal with. Whereas the Amish seek simply to be seen as an exception, and to be given protection from the harsh incidence of laws that fit the majority reasonably well, indigenous groups want full recognition as a people. As such, they ask more of the legal system than judges feel they can give, and than the political or legislative system is willing to provide. They want self-determination, an issue discussed in Chapter 2. Most of the solutions found to the Amish problem have been administrative rather than legislative: only legislation, and perhaps even changes to the Constitution, will adequately recognise the claims of indigenous peoples.

II. The French-Speakers of Belgium

The Story. In the early 1960s, several groups of French-speaking families living near Brussels, the capital of Belgium, challenged legislation dating back to 1932, and particularly some revisions made in 1963. The families all lived in the northern half of

---

9   Article 5 reads in part: "States Parties shall respect the responsibilities, rights and duties of parents ... to provide, *in a manner consistent with the evolving capacities of the child,* appropriate direction and guidance in the exercise by the child of the rights recognised in the present Convention." (Italics supplied.)

Belgium (the Flemish- or Dutch-speaking half).[10] They were opposed to the laws that had the effect of reducing government support for French-speaking schools in areas where the majority spoke Dutch. The challenges to the laws were made first in the European Commission on Human Rights. They were partially successful there, and the Belgian Government appealed to the European Court of Human Rights. The government succeeded in most areas of its defence of the 1932 and 1963 laws, but in two areas was required by the court to modify its position.

The case, which has become known as the Belgian Linguistic case, was heard by the commission in 1964 and by the court in 1965.[11] The 300 French-speaking parents challenged the legislation because of its effect on the schools they and other French-speaking families had established to provide their children with education in French in Dutch-speaking areas of Belgium.[12] The legislative arrangements are extremely complicated, and it is unnecessary for the purposes of this story to go into them in detail. However, they took effect by establishing linguistic districts throughout Belgium. Where the district was wholly or predominantly Dutch or French-speaking (the unilingual districts), that language was to be taught in the schools. Accordingly, Dutch was mainly taught in four northern provinces of Belgium, and French in four southern provinces.

One province, Brabant, in which Brussels, the national capital, was situated, was divided in half, with the northern half being mainly Dutch speaking and the southern half being mainly French speaking. Special arrangements were made for Brussels itself. It is situated in the Dutch-speaking (northern) area of Brabant, but is by majority French-speaking.[13] Under the

---

10 The Dutch speakers included a smallish proportion of Flemish, ie Dutch-dialect speakers, but for convenience the references are to the Dutch language.

11 For a note on the procedures of the court and the commission under the European Convention on Human Rights, see Chapter 15.

12 The reference to the French language is also somewhat misleading, as in the southern half of Belgium (often referred to as Walloonie), some Walloon dialects are spoken, although the French language predominates.

13 In 1969, measured by use of the mass media, some 53 percent of the population of Brussels was French speaking, only 7 percent Dutch speaking. Some 34 percent used both French and Dutch. See

arrangements for Brussels, the peripheral districts (in predominantly Dutch-speaking areas) were in most cases not to offer subsidies to French-speaking schools. In addition, French-speaking parents were not to be allowed to transport their children across a district boundary to enable them to be taught in a French-speaking school in a nearby district. A third aspect of the policy was to require pupils in minority schools to undergo a "homologation" process that required them, in effect, to sit their school certificate exams again, under state supervision, ie the minority school assessments were not accepted. It was these three points that formed the main basis of the challenge to the legislation.

The European Commission on Human Rights found for the parents and their 800 children on those three matters. First, they found the withdrawal of the subsidy to be a violation of Article 2 of the First Protocol[14] to the European Convention on Human Rights. Article 2 is phrased in the negative, in a way analogous to that of Article 27 of the ICCPR, discussed above in connection with the Amish story. Article 2 reads –

> No person shall be denied the right to education. In the exercise of any functions which it assumes in relation to education and teaching, the State shall respect the right of parents to ensure such education and teaching in conformity with their own religious and philosophical convictions.

Second, the commission found for the parents in relation to the embargo on transporting their children across district boundaries. It concluded that this restriction was both an infringement of Article 2 and discriminatory on language grounds. Dutch-speaking parents could transport their children to (majority) schools in another district, whereas the French parents could not. Third, the commission found the "homologation" rule to be discriminatory on grounds of language because it placed an unfair and unreasonable burden

---

McRae, *Conflict and Compromise*, referred to in Further Reading, pp 44-5.

14 A Protocol in this sense is an addition to the original agreement. There are now nine Protocols to the European Convention on Human Rights and they cover a range of procedural and substantive matters, such as the handling of complaints, the conferring of a right to property and the abolition of capital punishments.

on French speakers. As such, it offended against the general anti-discrimination provisions in Article 14 of the Convention. Article 14 reads –

> The enjoyment of the rights and freedoms set forth in this Convention shall be secured without discrimination on any ground such as sex, race, colour, language, religion, political or other opinion, national or social origin, association with a national minority, property, birth or other status.

The European Court was not so sympathetic to the French speakers' case. It found for them in only two respects. It agreed with the commission that the refusal to allow French speakers to transport their children across district boundaries was discriminatory in terms of Article 14. However, it did not, for reasons which will be mentioned below, agree with the commission that the refusal also breached Article 2 of the First Protocol. Also, it partly agreed with the commission on the homologation aspect. It did not fully agree, because it considered the requirement for additional accreditation could, in many cases, be a reasonable way of achieving the objects of the legislation. However, it did agree that in some cases the refusal would not be a reasonable, or proportionate, way of achieving the desired purposes –

> ... [the] inequality in treatment [between the French and Dutch schools] in general results from a difference relating to the administrative system of the school attended: ... [the French schools are] not subject to school inspection; ... [the Dutch schools are] subjected to such inspection. ... The exercise of the right to education is not therefore fettered in a discriminatory manner within the meaning of Article 14. It is not, however, impossible that the application of the legal provisions in issue might lead, in individual cases, to results which put in question the existence of a reasonable relationship of proportionality between the means employed and the objective aimed at, to such an extent as to constitute discrimination. (p 335 – words in parenthesis supplied)

The court disagreed with the commission on the matter of the withdrawal of the subsidy to minority language schools in certain districts. It reviewed the policy of the Belgian Government and Parliament, which was to encourage use of the

Dutch language and to move towards greater uniformity of language in the two main parts of Belgium, while rationalising the situation in Brussels. It took the view that the policy, in its broad aspects, was a reasonable one for a democratically elected government to pursue, and that if the general objectives were acceptable it should be wary of upsetting particular details. Further, it noted that the commission's decision on the subsidy aspect would require additional expenditure, and considered that it was not the role of the court to reach conclusions that would result in increased outlays by the government. It was particularly aware of the negative phrasing ("shall not be denied") of Article 2.

Discussion. The language controversy has been particularly acute in Belgium, and has had its ramifications in education, as described above; in the political structures of the country, as will be illustrated below by reference to a case decided 22 years later than the Linguistic case; and in the socio-economic area.

To understand the complexity of Belgium's language policy, and the fine tuning that has occurred, it is necessary to note Belgium's long and involved history, and the nature of the linguistic issue. Belgium has for most of its history, since the era of the city states in Flanders in the 12th century, been under the rule of an alien country. This has been at times French, Spanish and German (the latter during the two World Wars of the 20th century). Despite, and perhaps in part stimulated by, these periods of dominance it has remained a self-conscious entity notwithstanding the economic, linguistic and to some extent cultural differences between north (Flemish) and south (Walloon). It seems that the large capital city Brussels, where French has been the normal language of communication, has also provided a moderating influence. Another feature of Belgian life has been the substantial increase in the proportion of the population speaking both languages – from 5-6 percent in the mid-19th century to 15-20 percent now.

The importance of the language factor has increased greatly in the 20th century. Whereas until 1830 the language situation could be described as *laisser faire* or unregulated, it is now highly regulated, as evidenced by the details of the Linguistic case. It may be partly this history that led the European Court to stand aside in that case.[15]

But why has the language factor been so significant in Belgium? It is partly that the two groups are relatively equal in size. Thus there is no clear minority status for the French speakers. While Dutch speakers represented about 53 percent of the population in 1947,[16] French speakers represented about 42 percent.[17] Both groups fear, and would be threatened by, any pronounced change in the position of the other group. A complicating factor is that, although Brussels (with 1 million of Belgium's 10 million population) is situated in the Dutch-speaking area, it is predominantly French speaking. The Dutch group in the Flemish (northern) half feel the French have something of a grip on the capital, and on the apparatus of central government administration that is located there, and they fear increasing French dominance. Hence the 1963 legislation relating to French schooling in the outer areas of Brussels. Perhaps all that can be said is that language and what it entails represents an important element in the make-up of Belgian society, and that the objective seems to be to keep the two languages on a basis of equality by legislating when or where one side seems in the ascendant.

If the European Court decision is lined up against Article 27 of the ICCPR, one would probably conclude that it represents a reasonably fair implementation. The French minority (in this case) is not *denied* the right to speak or be educated in their own language. Although the court refused to find withdrawal of the subsidy a breach of the European Convention, it did hold the cross-district embargo to be inconsistent with Article 14. The

---

15 It may be noted that, as the case was proceeding through the European Convention system, the Belgian Government was reportedly considering withdrawing its consent to the jurisdiction of the court in relation to complaints against Belgium (the jurisdiction, under Article 46 of the European Convention on Human Rights, is optional).

16 The latest year of census figures on language matters. The estimate for the 1980s is of the same general order. In 1846, a century earlier, the Dutch-speaking proportion was higher at 57 percent, the French-speaking proportion was almost exactly the same.

17 German speakers hover constantly at about 1 percent – they are located primarily south of the Flemish/Walloon divide, and in the northeast of the Walloon area, south of Aachen.

result would probably have been the same, though for slightly different reasons, if the court had been using the ICCPR.

The fine-tuning of the linguistic balance in Belgium is, as mentioned above, a continuing phenomenon. Under Prime Minister Martens, elected in 1979, a federal structure was introduced, allowing a significant measure of self-government to Dutch-speaking Flanders, French-speaking Walloon and bilingual Brussels. In 1987, after the *federal* structure had been introduced, the question arose of how to accord political representation to the French-speaking voters in the federal Parliament. In *Mathieu-Mohin and Clerfayt*, European Court of Human Rights 1987, Series A, No 113, the European Court of Human Rights rejected a claim that aspects of the new electoral law discriminated unreasonably against the French speakers in the Brussels area. The two applicants had been elected to represent *Flemish* regions of Brussels. They took their oath in French, ie identified as French rather than Dutch speakers, and so could not be members of the Flemish Council, which was given legislative powers over Flemish areas. They claimed they had been deprived by the law of the right to participate in the governance of Flemish Belgium, including the area they represented. The commission agreed.

The court, however, dismissed the claim, thus reversing the view of the commission. It examined the requirement in Article 3 of Protocol No 1 of the Convention that "elections [will be held] at reasonable intervals by secret ballot, under conditions which will ensure the free expression of the people in the choice of the legislature". It held by majority that Article 3 must be seen not so much as an "institutional" right (to certain machinery provisions relating to the holding of free elections) as a "subjective" right – a broad purposive right – to full participation in the political process.[18] As such, the question was whether Mathieu-Mohin and Clerfayt had been deprived of that right. The majority decided they had not, referring to the complex and continually changing arrangements by which the Belgian Government and Parliament were adjusting the linguistic balance. They judged the departure from strictly full participation to be within the

---

18   Note the correspondence to Article 25 of the ICCPR, which provides that every citizen is to have the right "to take part in the conduct of public affairs".

"margin of appreciation" allowed to member countries to take account of their peculiar circumstances. Accordingly, there was no need to consider whether Article 14, the anti-discrimination article, applied. On the other hand, the minority felt the departure from full participation required by Article 3 was too wide, and that Article 14 did apply – there was an unacceptable discrimination on linguistic grounds.

The conclusion to be drawn is that some linguistic discrimination is still considered acceptable by the European Court in the case of Belgium. However, it is a fine-run question, and five members of the court, as well as the commission, felt the arrangements had gone too far.

The situation of the French speakers in the Canadian Province of Quebec has some similarities to that in Belgium. Taking Canada as a whole, the French speakers there could clearly be considered a minority.[19] The French speakers in Belgium (and certainly in Quebec) hardly qualify for minority status. But language is a main issue in Canada, and the Quebecoise, who are indeed a minority in Canada taken as a whole, feel strongly enough about it to be moving towards secession. In that, they are much more extreme than the Walloons, who do not appear to be contemplating a break-up of Belgium: they perhaps fear more, incorporation in a much larger France. It is surprising the Quebecoise do not fear a similar fate with the United States, even though the language of the United States is English, as in the rest of Canada.

The concern about language is, however, great among people whose native tongue is not that of the majority. In this respect, the ICCPR has been perceptive in including language, along with religion and ethnic origin, as significant identifying features, and rallying points, for minority groups.

Language is not a criterion that most would think of when considering what kinds of minorities should be singled out as deserving of special protection. However, language is much

---

19 Out of a total population of nearly 27 million, French speakers total some 6.5 million, ie less than one quarter. The difficulty is that in *Quebec*, with a population approaching 7 million, French speakers total 5.5 million, ie about 85 percent. The only other Provinces in which there are significant numbers of French speakers are Ontario (0.5 million – about 5 percent) and New Brunswick (0.25 million – about one third).

more than a pattern of sounds, or of marks on a page. It is the embodiment of the way people see each other and the world, and carries within it the whole of their culture, their life as a community. Thus the loss or repression of language strikes a blow at life itself, in any but the barest biological/physical sense. The Australian Aborigines feel this with acute agony, as they see, one after another, their ancient languages dying out. The whole of their culture and their religion, and of the significance of groups and individuals, is lost when language disappears, or is not given the opportunity to be used and to develop as times and circumstances change. This is why language is so important to groups and individuals: it is not only a means of communication, it is a symbol for and expression of the whole of life as they have come to know it.

III. OVERVIEW

As the era of the self-contained, sovereign and largely autonomous nation state wanes, the two-pronged challenge to the state gathers momentum. The first prong is the drive of peoples towards self-determination, discussed in Chapter 2. The second prong is the increasing assertiveness of minorities within the state. The first gives rise to a need to develop more effective international agencies and more regional style co-operation, in which the European community has been giving a lead for the past four decades. The second gives rise to a need for more sensitive internal ordering of the legal and political system, so that the majority does not crush the minority, but respects and allows it to flourish, to enjoy its entity as a group. The cases of the Amish and of the French speakers of Belgium illustrate different responses to this need.

The concept of minorities is not, however, easy to grasp. Here again, the international community has given a lead. In a six-year study of the question, based on an investigation of the implementation of ICCPR Article 27, Francesco Capotorti reported in 1977 that there is wide variation in the interpretation governments give to the concept of "minority".[20] The proportion within a state, of persons claiming to be a minority is clearly

20 Capotorti, *The Rights of Minorities*, referred to in Further Reading.

important. The general view expressed to Capotorti was that the number should represent a fairly small proportion of the total population – smaller than in a state such as Yugoslavia, which is made up of a number of relatively equal groups, none of which contains a majority of the population. On the other hand, smallness is not the only criterion. The small dominant white groups in former colonial countries, for example, should not be regarded as minorities for the purposes of the Article. There was also, it was felt, a need for a subjective test, rather than a purely objective one such as those based on language (the test most commonly used in laws), or religion, or a clearly distinctive or original way of life (such as for indigenous peoples).

Capotorti proposed the following working definition of "minority" for the purpose of ICCPR Article 27 –

> A group numerically inferior to the rest of the population of a State, in a non-dominant position, whose members – being nationals of the State – possess ethnic, religious or linguistic characteristics differing from those of the rest of the population and show, if only implicitly, a sense of solidarity, directed towards preserving their culture, religion, traditions or language.[21]

Most of the special features of this definition have been mentioned above. It seems to be an effective formulation, and to have been accepted by the international community as a valuable contribution to the understanding of Article 27 and the concept of minorities. It emphasises the subjective – self-identifying – nature of a minority. By referring to "implicitly" it neatly avoids the problem of excluding the hidden or emerging minority. It would include Australia's Aborigines, and other indigenous peoples. But, as mentioned earlier, Article 27 may be too negatively framed to require the positive action – affirmative action or special measures – they may need for their preservation as peoples.

The two cases discussed in this Chapter also prompt another comment. It is that the size of the minority group, and the extent to which its members are dispersed, may have a bearing on the extent to which its position, and that of its members, can be protected. In a democratic society, a substantially sized minority may, particularly if its members are concentrated in an

---

21 Ibid, p 96.

identifiable area or areas, be expected to be able to assert its rights through the normal electoral processes. This seems to have been the case in Belgium, where the French speakers, although they were in a minority in some (Dutch-speaking) areas, had a reasonable representation in Belgium taken as a whole. It was otherwise in Wisconsin and Iowa, where the numbers of Amish – and of Mennonites generally – were small, and were also small elsewhere. There, the United States Supreme Court was well justified in according the Amish virtually all they asked, although what they wanted was substantial: exemption from the entire high school system. There would have been little remedy for them through the normal political processes.

On the other hand, it is hard to see such a privileged position being accorded a large minority of any kind. The remedies for the larger group would be, as suggested above, through the normal political processes; or through claiming that specific rights, such as the right to freedom of religion, or to liberty and security of person, or to education or health care, were being infringed. Their remedies would be as for any other member of the population who suffered the same or similar violations. The more homogeneous a community is, and the more it has rights-protecting arrangements in place, eg through a bill of rights, the less there will be a need for special measures to protect minorities. The general law will provide fair recourse for any individual whose rights are not being adequately respected.

On a broader plane, it can be expected that governments will, in the coming years, have to grapple with the claims of increasing numbers of minority groups. New religious, ethnic and even political groups will emerge, and make their claims for special treatment. It will be important to distinguish genuine minorities – those of long standing, with self-identifying features and with continuing self-awareness – from ephemeral pressure-groups wanting to achieve specific goals, such as the repeal of a particular law (eg compulsory breath testing, provision of rights for animals, or censorship of certain publications), or the modification of a particular administrative system (eg paternity leave for fathers, protection of native forests, or new ways of paying benefits). These groups have an important place in the life of a community, but their claims should be handled through the normal political processes, and not through the special rights accorded to self-aware and continuing minority communities that have a life, culture, religion and often language of their own.

For Further Reading

Two good books on the Amish are *Amish Society*, by J A Hostetler, John Hopkins, 1980 for a general overview, and *Community Conflict, Public Opinion and the Law: The Amish Dispute in Iowa*, by H R Rogers Jr, Merrill, Columbus, 1969. There is also a useful update by MaryAnn Ruegger "An Audience for the Amish: A Communication Based Approach to the Development of Law" in (1991) 66 *Indiana Law Journal* p 801.

There is a very useful survey of the human rights of minorities under the ICCPR by Professor Sohn, "The Rights of Minorities" in L Henkin (ed), *The International Bill of Rights: The Covenant on Civil and Political Rights*, West, 1981. The report by Francesco Capotorti, which was commissioned by the Sub-Commission on the Prevention of Discrimination and the Protection of Minorities, is *Study on the Rights of Persons belonging to Ethnic, Religious and Linguistic Minorities* and was published by the United Nations, New York, in 1979. It contains a good survey of the problems of definition, and proposals for improving the protection of minorities, though these have not yet been taken up.

The most comprehensive book on the Belgian situation is *Conflict and Compromise in Multilingual Societies* by Kenneth McCrae, Wilfrid Laurier, Canada, 1983. It is in effect a case study of the Belgian situation, but sets it in a broader context. A more specific study, focusing particularly on Brussels and the languages used, is *Interdisciplinary Study of Urban Bilingualism in Brussels*, edited by Els Witte and Hugo Beardsmore, Philadelphia, 1987.

PART II

"Life Problems" – Euthanasia, Privacy and the Environment

No man is an Island, entire of it self; every man is a piece of the Continent, a part of the main; if a clod be washed away by the sea, Europe is the less, as well as if a promontory were, as well as if a manor of thy friends or of thine own were; any man's death diminishes me, because I am involved in Mankind; And therefore never send to know for whom the bell tolls; it tolls for thee.

From Meditation XVII of John Donne (1571-1631), on the ringing of a bell for the death of another.

The central issues in this Part are who decides when a person's life is to end, what rights we have "to be let alone" by the state and others in authority, and whether we have a right to some kind of sustainable environment. Each of these rights is vital to human wellbeing. What rights do we have as individuals to protect ourselves in the whole context of our environment?

Chapter 4

Baby J and Karen Quinlan

The Right to Life (1) – Euthanasia for Persons Who Cannot Make Their Own Choices

I. BABY J

The Story. Baby J was born 13 weeks early, on 28 May 1990. He weighed 1.1 kilos (2lb 8oz) and was not breathing. He was put on a ventilator[1] and was fed by a drip. His condition was very poor for the first few days, but he was able to be taken off the ventilator when he was about a month old. Unhappily, he had a series of convulsions which required further use of the ventilator, each use involving some overall deterioration in his condition.

When he was about three months old – at the end of August – Baby J was allowed to go home. He choked three days later, on 1 September, and became cyanosed. He was taken back to hospital and there had a series of fits, which prevented his carers taking him off the ventilator. About three weeks later, after a series of unsuccessful attempts, it became possible to wean him from the ventilator.

J's condition and prospects were carefully assessed by an experienced paediatrician. His advice was that J was now so seriously weakened by his troubles that if he were again to stop breathing, another episode on the ventilator would not be in his

---

1   Putting a person on a mechanical ventilator, which was what was involved here, is an intrusive process. It involves insertion of a naso-gastric tube, drips which need frequently to be resited (relocated), and constant blood sampling.

best interests. However, the doctor added that if he were to pick up a chest infection, manual ventilation, and antibiotics, might be appropriate, provided the ventilation was not prolonged.

J was now a ward of court, for "extraneous" reasons which the court did not explain. The initial judge decided on 11 October, on application by the local government authority in the area in which J and his parents lived, to order treatment as proposed by the paediatrician. That involved deciding that it was not necessary to make every effort to maintain J's life. On 19 October the case was taken to the Court of Appeal.[2] The court observed that, despite all the efforts by his carers and parents, his prospects seemed poor. He had irreparable brain damage because of lack of oxygen and was likely all his life to be quadriplegic,[3] and unable to sit by himself. He would almost certainly be blind, and probably deaf and unable to speak at all. He might be able to show pain, but probably would have no way of showing pleasure. His life expectancy was likely to be short – he could hardly survive beyond his late teens.

The court unanimously agreed that the doctor's proposal for treatment should be followed. It said that, in the normal course, such a decision would be taken by the doctors and the parents. The obligation of parents is to make their decision in the best interests of the child "and without regard to their own interests". When a child is a ward of court, the only difference is that the doctors will look to the court, rather than to the parents, for any necessary decisions. But, said Lord Donaldson of Lymington, the Master of the Rolls –

> No one can dictate the treatment to be given to the child – neither court, parents nor doctors. ... The ... inevitable and desirable result is that choice of treatment is in some measure a joint decision of the doctors and the court or parents.

Discussion. An unfortunate side effect of the greatly increased skills of doctors and hospitals is that it will be possible, with great and costly effort, to keep alive more babies with really terrible disabilities, at least where modern medical technology is

---

2   The case was written up in the British *Daily Telegraph* of Saturday October 20. It is reported as *In re J (A Minor) (Wardship: Medical Treatment)* [1991] 2 WLR 140.

3   This means that he would have had no control of his legs or arms.

available. The question is whether, as is argued by some right to life advocates, these unfortunate children have an unqualified right to life, or whether Clough's words[4] more accurately summarise the position –

> Thou shalt not kill; but needst not strive
> Officiously to keep alive.

The Court of Appeal in England has taken the position described by Clough.

In discussing J's case, the court referred to two other cases, those of *In re C (A Minor)* [1989] 3 WLR 240 and *In re B (A Minor)* [1981] 1 WLR 1421. Baby C was dying, and the court authorised that she be given palliative care only. Baby B was seriously disabled, but had the expectation of life of a Down's syndrome child, and the court ordered that her life be sustained.

Baby C was born in December 1988 and when the court, which had become C's ward, heard the application she was 16 weeks old. She was suffering from congenital hydrocephalus, and was assessed by her doctors to be incurable – treatment would only prolong the dying process. The social workers, on the other hand, felt she should be treated as any sick child and have another operation to drain the fluid from her head. The court decided that any treatment should be designed to "ease the suffering ... rather than to achieve a short prolongation of her life". "Baby C is dying" said Lord Donaldson.

Baby B[5] had Down's syndrome. Her life expectation was perhaps 20-30 years. Lord Templeman said the important question was not what the parents or doctors wanted (the parents did not want to save her) but –

> ... solely what was in the best interests of the child ... it was not for the court to decide that the child should not have the chance of the normal life span of a mongoloid child with the handicap, defects and life of such a child.

He said no court would order cessation of treatment unless the prospects were "demonstrably awful".

So the British courts have focused on the joint nature of the decisions to be taken They have emphasised the importance of

---

4   Arthur Hugh Clough (1819-61), in "The Latest Decalogue", published in *Poems*, 1862 and referred to in the judgment of Lord Donaldson in *Re J*.

5   *In re B (A Minor)* [1981] 1 WLR 1421.

deciding for the child him or herself, not simply for the concerned adult, parent, doctor, court or social worker. Different approaches have been developed in accordance with the different circumstances of the case. Where there is no future, as in Baby C's case, they have recognised that palliative rather than curative treatment is appropriate when life itself is ebbing. That is, they do not order treatment at all costs. Where however there is some future, however bleak, as in Baby B's case, they have protected the right to life by holding that once it can be established that the child has some expectation of life, no court can order steps which would lead to its death.

In between comes the case of Baby J. The decision is significant, because for the first time a court has been willing to make judgments about the likely quality of life of the child: if that is not adequate (as would have been the case if another mechanical ventilation episode was required to maintain J's life), then sustaining treatment need not be continued.

The agonising problem all the cases give rise to, relates to the decision on how strictly the "demonstrably awful" test will be applied. In Baby J's case we see the court deciding that, for the time being, the "demonstrably awful" situation was not present; but also prepared to make the decision that, if further mechanical ventilation proved necessary, it would be, and the baby could be allowed to die.

Taking a wider perspective, all countries, in their homicide laws and sometimes in their Bills of Rights, recognise that life is extremely precious and must be protected. As Article 6 of the ICCPR says –

> Every human being has the inherent right to life. This right shall be protected by law. No one shall be arbitrarily deprived of his life.

Gravely disabled children have not, as the stories show, been treated as having an absolute right to life. Precious as life is, it is difficult to claim for it an absoluteness that rules out other considerations such as suffering, a person's own clear decision that he or she no longer wants to live, or the need to choose when hospital equipment and other resources are limited and are needed for someone else. An absolute right would, in such circumstances, lead to consequences that most would view as undesirable, such as the possibility of bringing actions against the state, a hospital or a doctor, for preferring to save one person's life over another's. The important objective is, as the ICPPR says, that every individual's "inherent" right to life be respected, and protected by law.

The case of the disabled infant inevitably raises the question who it is that should make the decision about the child's future. As mentioned above, the British courts have left the matter to collective decision. On the other hand, the courts in the United States have tended to place more emphasis on the family. In *Bowen v American Hospital Association* 476 US 610 (1986), the Supreme Court decided that the parents were the ones who had the power to decide whether their child was to be supported or allowed to die. It said that the federal authorities could not interfere in the decision and that the privacy of family life should be respected. However, in both Britain and the United States the formal legal position is that, notwithstanding the case of Baby J, it would be a criminal offence to determine to kill the child. The law distinguishes between *motive* and *intent*. It focuses on intent. Under the law, if you *intend* to kill, no matter what your motive (with some exceptions such as self-defence), you are guilty. In *morals*, motive is the more important: if you kill to save further extreme suffering, that is acceptable. It seems to the author that the law has to preserve the principle that people may not kill others, ie may not have as their main motive the killing of another. However, recognising that modern medical magic can extend the powers we have over life and death and the processes between, the law must refine the exceptions in a way that gives primacy (but not absolute primacy) to the interests of the suffering person, ie may need to allow a killing when there are extreme degrees of suffering or disability, or when the situation of another person is judged to have greater claims to the scarce resource required, eg a ventilator.

II. THE CASE OF KAREN QUINLAN

The Story. On the evening of 15 April 1975 Karen Quinlan, then aged 22, ceased breathing for at least two 15-minute periods. She lived in New Jersey, not much more than 100km northwest of New York City. Despite the efforts of her friends, she remained unconscious. Although she was taken to the Newton Memorial Hospital, and later to Saint Clare's Hospital, Denville, she failed to recover consciousness. The cause of her collapse was never diagnosed. She showed signs of brain stem (cortex) damage and needed a respirator. After several days, her doctors assessed her as being in a "chronic vegetative state".[6] Although not "brain dead", her prospects of recovery to any kind of "sapient" state, when she could see, feel, talk or think, were negligible. On the other hand, supported by a respirator and by a nasal-gastro tube and an intensive care staff, it seemed that she could remain in the lower, non-sapient or "vegetative" state for years.

After she had been in hospital for nearly 8 months, her father appealed to the Supreme Court of New Jersey to have her declared incompetent and to confer on him the power, as her guardian, to discontinue all extraordinary medical procedures. The Supreme Court decided, contrary to the earlier decision of the Superior Court, to issue the order sought. The order was to the effect that, after consultation with the attending physicians and with the Hospital Ethics Committee, and agreement that no reasonable possibility of recovery to the sapient state existed, the life-support systems could be withdrawn. They were, in the end, withdrawn but Karen Quinlan remained alive, in the "vegetative" state, for some 10 years.

The court based its decision to allow withdrawal of the support systems on two grounds. The first and primary ground was the constitutional right to privacy. The second and less significant was based on the ancient common law right of each individual to self-determination – to decide whether to accept and continue with medical treatment.

Discussion. Since the path-breaking case of Karen Quinlan, many State courts in the United States have considered these issues. Gradually, it seems to have been accepted that one of the most important questions is whether the patient did actually express the wish at an earlier time not to be maintained in a vegetative state. This invokes the right of the individual to self-determination, and that was affirmed in *Gray v Romeo* 697 F

---

6   This is a condition in which body temperature, breathing, chewing and swallowing, sleeping and waking and to some degree heart rate and blood pressure are controlled, but none of the "higher" or "sapient" functions.

Supp 580 (DRI 1988). Marcia Gray, a married woman and mother of two children, who was in her early forties, collapsed in January 1986 with a major brain haemorrhage, while shopping at a Rhode Island store. For 16 months, efforts were made to bring her back to consciousness. In May 1987 her family, in despair and accepting the medical verdict that there was no reasonable likelihood that she would recover consciousness, sought an order from the court that nutrition and hydration should cease, thereby leaving her to die with whatever palliative care could be given. The main ground for the decision was her basic right to self-determination, rather than the constitutional right to privacy, which had been the primary ground in the Quinlan case. Marcia had, in conversations with various members of the family, criticised keeping Karen Quinlan alive by artificial means, and evidence to this effect was given in, and accepted by, the court.

The hospital and the caring staff – management, nurses and doctors – were not happy with the proposal. They did not wish, on religious or moral grounds, to embark on a procedure that they saw as in effect killing Marcia. They opposed the proposal and asked to be permitted to continue caring. They pointed to the state interest in the right to life. They identified the state interests as being to preserve life, to prevent suicide, to protect innocent third parties and to maintain the integrity of medical ethics. They felt these outweighed the interest of the patient in self-determination.

The court reached an ingenious compromise. It said it would respect the right to practise one's religion and beliefs and so would not order the hospital to withdraw the treatment. However, if the hospital was not willing to withdraw the systems, it must transfer the patient to a hospital that would. If it would not do this, it must accede to her wishes that her life not be prolonged. Thus the weighting – the balancing of the rights of those involved – was more in favour of the right of the individual to self-determination than of the rights of the carers to act according to their religion or beliefs. Unless the hospital clearly expresses its position (when a move of a patient may occur, as with Marcia Gray), the right of the individual will, it seems, prevail over that of the medical personnel.

The only case on these issues that has so far reached the United States Supreme Court involved a young woman, Nancy Cruzan, who was injured in a motor accident in Missouri. She was reduced to the "vegetative" state. The Missouri legislature, wanting to protect life if at all possible, had made it unlawful to terminate treatment unless there was "clear and convincing evidence" that the patient would have wanted this. Accordingly, Ms Cruzan's parents asked the court (*Nancy Beth Cruzan by her parents and co-guardians v Director, Missouri Department Health* (1990) 58 Law Week 4916) to declare the legislation invalid because it infringed her rights to privacy and autonomy.

The majority, led by Chief Justice Rehnquist, emphasised the right of the state to regulate matters in this difficult area and pronounced the legislation to be within power.

The minority, led by Justice Brennan, said a vital right of the individual was being eliminated by the majority decision. He mentioned two main grounds for his view. The first was that "no State interest could outweigh the rights of an individual in Nancy Cruzan's position". The second was that the legislation was "markedly asymmetrical" in that it placed a much heavier burden of evidence on the supporters of the patient than on the carers. Those wanting to have the treatment terminated had to show clear evidence of the patient's wish. Those wanting to maintain the treatment did not: "No proof is required to support a finding that the incompetent person would wish to continue treatment".

The need of the state to protect the lives of its citizens is here starkly opposed to the right of individuals to lead their own lives and, *in extremis*, to decide whether to live or die. It is not so much a question whether one has a right to die. The author believes one does not. First, a right to die is in a sense opposed to a right to life. Second, there are dangers of misuse to which a claimed right to die might be put in the hands of ill-disposed governments and authorities. Third, the right to life itself is comprehensive enough to allow for a dignified ending. The real question is how to balance the obligations of the state and the rights of the individual. On this matter, the author would see the preferable course as being to give the unfortunate individual rather more scope, for example through enabling legislation and a register of a person's wishes to determine, for him or herself, whether continued vegetative existence is desirable. But the message is clear: if one wants to be sure, one should write something down, and preferably consult one's lawyers first.

III. OVERVIEW

The several stories briefly told show how difficult are the problems of ensuring that the incompetent person is guaranteed his or her right to life and of balancing that against the rights of others involved. It does not seem tenable to argue that the incompetent person has an absolute right to life. Too many other people have rights, such as those of carers to express their religion and of families to protection from disruption. At the same time, the incompetent person must be protected from the many often seemingly persuasive reasons for putting an end to his or her life. Relatives and friends can too quickly tire of the burden, often financial as well as emotional, of sustaining the life of an incompetent person. The state also could raise the point – though this does not yet seem to have happened – that the cost of maintaining a half-life existence is not justified in the interests of efficient use of the health dollar.

What we have seen is a painful, step-by-step, but not always consistent, development by the courts of the United States and the United Kingdom of a rational basis for dealing with the problems that occur at the margin. The British courts have been more willing to state absolutely that no action may be taken to terminate a life. The American courts have been more ready to recognise the religious and moral problems of the carers. American state legislatures have attempted to lay down some principles, as in the Gray case. All have been willing, if hesitantly, to consider quality of life issues, though not as the principal determinant.

Three main professional disciplines, each with its own role and standards, are involved in these issues. The medical profession has its role as carer, the religious as guardian of values and the legal as protector of rights. On the more personal side, the incompetent person him or herself, and his or her near relatives and friends, have an interest primarily in autonomy and quality of life issues, and the state has interests in ensuring observance of the right to life. It has been suggested that the legal framework is unsuitable for solving medical questions?[7] While this may be too sweeping, there is a case for taking the view that the courts have now gone a substantial way toward stating principles to guide the principal actors in the situation – parents or near friends, doctors and other carers, and the state. The principles seem to strike a fair balance between the rights to life (including the right to surrender that life) and to privacy of the incompetent person, and the general protection of the right to life by the state. Once the principles can be stated, the carers will be liberated to work within them, and the courts will be able to withdraw to their traditional role as protectors and enforcers.

One other issue needs mentioning. It relates to the old and respected proposition that where life is at the margin, only "ordinary" and not "extraordinary" measures should be adopted. That was a doctrine developed primarily by the Catholic church. But it is no longer capable of clear application, as indeed the Sacred Congregation for the Doctrine of the Faith observed in its penetrating and helpful Declaration on Euthanasia in 1980. Nor, really, is the "proportionate-disproportionate" criterion for treatment it suggested as a substitute. The ordinary/extraordinary criterion is no longer really helpful because of the difficulty of determining what is an "ordinary" measure. Where does one stop – at drips, at mechanical lungs, at heart-lung machines, and in what combination? The proportionate/disproportionate criterion is not satisfactory because it risks an oversimplified economic assessment of the worth of life. What seems to be emerging is the need for a clearer statement of the implications of the main principles involved – privacy, personal autonomy (if these two are not the same – see Chapter 6) and the sanctity of life. As David Suzuki said, "Aiming for life at all costs, *regardless of its quality*, simply does not take into account the reality of today's technologically sophisticated world, where issues are far more profound and difficult than they once were". (Emphasis added.)

What the courts have slowly, and on the whole consistently, been doing, as cases have come to them, is to work out the best way of ensuring that enjoyment of each of the fundamental

---

7   See, for example, Lerwick P, "Withdrawal of Life-sustaining Treatment: Patients' Rights – Privacy Rights" in [1990] 42 *Maine Law Review* 193, at 214.

rights involved is maximised, without disregarding the human and political elements in the situation. Thus in the case of Re J, taken with the cases of Re B and Re C, it is now clear that the sanctity of life is of high, but not absolute, value; and that account can be taken of *quality* of life – surely a very important principle if one is thinking of rights as enabling mechanisms. In Quinlan, the importance of personal autonomy is recognised, along with the role of the state in protecting the right to life. In Gray, the rights of the carers are articulated. The "inherent right to life" provided for in the ICCPR is steadily and sympathetically being clarified and applied.

For Further Reading

The cases referred to in the text contain a wealth of discussion of the issues. Particularly in the case of Nancy Cruzan, where the Supreme Court divided, there are both an interesting expression of differences, and two very lively dissenting opinions by Justice Brennan (with whom Justices Marshall and Blackmun joined) and Justice Stevens.

The author's text, *Human Rights: Australia in an International Context,* Butterworths, 1990, contains in Chapter 9 an analysis of the right to life, and a study of the problems and rights involved in the case of the severely disabled newborn infant. A more comprehensive, and really illuminating study is contained in the book by Helga Kuhse and Peter Singer, *Should the Baby Live?*, Oxford, 1985, a paperback by two Australian authors.

On more specific issues, the article by Patricia Lerwick referred to in footnote 7 is good in its analysis of the principles involved in the mid-life case, and Irene Prior Loftus examines the carers issue in "I Have a Conscience Too: The Plight of Medical Personnel Confronting the Right to Die" (1990) 65 *Notre Dame Law Review* 699. She also considers whether the courts should order institutions, as distinct from individuals, to perform actions such as directing their staff to remove life support systems.

The Nancy Cruzan and Mary O'Connor cases are analysed carefully by Sandra H Johnson in "From Medicalization to Legalization to Politicization: O'Connor, Cruzan and Refusal of Treatment in the 1990s" (1989) 21 *Connecticut Law Review* 685.

Chapter 5

The Cases of Debbie and

Mrs Janet Adkins

The Right to Life (2) – Euthanasia for

Persons Capable of Choosing

I. DEBBIE

The Story. Debbie, aged 20, was dying of an ovarian cancer. She was in her hospital bed wracked with pain and having difficulty breathing. As she breathed, her whole frame heaved. It was late at night, and standing beside her was a middle-aged woman, holding her hand. Debbie had not eaten or slept for two days, and was being maintained by intravenous drip and oxygen by nasal tube. The alcohol drip she was being given for sedation was apparently causing repeated vomiting. She looked older than her 20 years, and her weight had reduced to 36 kilos.

A resident doctor in the hospital was woken from sleep to give her assistance. He or she was not happy to be woken, knowing that the next day would not be easy to get through. As the doctor, who had not seen Debbie before, looked at her card, it was apparent that she had not long to live, that she had not responded to chemotherapy, and that she was being given supportive care only. What should be done?

At this moment, Debbie managed to gasp "Let's get this over with". The doctor left the bedside and, at the nurse's station, reflected on what should be done. The patient was tired and needed rest, and the case was terminal. A course of action was decided. The nurse on duty was asked to draw 20 milligrams of morphine sulphate into a syringe, which the doctor then took to the room and administered to Debbie. Within a few seconds her breathing eased. Her eyes closed, and she began to look less strained. The woman beside her bed stroked her hair and within four minutes her breathing slowed, became irregular and ceased. It was over.[1]

Discussion. We do not know the name, age or sex of the doctor, or whether the woman beside Debbie's bed was her mother or someone else. However, we do know that there was an outcry in the United States that a doctor not in charge of Debbie's case had decided, alone and in the middle hours of the night, to give her a dose of morphine that was calculated to bring her life to an end. We also know that the doctor, while apparently acting in accord with Debbie's wishes, had not seen her before and did not consult with her own doctor, or her relatives or friends. Four doctors who signed their names wrote in protest to the *American Medical Association Journal* and offered the view that "on his (sic) own admission, the resident appears to have committed a felony: premeditated murder".[2]

The doctors' view of the law is almost certainly correct. Even if Debbie's mind was sufficiently clear to enable her to give consent to cessation of treatment, and the message as the doctor had received it was to that effect, it was still murder. The law as it stands in countries deriving their law from Britain still mostly defines any act of deliberate killing as murder, no matter what the motive (the only exceptions being killing enemy combatants in time of war and killing in self-defence).[3] Thus the right to life as an inherent and inalienable right is respected. Indeed, it is only fairly recently that the decision of the autonomous person to commit suicide has ceased to be a criminal offence.[4] In law,

---

1　The story is based on the article in (1988) 259 *Journal of the American Medical Association*. It is also told in Baird R M and Rosenbaum S E, (eds), *Euthanasia*, Prometheus, New York, 1989 and in Van J, "It's over, Debbie: A Doctor confesses to mercy killing", *Canberra Times*, 10 February 1988.

2　The letter was reproduced in *Euthanasia*, cited fn 1, p 25.

3　As to the distinction in law between "motive" and "intent", see Chapter 4, p 55.

4　In fact, of course, the crime was really only to *fail* in a suicide attempt, although undesirable consequences followed a *successful* attempt eg in relation to burial in a church cemetery.

recognition of the right of a person to take his or her life, ie to surrender the right to life, does not extend to others who might be willing to assist. The law is clear: another may not assist in a suicide. Nor may another intentionally kill, either by refraining from an act, eg by not giving available care, or by doing an act, as in the case of the doctor in Debbie's case.

The question arises: have we got the balance right? It is a fearful thing to kill another, even at that other's request. It is easy to see the dangers in the kind of action that occurred in Debbie's case. Did she really want to die then? Was her mind sufficiently clear? Should her own doctor, or her relatives, have been consulted? The answers to all those questions are probably not in favour of what the doctor did in her case. But are there circumstances in which a person should be able to get help in having his or her own life brought to a close?

Increasingly, popular polls seem to show that people believe a person with a terminal illness and who is in torment, as Debbie was, should be able to have relief through death. In some countries, there is now "living wills" or "natural death" legislation[5] that allows a doctor to refrain from further treatment if a person has a terminal illness and has clearly stated a desire to die.[6] In Victoria, an enduring power of attorney allows a named person to make a decision to prevent further treatment if the person executing the power is terminally ill and not himself or herself competent to decide.

But as yet in Anglo-American law there is no measure that allows the next step to be taken. The next step is the one the doctor took in Debbie's case. It is by a *specific positive action* to terminate the patient's life (or, if one wants to use that hard word, to "kill"), at the patient's request. People are properly

---

5   Living wills legislation exists in California and in several other states in the United States. In South Australia, the Natural Death Act 1983 allows a person to make and lodge a declaration that will allow the doctor to terminate treatment in the event of a terminal illness. In Victoria, the Consent to Medical Treatment Act 1985 makes it a tort, ie a wrongful but not a criminal action, to treat a person if consent is refused, and also, as mentioned in the text, allows execution of a continuing power of attorney.

6   The English/Australian phrase is "terminal illness", but the situation is sometimes termed "incurable illness". The phrase "terminal illness" will be used because it carries the meaning of the phrase more accurately – that the person has an illness from which there is no recovery, and that his or her condition is such that there is no prospect of even brief recovery.

cautious about pressing for this. If it can be said that refraining from further treatment is not euthanasia, but simply recognising the futility, and perhaps even the cruelty, of striving to maintain a life by further treatment, then this form of "killing" would be euthanasia in its least objectionable form. It would go beyond what the Catholic Declaration on Euthanasia would allow? That document accepts that –

> When *inevitable death is imminent* in spite of the means used, it is permitted in conscience to take the decision to *refuse* forms of treatment that would only secure a precarious and burdensome *prolongation* of life, so long as the normal care due to the sick person in similar cases is not interrupted. In such circumstances the doctor has no reason to reproach himself with failing to help the person in danger. (Emphases added.)

However –

> It is necessary to state firmly once more that nothing and no one can in any way permit the killing of an innocent human being, whether a foetus or an embryo, an infant or an adult, an old person, or one suffering from an incurable disease, or a person who is dying. Furthermore, no one is permitted to ask for this act of killing either for himself or herself or for another person entrusted to his or her care, nor can he or she consent to it, either explicitly or implicitly.[8]

In some European countries, and also in China and Japan, the need for a degree of flexibility in the difficult area of taking actions that will hasten the dying process has been recognised. Without going into details, the homicide laws in those countries have been brought into a form of harmony by refining the categories of killing. Premeditated murder is the crime most severely punished. In the middle comes often an offence of assisting in a suicide. At the other extreme, Norway makes it an offence, but provides no specific penalty, for killing a terminally ill person at his or her request.[9] Suicide itself is not made an offence. For the offence of killing a terminally ill person, the judge is left to determine what the penalty should be. In the Netherlands, there is now a willingness to allow euthanasia for

---

7   *Declaration on Euthanasia*, Sacred Congregation for the Doctrine of the Faith, 1980, p 9.
8   Ibid, p 5.
9   The information here is contained in an article by Helen Silving, and the full reference is given in Further Reading.

the terminally ill. The situation there is discussed in Section II below, in relation to the case of Mrs Adkins.

For countries whose law draws on British legal tradition, there is no underlying recognition that there are different kinds of killing and that only some of them should be regarded as criminal offences. Any change in this direction would have to be taken only after much careful discussion. Any killing for its own sake is a grave step, and all one can do is to explore carefully what changes could be made in the interests of just treatment of those who kill for responsible reasons. The author believes it is time for discussions to start on the process of exploring possible alternatives to the present law. Although any act as unilateral and uninformed by consultation as that of the doctor in Debbie's case seems unacceptable, it should stand as a warning and not as a total impediment to careful revision of the law, perhaps based on European precedents.

II. The Case of Mrs Adkins

The Story. Mrs Janet Adkins, formerly a teacher of English, lived in Portland, the largest city of the State of Oregon. Oregon State is in northwestern United States, just south of Washington State and north of California. Mrs Adkins was diagnosed in 1989 as having Alzheimer's disease. She greatly feared the gradual deterioration that would follow, and the burden that she would place on her relatives and friends. Although life expectancy for people developing the disease in their early fifties is reasonably substantial (Mrs Adkins was 53 at the time of the diagnosis), there is no known cure for it. As the mental faculties of the sufferer deteriorate, those who have to care for the person find the task increasingly difficult (the sufferer may stray from home, lose things, forget things). Caring also becomes increasingly distressing particularly if, as often happens, personality changes occur. Since Alzheimer's disease tends to run in families, Mrs Adkins may have had to watch her own parent or elder relative, and the family, go through the torment on other occasions. Was it not reasonable that she should want to surrender her life to avoid her own inevitable deterioration, and the pain and hurt that would follow for her closest family and friends? What she wanted was euthanasia in the least awful form – to prevent an incurable illness taking its inexorable, distressing path.

So Mrs Adkins decided to fly, with her husband, to Detroit to seek the assistance of Dr Jack Kevorkian, a physician aged 62. Dr Kevorkian had made known the facilities he was willing to make available to people wishing to end their lives quickly and painlessly. He believed it was important that people should have a way of terminating their own lives in that way.

Dr Kevorkian had the intention, it seems, of taking some care to ensure that the people he assisted were suffering from an incurable illness, that they were fully aware of the finality of the process, and that they had the firm intention of terminating their lives. He himself did not activate the apparatus he had constructed. He joined his patients to it, and told them that, when they pushed the relevant button, a lethal combination of chemicals would enter their bloodstream. It would kill them quickly and without pain. For that purpose, he had equipped a 1968 van in a park about 65km north of Detroit, to which his patients could come. He videotaped an interview he had with Mrs Adkins before proceeding to link her to the machine. Then, on 4 June 1990, he linked her to the device. There, watched by him, she pressed the button and quickly lapsed into unconsciousness. Shortly afterwards, death followed.

The authorities in Oakland County announced in December that they would charge Dr Kevorkian with murder. Prosecutor Richardson commented that "For me not to charge Dr Kevorkian would turn Oakland County into the suicide mecca of our nation". However, later in the month, a District Court judge refused to allow the charge on the ground that Mrs Adkins had caused her own death. This put the authorities in a dilemma, because in Michigan, unlike most states, it is not an offence to assist suicide. What they sought instead was a civil remedy, by way of an injunction, to prevent Dr Kevorkian using his machine again. The court granted that injunction on an interim (temporary) basis. On 5 February 1991, Judge Alice Gilbert of the Oakland County Circuit Court made the injunction permanent.

Judge Gilbert did not disguise her dislike of what had occurred. She commented that, in the way the suicide had been assisted – without lengthy and careful interviewing and in hardly suitable surroundings – the standards and codes of medical practice appeared to have been "flagrantly violated". At the trial, she noted that what was being offered was a "crude, homemade device". She said that although a videotape had been made of Mrs Adkins' discussion of her suicide with Dr Kevorkian, it did not reveal either that Mrs Adkins' desire was firm or that any of the available alternatives had been properly explored.[10]

In the year that has followed the proceedings related to Mrs Adkins, four more people have been assisted to die. On 23 October 1991, Ms Marjorie Wantz, 58, and Ms Sherry Miller, 43, died. Neither of them suffered from a terminal illness, though both were sufferers: Ms Wantz from chronic pelvic pain and Ms Miller from multiple sclerosis. On May 15 1992, Ms Susan Williams, 54, a multiple sclerosis sufferer, also died with Dr Kevorkian's assistance. The fifth person was Ms Lois Hawes, aged 53. She was afflicted with terminal lung cancer. She died on 26 September 1992.[11] These arrangements were made despite a court order in March 1992 to desist, and despite his being struck off the medical register in November 1991. In the courts, the murder charges relating to Ms Wantz and Ms Miller were dismissed, along the same lines as the charge in relation to Mrs Adkins.

Discussion. What is first to be noted is that, in Mrs Adkins' case, the doctor enabled her to terminate her life before it got to the "terminal" stage. So in one respect it went beyond what the doctor did in Debbie's case: Debbie was in the terminal stages of her cancer, while Mrs Adkins still had an expectation of perhaps some years of reasonably viable, though admittedly deteriorating, life.[12] Mrs Adkins' illness, although fatal and incurable, was not, in the sense used in discussions of these issues, terminal. Dr Kevorkian went even further with the cases

---

10   The information for this story comes from reports in the *Canberra Times*, 5 December 1990 and in Edward Walsh, "Court Bars Use of 'Suicide Machine'", *Washington Post*, 6 February 1991, Final Edition. I am indebted for the latter article to Dr Bill Andreen, a member of the Faculty of Law, University of Alabama.

11   A sixth person has also used Dr Kevorkian's machine – the *Canberra Times*, 25 November 1992.

12   In another respect, it did not go as far: the doctor in Debbie's case in effect decided actively to terminate her life, whereas Dr Kevorkian simply assisted Mrs Adkins to terminate her own life by providing facilities.

of Ms Wantz, Ms Miller and Ms Williams. Their ailments were not even fatal in the same sense as Mrs Adkins'.

In the Netherlands, there has been active discussion, for over two decades, and some litigation, about active as distinct from passive euthanasia. The terms "passive" and "active" euthanasia are used to distinguish between allowing a patient to die (passive), and actually accelerating, or even initiating, death (active). Assisting a suicide falls between, because it is now recognised in most legal systems that a person may take his or her own life (suicide). But for obvious reasons, there has been much more caution, as mentioned above, about persons assisting in a suicide: it is so easy for malpractice to occur.

"Active" euthanasia would have occurred in the action of the doctor in Debbie's case, assuming he acted of his own volition and was not in effect assisting a suicide. There is no evidence of the latter, even if he was motivated simply to do what she wanted – which was that her suffering be brought to an end. On the other hand, Dr Kevorkian, although making the suicide facilities available to Mrs Adkins and others, clearly did not himself kill her. But one can see how dangerous it could be to regard the mechanistic provision of suicide facilities as being altogether outside the scope of homicide laws.

In the Netherlands, and indeed in many other countries, passive euthanasia – the stopping of treatment – has been practised for some time, provided there has been an active and well-informed request by the patient. Indeed, as mentioned in Section I above, there is now legislation in some jurisdictions that allows "passive" euthanasia at the patient's request.

In the Netherlands there has also been some practising of "active" euthanasia. What has been happening suggests that doctors, the community and the judges there are, to a degree, willing to take or allow active euthanasia. But the steps have been careful: "active" euthanasia is practised by doctors and condoned by the courts only when the patient is informed, "earnestly requests"[13] cessation, and is terminally ill.

---

13   "Earnestly requests" is a phrase often used in discussions of euthanasia for terminally ill patients and is designed to emphasise the need for a patient to be altogether clear in his or her own mind that euthanasia is wanted, and wanted urgently or pressingly.

The matter was tested in the Dutch courts in 1984 in the Alkmaar case. Dr Alkmaar gave his patient, a 95-year-old woman, a series of injections that resulted in her death. She was seriously ill, and there was no prospect of improvement. She suffered a deterioration in her condition and when she recovered consciousness pleaded that her life be terminated, as she had done on earlier occasions. After consulting his assistant physician and the patient's son, both of whom agreed that he should give the injections, he administered them. Apart from the patient's own wishes, Dr Alkmaar had formed the clear view that her suffering was unbearable and that he should accede to her clearly expressed desire.

In the Court of Appeals of Amsterdam, Dr Alkmaar was convicted of murder, but no sentence was imposed. The High Court, to which Dr Alkmaar appealed, reversed the decision. It did this on the ground that the Amsterdam Court had not sufficiently taken into account a number of circumstances. It mentioned specifically the need for a court with such a case before it to consider what the consequences of sustaining the patient's life would have been for her; whether there was any way her suffering could have been alleviated; and whether, if the doctor had refrained from the action she wished, she would have reached a stage where she could no longer die with dignity.

At about the same time (in 1985), the Netherlands State Commission on Euthanasia, which had been appointed in 1982, produced its report. It recommended that a doctor or other person terminating a person's life at that person's explicit request should be punishable, but that an exception should be made for a doctor who took the action on the basis of the desperate, unbearable and irreversible situation of the patient. In other words, it advocated the recognition of active euthanasia at the request of a terminally ill and severely suffering person. However, because of elections that followed soon after, and the return of the conservative Christian Democrats, no legislation was produced, despite the decision of the Dutch Medical Association to support reform along these lines.

III. Overview

Thus no major Western European country has yet legislated to allow active euthanasia to take place, even if the person wishes it and is suffering from a terminal illness. On the other hand, passive euthanasia is sanctioned both by law in many countries and by the Declaration on Euthanasia of the Catholic Church referred to in Section I, provided the person clearly wishes it and is in the terminal stages of a fatal illness. Nonetheless, in the Netherlands, it is clear that practice has moved ahead of the law – and it has probably done so to some extent in most Western European countries. Doctors, convinced of the wishes of their suffering and terminally ill patients, have decided to intervene in as humane a way as they know how, to end the patient's life more quickly and less painfully. After all, from a doctor's point of view, there is little to choose between "allowing" a person with a terminal illness who so wishes to die, ie practising passive euthanasia, and "hastening" that same person's death in a humane way, ie practising active euthanasia. Nor is there a distinction in moral terms. The motive in either case is the same – to reach the moment of dying as painlessly and quickly as possible. Indeed, the means available if passive euthanasia only is allowed may lead to more suffering and indignity than would active euthanasia in the same circumstances.

In terms of the right to life, the international standard set out in both the International Covenant on Civil and Political Rights and in the regional human rights conventions is that every person has the inherent right to life and that this right should be protected by law. The author believes this standard is met by providing that a terminally ill person be able to request, and a qualified doctor to administer, either passive or active euthanasia, with the choice between the two being made in the light of the patient's own wishes and best interests. There are dangers, such as we have seen in the case of Debbie. It may, however, be better to attempt to avoid them by allowing carefully controlled processes that respect each person's inherent right to have and to surrender his or her life, rather than by attempting to prohibit altogether the achieving of a merciful and quiet death.

On this question, there is much to be said for the view of Dr Pieter Admiraal, a well-known and respected doctor in the Netherlands who has for many years advocated "active" euthanasia in the circumstances outlined above. He wrote that:

> Every patient has the right to ask for euthanasia. Every doctor has the right to perform euthanasia. Every doctor has the right to refuse it. One thing, however, is for certain: it is the patient who must make the decision. Neither the family nor the doctor have the right to make that decision for him.[14]

Dr Admiraal emphasises also the need to make the decision one in which there is full involvement not only of the patient and doctor but of the whole caring team. He considers it important that a decision about mercy killing should not be taken precipitately or secretly. As should be the case for all major decisions in life, it should be taken carefully, meditatively and collegiately. With that the author would agree, and also with Dr Admiraal's sage comment about the definition of euthanasia.

Dr Admiraal noted that he approved the definition of euthanasia given by the Dutch Health Council. The Council said that euthanasia involves:

> ... a deliberately life-shortening act or the deliberate omission of a life-lengthening act in respect of an incurable patient, in such a patient's interest.

Dr Admiraal noted that this definition would cover both active and passive euthanasia. He suggested that it should be supplemented by adding at the end that the act should be "carried out so that quick, peaceful death ensues".[15] Palliative care has greatly improved, and should be used where possible. But where a patient clearly and actively desires to die, and suitable procedures have been put in place to avoid malpractice, acceptance of the wish seems appropriate, and consistent with the individual's right to waive the inherent right to life when illness is incurable, and imminent.

On the other hand, the case of Mrs Adkins appears to present much greater difficulties. It seems that authorising *another* person to assist someone who is neither terminally ill nor

---

14   Admiraal P V, "Active Voluntary Euthanasia", in Downing AB and Smoker B, *Voluntary Euthanasia: Experts Debate the Right to Die*, Peter Owen, London, 1986, p 189.

15   Ibid, 190 and 192.

in great suffering to terminate his or her life may be going too far. This is a matter on which each person must reach his or her own conclusion. Very real dangers are involved. It may be too easy to use such an authorisation as a means of depriving a person of his or her inherent right to life. It may be, as suggested above for the case of Debbie, that a better process should be adopted. Suicide is one thing. To allow others to assist in suicide, except in the carefully defined situation of a patient's doctor and terminal illness, may be another.

However, the implications of accepting that suicide is both lawful and not a violation of the inherent right to life (because an autonomous person is involved) need to be thought through. Logically, if it is not illegal to kill oneself, it is not illegal to assist. It would follow that, as the courts found, Dr Kevorkian's actions, though perhaps crude, were not illegal. On this basis, the best course may be to accept the logic of the situation, but, on moral grounds, to institute measures that prevent the aspects of Dr Kevorkian's actions that many find offensive. The object of the measures would be to ensure a respectful, collegiate process, designed to ensure that the suicidal person had a clear perception of the issues and a firm intent, that a medical or counselling team accepted this, and that there was no suggestion of influence by the "facilitators".

If discussions do start with the object of enabling terminally ill patients, or even suicidal persons, to have their lives "actively" terminated lawfully and of protecting doctors from the risk of prosecution, two approaches could be adopted. One would be to define the laws of homicide (unlawful killing) so that they simply do not apply to mercy killing. This would be the same as the law relating to foreign enemies of the state when there is a war in process: killing the enemy is not a homicide. The law is known not to cover killings of this kind, and the homicide laws when stated make no reference to it. Following this approach would have the consequence of removing mercy killing from the aura of criminal actions, and in effect of giving it a positive endorsement.

The other approach would be to continue to recognise mercy killing as a homicide, but to allow courts to reduce the sentence to a minimum or to refrain from any punishment. This approach would involve the courts in finding guilt, but then in determining that no sentence, or a low one, would follow. The sense of no killing being lawful would be retained, but the court would be able, in special circumstances, to determine that no punishment be meted out, despite a finding of "guilty".

Some will prefer the first, some the second approach. The first is far bolder, and certainly ahead of current thinking. The second seems likely to protect more fully the inherent right to life of each individual. If it were to be followed, the risks of malpractice would be less. The courts would need to be given adequate power to supervise what was happening, and to balance and protect as appropriate the rights of patients, families and doctors.

Finally, there is the question of the right to die. Some have claimed that, in addition to a right to life there should also be a right to die. As a first step, it could be said that a right to die as such makes no sense. How can we have a right to something that is inevitable? Accordingly, the appropriate question for discussion might be whether a right say "to die with dignity" should be recognised. It would, presumably, be complementary to the right to life, and could perhaps be used among other things to assert the right of all people to have proper recognition of their death, whether AIDS victims, of alien origin, criminals or whatever.

On the other hand, it hardly seems necessary to assert the existence of some kind of a right to death if the comprehensiveness of the right to life is adequately recognised. There is no reason why, as *part* of one's right to life, there should not be a right to end one's life in dignity. It is just another aspect of the right to life that asserts in the first place that all people should be treated with dignity and respect; and in the second place that people may preferably not be killed at any time (even for the most serious offences) and that they have at all times a right to protection of their life and liberty. The hospice movement in effect bases itself on the right to life, and not on the "right to death". It claims that there comes a time when a person whose life is drawing to a close needs peace, skilled care and an opportunity for reflection and quiet. It vests in those last stages of life a dignity and a value that is wholly in accord with a rich and deep perception of the meaning of a right to life. No "right to death" is needed, particularly when one contemplates what terrible travesties could be wrought by tyrants, or by people with perverted senses of reality, who could administer torture or other forms of cruel or inhuman treatment to another person (not necessarily a dying patient). One need only contemplate the case of Monica Mignone – see Chapter 11 – to see how convenient a "right to die" might have been to her torturers. The hospice vision of a substantive period of life that needs to be given meaning in itself, as a final stage in life, and which is followed by the end of that life, seems all that is necessary, and an objective worth pursuing in giving the right to life its most comprehensive significance.

For Further Reading

The story of Debbie is reproduced in Baird R M and Rosenbaum S E (eds), *Euthanasia: The Moral Issues*, Prometheus, New York, 1989. It contains a number of stories, including that of Max Cowart, who was saved from death as a result of burns despite his wish to be allowed to die, and many comments.

The story of Mrs Adkins is found in newspaper reports, particularly the *Canberra Times* of 5 December 1990 and in a *Washington Post* article of 6 February 1991 and in many notes since then. But because the case arose so recently, and is still in process by way of an appeal against the injunction, there has not as yet been a detailed published analysis of it.

More generally, one of the best books is edited by Downing A and Smoker B, *Voluntary Euthanasia: Experts Debate the Right to Die*, Peter Owen, London, 1986. The experts include Professor Glanville Williams and Dr Admiraal, a series of notes on the voluntary euthanasia movement, and the text of two British Voluntary Euthanasia Bills and of the 1980 Vatican Declaration on Euthanasia.

On the legal side, a very good introduction to the issues is contained in Robertson J A, *The Rights of the Critically Ill*, Ballinger, Cambridge, Mass, 1983. From there one has to go either to a criminal law textbook or to articles in legal or medical journals, such as the *Journal of the American Medical Association* and the *Journal of the British Medical Association*. The Law Reform Commission of Canada has published Working Paper 28, *Euthanasia, Aiding Suicide and Cessation of Treatment*, 1982 which reviews the law and reaches some conservative conclusions. Finally, a very comprehensive, even if now old, paper on the law relating to euthanasia in European countries and China and

Japan appears in Silving H, "Euthanasia: A Study in Comparative Criminal Law" in (1954) 103 *University of Pennsylvania Law Review*, 350. There is a good account of the situation in the Netherlands by Gevers JKM, "Legal Developments Concerning Active Euthanasia on Request in the Netherlands", (1987) *Bioethics*, Vol 1, 152.

Chapter 6

The Cases of Jane Roe and James Malone

The Right to Privacy

I. THE CASE OF JANE ROE

The Story. In 1969, when this story begins, Norma McCorvey had returned to Dallas, Texas from work in the south of the United States. She had been selling tickets for an animal side-show in a carnival that travelled where opportunity offered. She enjoyed the work, because it put her in touch with people who were in live theatre and set out to entertain and amuse the visitors to the carnival. It accorded with her own spirit and approach to life.

However, one night, after a disturbance at the carnival, which was then near Augusta, Georgia, she was raped on the way back to the motel room she was sharing with two other women. She said she remembered little of the incident, or of the ensuing hours, or of how she missed the carnival as it left for another town. All she could remember was that she felt ill and alone. After managing to borrow just enough for a bus ticket back to Dallas, she found a job as a waitress. Not long afterwards, she discovered she was pregnant. She thought of returning to live with her father, but this was not successful. He was more than unkind when he had drunk too much, and had just separated from his second wife. Nor was her mother receptive, certainly not wanting another child to care for. Norma was alone in the world.

Norma had not had an easy childhood. Born in 1948, the family often moved home as her father, then in the Army, was given new postings. Her early teenage years were spent in Dallas, where her father, having left the Army, was working as an electrician. After a good deal of fighting between her parents, her father left home, but Norma stayed on with her mother and younger brother. Although the stress of the marital disputes ceased, Norma found home life difficult because of a bad relationship with her mother. She was in and out of trouble at school and with the juvenile authorities. She left school at the age of 16, after completing year 10, and found work in a drive-in restaurant. She joined up with a 20-year-old man and went with him to Los Angeles, where she became pregnant, was beaten up by him, and left to return to Dallas. Back with her mother, whom she perceived as cold and down-putting, she had the baby. Her mother adopted the baby and then, with her step-father, moved to Arkansas. Norma stayed on in Dallas. This was in 1964 and 1965.

In 1969, Norma did not want another child. She felt the only option was to have an abortion. But abortion was illegal in Texas, unless the life of the mother was in danger. The penalty on the doctor or abortionist for performing an abortion was 2-5 years' imprisonment (abortion laws often do not penalise the mother). If the mother should die, the offence was murder. Since doctors were unwilling to perform abortions, and Norma had no money to travel to a state that allowed abortions, she decided she would have to search for an abortionist. But the prospects were so awful that she began to contemplate arranging an adoption. She consulted a lawyer, who put her in touch with two young lawyers just beginning practice in the area: Linda Coffey and Sarah Weddington.

Coffey and Weddington had been looking for some time for a person around whose case they could build a challenge to the Texas laws on abortion. Because of the relatively advanced state of Norma's pregnancy, and her unfortunate past (not always helpful in a hard-fought court hearing) they had some doubts about whether to use Norma's case. However, they decided to proceed. They wanted to assist her, as a pregnant woman wanting an abortion, to challenge the validity of the century-old law.[1] They wanted the six Articles in the Texas criminal code

---

1   The Texas law was enacted in 1859. It was very "conservative": it did not contain two of the usual exceptions to abortion law – those relating to a child the product of rape or of incest. It was only in 1987 that, in a rare interview with a journalist, Norma revealed (to Carl Rowan) that she had

dealing with abortion declared unconstitutional so that Norma, and many other women, could have an abortion in Texas, have it performed legally by a qualified medical practitioner, and have it in safe surroundings. They warned Norma that, because she probably needed to be pregnant to be able to bring the case, she might not be able to have an abortion within the first 12 weeks, after which most abortionists would not operate because of the health risks.

Norma continued willing, so urgent action was taken to have the case brought on for hearing. Otherwise, a possibly unfriendly court might declare that the case was moot[2] since Norma was no longer pregnant. To keep her identity hidden, they decided to litigate in the name of Jane Roe. To Norma were added two other parties – a doctor on charges of criminal abortion (Dr James Hallford) and a young married couple, who went under the names of John and Mary Doe. The Does were active in the community, had advanced university degrees and were churchgoers. They wanted to challenge the law because Mary had a condition that made it unwise for her to have a pregnancy: she wanted to be able to obtain a legal abortion even if the consequence of carrying the baby to term was not certain to be fatal or seriously injurious to her health so as to bring her within the legal exception.

The case was heard in the Federal Court rather than the Texas District Court because it was of concern beyond the state and because it raised an important rights issue that related to the Federal Constitution. It was entitled *Roe et al v Wade*, Henry Wade being the District Attorney for Dallas County. It was heard on 23 May 1970. A month later, judgment was given for Roe, but the joined action by the Does was not successful. The Does' case was struck out because there was not a "justiciable" issue, that is a current matter the courts could decide upon. However, the court gave only what is known as declaratory, and not injunctive, relief. That is, it declared the Texas law unconstitutional, but it refrained from directing that the charges

---

not actually been raped, which meant that in any case the Texas law would have applied.

2   A moot case is one in which there is no current issue in respect of which the court can make a decision.

against Dr Hallford be dropped and that Norma be allowed to have her abortion.

Almost immediately, Norma's lawyers lodged an appeal direct to the Supreme Court. They gambled on getting an immediate decision from the highest court in the land. If they succeeded, not only Norma, but women all over the United States, would be able, if they wished, to obtain abortions without having to evade restrictive laws that at that time were operative in over 30 states. If they failed, they would have to find another case and start all over again.

Somewhat to the surprise of the anti-abortion groups, the Supreme Court decided to hear the case. The judges recognised that abortion issues had become contentious, and considered a decision by the court should settle matters for the nation as a whole. On 13 December 1971, 18 months after the Texas Court had issued its decision (Norma had of course long since had her baby), the Supreme Court conducted a first hearing, and a second on 11 October 1972. On 22 January 1973 the court, by a large majority[3], upheld the Texas Court's decision, except that it dismissed the case by Dr Hallford.

The Texas Court based its view of the unconstitutionality of the abortion laws primarily on the basic right of a woman – whether pregnant or not – to choose how to manage and control her own body.[4] The Supreme Court, however, relied on a number of rights contained in the Bill of Rights[5] Using five of the Articles in the Bill of Rights,[6] the court applied the "penumbra" right of privacy and the "due process" right in the 14th Amendment as they had been developed in *Griswold v Connecticut* 381 US 479 (1965). Blackmun J, writing for the court[7] held that this right to privacy extended to give a woman a right to determine how she would manage her pregnancy. He showed

3   Seven justices to two, the dissenters being Justices White and Rehnquist.
4   It based its reasoning importantly on the concurring judgment of Justice Goldberg in *Griswold v Connecticut* 381 US 479 (1965). Goldberg J drew on the Ninth Amendment, which provides that none of the rights in the Amendments are to deprive the people of other rights. He held that the Amendment guaranteed the ancient common law concept of marital privacy as part of the basic rights of the individual.
5   The Bill of Rights is made up of the first ten Amendments of the Constitution, made in 1791, and the Fourteenth Amendment, made in 1868.
6   The First, Fourth, Fifth, Ninth and Fourteenth Amendments.
7   Six other Judges concurred in his judgment.

that it had never been a common law offence to procure an abortion up to "quickening" (the first sign of movement and occurring about the 16th-18th week of pregnancy). Indeed, he suggested that the common law had probably not made abortion an offence until the foetus became "viable" at about the 24th-28th week.[8] Only with Lord Ellenborough's Act in England in 1803 was abortion before quickening made a minor offence, and after quickening a serious (capital) crime. Hence a woman had a "right" to an abortion in the early, pre-viability stage, or even later, unless that right was in some way reduced by statutory provision.

The specific question in the Roe case was whether the Texas statute was valid. Blackmun J recognised that, although a woman had a right to make a decision whether or not to have an abortion, the state legislatures also had a right (or power[9]) to regulate matters such as abortion in the public interest, on health and also on moral grounds. How then were the two – the interests of the mother and of the state – to be reconciled?

Blackmun J sought to reconcile them by identifying three stages in a pregnancy. He indicated that in the *first stage*, prior to "quickening" and following the lead of the common law, a woman has, in effect, full power to control her own body and the foetus within it. Subject only to the constraints on any doctor she might consult that related to medical practice generally, she could legally have an abortion and the state could not prevent or regulate it. In the *second stage*, he indicated that the state has a power to control, but only in a regulatory[10] way, matters relating to an abortion. That is, a woman could still have an abortion, but the state might regulate the situation by reference to health and medical standards and to what he described as "prenatal life". On the other hand, the regulations could not be such as to

---

8   Traditionally, the "viability" stage is reached when the baby, if born prematurely, has a reasonable chance of surviving. At that stage (viability) it was regarded as being a recognisably formed human being capable of surviving outside its mother's body.

9   See the discussion of the distinction between a "power/liberty" and a right in Chapter 12).

10 Strictly, the state had a power to prohibit, or compel, certain action but it was to be "narrowly drawn" and therefore had to be regulatory rather than prohibitive in nature.

prevent the woman making a free decision.[11] In the *third stage*, commencing with "viability", that is at about the 24th week, the state has a "compelling" power, which would even extend to prohibiting an abortion in the interests of the unborn child.

So by 1973 the United States Supreme Court had handed down a fateful decision. In the words of Blackmun J in the later case of *Webster v Reproductive Services* (discussed below), it had asserted "the fundamental constitutional right of women to decide whether to terminate a pregnancy" and gave "liberty and equality [to] millions of women who have lived and come of age in the 16 years since Roe was decided".[12]

To complete the story, Norma McCorvey's baby was carefully adopted out. Norma withdrew into relative solitude, though occasionally she gave an interview to a selected journalist or writer. She lives her life as privately as she can, without the trappings of the victor in a warlike cause but with the silent gratitude of many ...

Discussion. On many occasions, a decision by the United States Supreme Court has the effect of settling the dust. The guardian and arbiter of the Constitution has spoken, and the parties are prepared to let the matter rest. But in the case of Norma McCorvey, the matter has not been allowed to rest. In the years since 1973 the battle has continued to rage, both in the courts and at federal and state political level, between the so-called pro- and anti-abortionists. The appointment by successive Republican Presidents[13] of more conservative judges has meant a gradual swing towards conservatism of the attitude of the court as a whole.

In addition, advances in medical science have affected both sides of the debate. On the "pro-abortion" side, it is now *on medical grounds* as safe to have an abortion up to "viability" as it

---

11 Many subsequent cases have been brought to determine just what is acceptable "regulation" and what unacceptable prohibition. See the review of Webster and Casey in the Discussion section below.

12 From *Webster, Attorney-General of Missouri v Reproductive Health Services* (1989) 57 Law Week 5023 at 5035, 5036.

13 Nixon, Ford, Reagan and Bush, with only the one term of Carter between Ford and Reagan.

is to have a full term birth.[14] So the need on health grounds to make special regulations to prevent women having pre-viability abortions has diminished, if not altogether vanished. That would argue for less power in the state to regulate, at least before "viability". On the anti-abortion side, it seems that the date of viability is becoming earlier, meaning that *on medical grounds* there is a case for the state to have an earlier "compellability" date than envisaged in the Roe case. However, the risks to the future health of the child born in the earlier stages of the "viability" period are measurably greater than for those born nearer to natural term.[15] This means that the case for earlier compellability based on "viability" is not as strong as the case for longer freedom from regulation.

The most recent cases in which the abortion issue has been definitively addressed are *Webster v Reproductive Services* and *Planned Parenthood of Southeastern Pennsylavania v Casey* (1992) 60 Law Week 4795.[16] The decision in Webster was issued in June 1989. In it there was a clear majority in favour of the validity of a Missouri statute. The statute was designed to require a doctor to test for viability of a foetus before performing an abortion, if he (sic) thought the woman was 20 or more weeks pregnant. Three judges, led by Chief Justice Rehnquist, went further and expressed doubts about the decision in the Roe case. Essentially the objection was the same as in Rehnquist J's dissent in Roe, that the decision amounted to "judicial legislation" and that in any case the trimester test was "unworkable in practice".

The minority judges, took the view that any watering down of Roe would threaten the rights of women to control their own bodies and preserve their own privacy. The main opinion was written by Blackmun J, writer of the majority judgment in Roe. He pointed out that the trimester dates were never thought of as absolute, but were guides to the points at which the relative strength of the various interests should be seen as changing, and that to tamper with them was dangerous. The proper position, when strongly held views were involved, was to give people as

---

14 Further issues are raised by the new situations created by "test tube" babies, but for reasons of space these are not discussed in this book.

15 See particularly the interesting article by Paul Reidinger, "Will Roe v Wade be Overruled?" in (1988 – July) *American Bar Association Journal* 66, esp p 69.

16 See fn 13 above for the Law Weekly report of *Webster*. The US Reports have not yet been issued.

much freedom as possible, and not to impose one particular moral view on others. The court must hold to the role of protecting rights, and particularly the rights of poorer women such as Norma McCorvey, who could not afford expensive tests or to travel to a state where abortion was available. To deny abortion rights as defined broadly in Roe and refined in later decisions would, said Blackmun J, be disastrous –

> The result, as we know from experience, ... would be that every year hundreds of thousands of women, in desperation, would defy the law, and place their health and safety in the unclean and unsympathetic hands of back-alley abortionists, or they would attempt to perform abortions on themselves, with disastrous results.[17]

In a situation where opinion is very deeply divided, the fairest way to proceed is to attempt some balance between the opposing views. In the case of abortion, there are on the one hand those (including many women and substantial numbers of men) who wish the law to protect women's right to choose. On the other hand, there are those (again both women and men) who hold the firm belief that the law should prevent women having an abortion, perhaps with a few exceptions such as for pregnancies that threaten the life of the mother (as in the Texan couple's case) or are the result of incest or rape.

In Casey the Supreme Court, in its most recent decision, has attempted to balance the opposing views.[18] By majority, it upheld the principle of Roe, in that it has continued to recognise the right of a woman to make her own choice before viability. The state cannot legislate to impose a prohibition, or even to impose a "substantial obstacle"[19] on abortion. Some regulation is permissible, such as the provision to require testing for viability (Webster was thus upheld). Also permissible are requirements that the mother be given information about abortion at least 24 hours before the abortion, and that one parent's consent be given for a minor (there is a possibility of approaching a court if a parent is not available or will not consent). But a requirement to notify a husband of an intended abortion is not valid – it would

---

17 Ibid, p 5041.
18 *Planned Parenthood of Southeastern Pennsylvania v Casey* (1992) 60 Law Week 4795.
19 Ibid, 4810.

represent an "undue burden"[20] on the woman. So a new balance has been struck between the now confirmed right of a woman to make her own private choice and the power of the state to intervene in a not unduly burdensome way to protect "the health of the woman and the life of the fetus that may become a child".[21] The trimester framework itself, however, has been abandoned as being "not part of the essential holding of *Roe*"[22]

This position will not satisfy people implacably opposed to abortion, but they will need to realise that it is not appropriate in a democratic society for one group – whether it be a majority or a minority – to impose its will on another when that results in a material reduction in the enjoyment of rights. No rights are absolute, and what must be sought is the maximisation of the enjoyment of rights by all. The Supreme Court's decision appears to be a reasoned response to scientific developments and basic rights. The question will be how it interprets, when considering the validity of restrictive legislation, what is "unduly burdensome". Some apprehension seems in order.

Giving the foetus "personhood" from conception will not resolve the problem. This was what was argued by the Texas Government in Roe. The Supreme Court avoided determining precisely when a "person" exists, but noted that the references in the Constitution to a person imply either one who has been born or, more often, one who has attained the age of legal capacity, ie, 18 years. It took the view that "the pregnant woman cannot be isolated in her privacy. She carries an embryo and, later, a fetus."[23]

An unborn child is so different from a live, separated individual that new rules would have to be developed about what rights should be given to it. It cannot itself exercise any rights. Birth is still a major event in life, and it seems best to reserve "ordinary" rights for born and living people. But that does not prevent the unborn child from having rights of some kind. These are already recognised, for example in the remainder laws relating to the transfer of property, and in the possibility of bringing actions after birth for damage caused to the unborn

---

20   Ibid, 4806, 4807.
21   Ibid, 4798.
22   Ibid, 4806.
23   410 US 113 at 159.

child. Some balancing of the rights of the mother and the unborn child – and of the father – is important. None are or can be absolute. Resolution of the conflicting views can only be achieved by careful thought, full consultation and sensitive action. It can never be good to destroy life, but in the early stages of pregnancy the person bearing the unborn child should be the one to make the decision, without interference but hopefully within the caring and supportive framework of family, friends and medical advice.

II. THE CASE OF JAMES MALONE

The Story. James Malone, aged 40, was an antiques dealer working in Dorking, some 40km south of London. In March 1977, officers of the Metropolitan (greater London area) Police entered and thoroughly searched his house in Aldebert Terrace. They had warrants for the search and they took away with them a large number of goods which they suspected of having been stolen, including the movement of a grandfather clock. With the clock, which was found in a concealed cupboard, and was later found to have been stolen, were also Bank of England notes to the value of about £7000 and United States dollars and Italian lira to the value of about £3000. The money was not identifiable as stolen, or as being the proceeds of sales of stolen property. The goods and the money were retained by the police, but £1419 found on Malone's person were returned to him the following week.

Mr Malone and his wife were arrested and, along with five others, were charged with handling stolen property and with conspiracy. In August 1978 a jury found him not guilty of stealing the clock movement, but disagreed on the other charges. The jury was discharged and there was a further trial in May 1979. The jury again failed to agree. Later, he was formally arraigned,[24] but the prosecution offered no evidence and so he was acquitted, as is required by law when no case is presented.

Mr Malone brought two actions in the courts, one for restoration of his property before the trial processes were

---

24 Formally brought to the bar for charging.

complete (which was refused[25]) and one for breach of privacy. The first case is only relevant in that it shows how actively Mr Malone pursued his legal rights in the courts. The second action, on invasion of his privacy, was heard in the Chancery Division of the High Court. Mr Malone claimed that his telephones in his former residence in London, and also in Dorking, had been tapped unlawfully by the police. He was unable to produce any evidence that showed conclusively that the phones were tapped, although he claimed that the police knew of events they could not otherwise have become aware of, and that there were suspicious clicking noises on the phone. He was also able to point to a statement in a police officer's diary, produced at his first trial, that contained details of a telephone conversation. In response to this, counsel for the Crown said he was authorised to admit that an interception had taken place, but that he would make no other statements or admissions.

Mr Malone also claimed that the fact that, when he was arrested, some 20 people he had recently telephoned were subjected to inquiry and search, led to the conclusion that his phone had been "metered".[26] Finally, Mr Malone claimed that his correspondence had been interfered with. He produced a number of letters with envelopes that had been sealed with similar tape, or were unsealed, and said that the senders had not sent the letters in that condition. He added that the letters were often delayed, and that parcels addressed to him were invariably delayed for up to a month and had clearly been opened and resealed.

The case was heard by the Vice-Chancellor, Sir Robert Megarry. It was long, taking up eight hearing days during January and February 1979.[27] It was agreed between the parties that the facts would not be disputed. What the court was asked

---

25   See *Malone v Metropolitan Police Commissioner* [1980] 1 QB 49, reporting the reversal by the Court of Appeal of the decision by Wien J.

26   Metering involves a process that the Post Office uses when a client asks for a check on charges. The Post Office said no request for metering had been made, so there would have been no metering, but the Post Office Engineering Union (POEU), in a separate submission to the European Court, pointed out that metering is also used for other purposes: see POEU submissions in *Publications of the European Court of Human Rights, Series B*, Vol 67 – Malone Case, at pp 72 and 132, and esp 146.

27   The case is reported as *Malone v Metropolitan Police Commissioner* [1979] 1 Ch 344.

to resolve was whether there was in British law any protection from phone tapping and inspection of correspondence and whether, if not, the actions were unlawful because of the requirements of Article 8 of the European Convention on Human Rights (ECHR), to which the United Kingdom is a party.

Sir Robert Megarry, in a lengthy judgment, said that the ECHR was not part of English law, and that he neither had power to enforce the provisions of the ECHR, nor to interpret them. He would take note of the relevant provisions, and in particular of the decision by the European Court of Human Rights in the Klass case[28] when construing and applying English law, but only Parliament could make the Convention part of English law.

Addressing the question whether there is a right to privacy in British law, Sir Robert said there is not. He noted that some aspects of privacy are embodied in the law. For example, the old adage "an Englishman's home is his castle" comes directly from the case of *Semayne v Gresham* (1604) 5 Co Rep 91a, 77 ER 194, and the law of trespass prevents invasion of body space and of property. Although he held the practice of authorising telephone tapping to be a valid exercise of executive power, he permitted himself the following observation on the process –

> Even if the system were to be considered adequate in its conditions, it is laid down merely as a matter of administrative procedure, so that it is unenforceable in law, and as a matter of law could at any time be altered without warning or subsequent notification. Certainly in law any "adequate and effective safeguards against abuse" [a quotation from the Klass case] are wanting. *In this respect English law compares most unfavourably with West German law: this is not a subject on which it is possible to feel any pride in English law.*
>
> I therefore find it impossible to see how English law could be said to satisfy the requirements of the Convention as interpreted in the Klass case. ... But I see the greatest difficulty in the common law framing the safeguards required. ... Any regulation of so complex

---

28 *Klass v Federal Republic of Germany* (1978) 2 European Human Rights Reports (EHRR) 214. In that case the European Court found that the ECHR required protection against invasion of privacy in domestic *law*, and not just by way of *administrative* practice or arrangement.

a matter as telephone tapping is essentially a matter for Parliament, not the courts. ... [29]

Following Sir Robert's decision, the British Government reviewed the matter but decided not to introduce legislation. The Home Secretary, announcing this decision in Parliament in April 1980, relied on the protection provided by a democratically elected Parliament and Ministers responsible to it –

> The interception of communications is, by definition, a practice that depends for its effectiveness and value upon being carried out in secret, and cannot therefore be subject to the normal processes of Parliamentary control. Its acceptability in a democratic society depends on its being subject to Ministerial control, and on the readiness of the public and their representatives in Parliament to repose their trust in the Ministers concerned to exercise that control responsibly. ... There would be no more sense in making such secret matters justiciable than there would be in my being obliged to reveal them in the House.[30]

Having failed to get any satisfaction from the British courts or the Government, Mr Malone took his case to the European Commission on Human Rights established under the ECHR. The commission found the case admissible and, in a later report,[31] that Mr Malone's right to privacy, guaranteed by Articles 8 and 13 of the ECHR, had been violated. Because the British Government was unyielding, the commission took the case to the European Court of Human Rights.[32] The court endorsed the findings of the commission.[33] The court noted that, although there was technically a means in law of having the Secretary of State revoke a warrant improperly issued, the process of review was internal and that "According to the Government, there never has been a case where a complaint ... has proved to be well-founded" (p 36).

---

29 Malone's case, quoted above, 379-80. Italics supplied.
30 Quoted in *Malone v United Kingdom* (1981) 4 EHRR 330 at 338 – this was the report of the findings of the *European Commission* on the question of the admissibility of the complaint. The court's judgment is referred to later.
31 See (1983) 5 EHRR 385.
32 Under Articles 44 and 48 of the ECHR, a complainant cannot take a case to the court – that is the prerogative of the commission or a government involved in the case, though a new Protocol is being considered that would, when operative, allow an individual to appeal to the court.
33 The court's judgment in the case, still entitled *Malone v United Kingdom*, is in (1984) 7 EHRR 14.

Discussion. In the course of its judgment, the European Court reached one conclusion that will have an important and continuing effect on much international human rights law. The conclusion concerns the meaning of the phrase "in accordance with the law". It occurs in Article 8 of the ECHR, which reads –

> 1. Everyone has the right to respect for his private and family life, his home and his correspondence.
>
> 2. There shall be no interference by a public authority with the exercise of this right except such as is *in accordance with the law* and is necessary in a democratic society in the interests of national security, public safety or the economic well-being of the country, for the prevention of disorder or crime, for the protection of health or morals, or for the protection of the rights and freedoms of others. (Italics supplied.)

The problem with the phrase "in accordance with the law" is that it could have the effect of entirely negating the protection otherwise given by Article 8. All a Parliament would have to do would be to pass a law that, in Malone's case, simply said that any phone-tap of an antiques dealer suspected of crime would be lawful. What the court said was that "in accordance with the law" does not refer only to the need to have domestic law on the subject, but "relates to the quality of the law, requiring it to be compatible with the rule of law" and with the human rights principle in question. Specifically, to be in accordance with the rule of law, the rules for restricting tapping would have to be publicly available and prevent arbitrary action. They would have suitably to respect the telephone user's right to privacy. The court found the law to be insufficiently clear, and also that the legal rules and the related administrative arrangements were insufficiently precise to avoid the challenge of arbitrariness (pp 41-4).

What we see in this case is the remarkable spectacle of a Government being criticised first by one of its own most senior judges, and then by both the commission and the Court of Human Rights, and still persisting in maintaining its unsatisfactory range of administrative arrangements. Even the Interception of Communications Act 1985, the UK Parliament's response to the criticism, was inadequate. The new law did not provide effective regulation of the "metering" of phone calls where crime was suspected. Nor did it give the Tribunal, established by the Act to investigate complaints, any effective powers where a tap is suspected but the Secretary of State advised that no warrant had been issued. Further, the actions of the Tribunal are not in any way reviewable in the courts, and questions such as those asked by Malone can no longer be asked in any court proceedings. It seems that the requirement that any invasion of privacy be "in accordance with the law" has not been met in the substantive sense.[34]

Malone's case shows the most effective of the international systems for the protection of human rights – the European Convention system – at its best in identifying and clarifying the requirements of the right to privacy in its application to a detailed and sensitive area of domestic law. It shows a national government at its obscurantist worst in responding to the challenge, and it leaves protection of privacy in British law lagging a long way behind what it is in many other countries, including in West Germany as revealed in the Klass case.

III. Overview

The Roe case illustrates two important aspects of the right to privacy. First, it shows how the United States courts, applying law based on precisely the same historical legal foundations as the British, have been able to derive a right to privacy from the Bill of Rights, even though it contains no mention of such a right. That they have been able to use the Bill of Rights in this way shows how a clear statement of objectives in a Bill of Rights can not only protect the rights it enumerates, but also liberate the courts in related areas to give individuals protection against the encroachment of the state.[35] Second, it shows the courts at work in what might be called the intimate personal area of privacy. As will be suggested, it is here that the core of the right to privacy, if such a core exists, is to be found.

---

34 For a compelling criticism of the new procedures, see Appendix C in David Feldman's learned and comprehensive book *The Law Relating to Entry, Search and Seizure*, Butterworths, London, 1986.

35 At the same time, it must be recognised that the court could also decide the other way.

The Malone case also illustrates important aspects of the right to privacy. It underlines first, the fact that states have strong interests in restricting the right of individuals to privacy. The more the right is protected, the harder it often proves for their police and security forces, their tax and customs agents and their health, social security, education and other regulatory agencies, to do their job without what they tend to see as obstructive protection of the individual. Second, the Malone case illustrates the potential weakness of the courts, if a government and Parliament refuse to heed what they say. A horrifying example of this appears in Chapter 11, in the story of Monica Mignone. At the same time, it highlights the importance of a free and independent judiciary, that can hear cases from individuals and pronounce on the law and bring its deficiencies to notice. Third, Malone shows that privacy is important to individuals in areas other than the immediately personal. It is relevant to *place* as well as person.

It may, indeed, be possible to clarify the notion of privacy by identifying the areas in which it can work. Following what has just been said, it could be suggested that privacy has three main areas of application. First, as in Roe, it operates in the close personal area. Second, as in Malone, it operates in relation to particular space or place – one's home, place of work, place of worship and so on. A third important area is that of relationships. It covers such situations as those of lawyer and client, doctor and patient, or banker and customer.[36] The use of the concept of privacy also needs consideration in the area of commercial dealings. These, however, seem really to relate more to business arrangements than to privacy as such. Examples are the often complex laws relating to business and trade secrets and intellectual property. Business and commercial dealings may be better regarded as in a separate category, and not as part of the general (personal) law of privacy.[37]

---

36 The division into place, person and relationship – oriented areas has been made by Dionisopoulos PA and Ducat CR in *The Right to Privacy: Essays and Cases*, West Publishing Co, Minnesota, 1976. They based their division on an analysis of cases decided by United States courts.

37 In Australia, the *Privacy Act* 1988 has, since 1990, applied to protect personal information in the hands of banks, companies, credit agencies etc (termed "credit providers" and "credit reporters") as well as in the hands of government agencies.

Somewhat related is the argument many have put forward that there is no "general" right to privacy. They say that privacy is a woolly concept, incapable of meaningful application in legal form. It would be better, so the argument runs, to apply the general idea involved in privacy in specific situations, without giving a general right. Thus it would be possible to protect business secrets by appropriate provision in company law; to protect space and personal privacy by for example trespass laws and making spouses non-compellable witnesses; and to protect relationship privacy by regulating dealings between doctor and patient, solicitor and client and so on. None of these, it would be said, need be regarded as "privacy" laws, although if one wished one could use that vague word. Rather, the content of each of the laws would be determined by the needs of the persons with interests in that particular situation, whether business, personal or relational.

The alternative view, which the author holds, is that it is not good enough to regard privacy as an unhelpful and undefinable general idea that cannot be given consistent expression in law. People do have a general sense of what is private, and will apply it in assessing particular situations, whatever the law says or does not say. Further, the international human rights movement has been unequivocal in asserting that individuals have a right to privacy. The first formulation of it was in the Universal Declaration of Human Rights of 1948. Article 12 provides that –

> No one shall be subjected to arbitrary interference with his privacy, family, home or correspondence, nor to attacks upon his honour and reputation. Everyone has the right to the protection of the law against such interference or attacks.

The International Covenant on Civil and Political Rights, in Article 17, closely follows this formulation. The main thrust is to prevent unreasonable intrusion into the life of an individual, and the means of protection is to be the law. The text of Article 8 of the ECHR has been quoted above. It is more positive, but interestingly does not refer to privacy as such. It is concerned with ensuring that everyone's "private and family life" is protected by law. Limits are put on the extent to which law may invade privacy, and the European Court and Commission have clearly treated the Article as conferring a right to privacy. Nonetheless, the adjectival use of "private" in the situational reference to personal and family life does suggest some attempt to confine the term.

Returning to the second view, namely that it is possible to identify the core of a general right to privacy, the question is what its scope should be. The two poles are the individual and the community. Just as the individual has to be restrained by criminal and other laws from harming the community and other individuals, so the community and other individuals have to be restrained from encroaching unduly on the individual. The relevant rights or interests have to be balanced. The author ventures the suggestion that the core of the right to privacy relates to giving each individual maximum opportunity to develop without unreasonable intrusion by others. For this, the individual needs a harmonious environment and the opportunity, without unreasonable restriction, to enjoy, respond to, and not be prevented from intimacy with others.[38] In such circumstances each individual, and the society as a whole, will flourish.

A core definition of this kind need not confine the right purely to the personal realm. Although its centre relates to the individual person and relationships between individuals, it would inevitably extend to at least some aspects of the activities the individual has in the business world. But as the spheres of business, commerce and so on are progressively entered, the personal development interest, and thus the centrality of the right, diminish and the requirements of the particular activity assume greater importance. Always lurking in the background will be the core personal right to privacy that could be invoked by the individual in protection of important personal and developmental rights.

---

38   This concept of development is fascinatingly expounded by Piaget – see Ginsburg H and Opper S, *Piaget's Theory of Intellectual Development: An Introduction*, Prentice-Hall, 1969, esp at p 14.

For Further Reading

There is a fascinating book, relatively recently published, by Marian Faux on the Roe case: *Roe v Wade: The Untold Story of the Landmark Supreme Court Decision That Made Abortion Legal*, Macmillan, New York, 1988. It tells in a readable and lively way the full story of the participants in the action, and gives useful background and extremely good assessments of the legal as well as the human issues. The court reports themselves are valuable documents, and they contain many references. There is also a forward-looking article by Nancy Rhoden in *The Yale Law Journal*, (1986) Vol 95, No 4, 639.

The Law Reform Commission of Canada has published a thoughtful analysis of the extent to which crimes against the foetus should be revised or introduced, and recommends a comprehensive code on the matter, though it stops short of a firm recommendation on the question of abortion during the first trimester: Law Reform Commission of Canada, *Crimes Against the Foetus*, Working Paper 58, 1989. The United States Reports and, for the more recent cases of Webster and Casey, the Law Week Reports, are worth looking at because of the full discussion, and active debate, the judgments contain. A humane article about the rights of the father in relation to abortion is contained in the extended commentary by Paul Ramsey "The Supreme Court's Bicentennial Abortion Decision: Can the 1973 Abortion Decisions be Justly Hedged?" in *Ethics at the Edges of Life: Medical and Legal Intersections*, Yale, 1978. The fourth footnote contains a superb summary of the development by the Supreme Court of the doctrine of "due process" – both formal and substantive.

The many court proceedings in which Mr Malone was involved, both in England and in the ECHR context, have been documented in the text. A useful but relatively brief discussion of the whole of the right to privacy is contained in Bailey PH, *Human Rights: Australia in an International Context*, Butterworths, Australia, 1990, Chapter 10. A book that takes a rather different view, arguing that privacy is essentially relevant only in the context of regulating the flow of information, is by Wacks R, *Personal Information: Privacy and the Law*, Clarendon, 1989. The Australian Law Reform Commission, which also comes down against any general right to privacy, produced a comprehensive two volume report *Privacy*, Report No 22, AGPS, Canberra, 1983.

Chapter 7

The Chernobyl Disaster and
the Forest-Dwellers of Brazil

The Right to a
Sustainable Environment

I. THE CHERNOBYL DISASTER

The Story. Just as the night-shift workers in Forsmark, a small town on the central east coast of Sweden, and about 80km west of the historic Aland Islands, were leaving their posts in the light of the dawn on Monday 28 April 1986, the meteorological station there detected an unusual increase in nuclear fallout. But there were no reports from any source of some special event, or of a nuclear explosion. During the day, similar readings were noted in other areas of Western Europe, but there was still no news from an authoritative agency.

The various observations made by recording stations in Western Europe clearly indicated a source within the Ukrainian region of the Soviet Union. However, it was not until 10 days later that the Soviet Union officially reported a serious nuclear explosion in the Kiev region of the Ukraine.

What had happened was that those in control of Plant No 4 at the nuclear power station near Chernobyl decided that some safety tests should be carried out on the plant on Sunday 27 April. The idea was to check whether sufficient power would be available, if the plant had to be shut down in an emergency, to complete the necessary procedures such as withdrawing the cores, closing doors and starting up alternative sources of power. In some stations, huge batteries are available, and diesel generators can be started up in under half a minute. For Plant No 4, the arrangement was for the turbines to provide the necessary power as they slowed down after the shutdown occurred. It was the adequacy of this provision that was to be tested. The tests started, but had to be delayed for 12 hours because additional power was necessary. The procedures were resumed during the evening. Then things began to go wrong. At 1.23am on the Monday morning, Reactor 4 "went into a searing and uncontrolled chain reaction. [T]he resulting steam explosion tore the concrete housing apart, blew the thousand ton 'safety cover' off the top of the reactor and spewed radio active materials into the atmosphere".[1]

The consequences of that explosion, the worst the world has experienced, are still not fully known. Those worst affected were the 46,000 people living at the special service town of Pripyat, 3km from the plant. Chernobyl, 15km away, with 12,500 inhabitants, was also seriously affected. Mercifully, Kiev, ancient capital of the Ukraine and some 130km away to the south, was not as seriously affected, but the fallout extended rapidly north and west so that 7 hours later Forsmark, 1300km to the northwest, noted unusual fallout, as did monitoring stations in the Swiss and Austrian Alps, and in Scotland and Wales. The children of Pripyat were the worst affected, because for the whole of Monday they went about their daily activities with no warning of what had happened, and while the fallout was at its worst. Burns for some, diarrhoea for others, and now severe and often irreversible leukemia, are their lot. The Lapps in Sweden and Norway have suffered directly, and through the compulsory destruction of more than half the reindeer, on whom they depend for much of their food and livelihood. The reindeer were contaminated through eating affected lichens. Sheep (between 12 and 4 million) were contaminated in Wales, and sheep and cattle (86,000 of the latter were destroyed) in other parts of Europe. Some of the children of Chernobyl have visited Australia in 1991 and 1992, to get away from their homes for a few weeks and enjoy sun, sea, food including icecream and the hospitality of Australian homes, before they return, many to a lingering death.

In short, we do not yet know, and probably never will, the full extent of the damage caused by the disaster. We do know that it was greatly more severe than the Windscale disaster in

---

1   Gould P, *Fire in the Rain – The Democratic Consequences of Chernobyl*, Polity Press, 1990, p 2.

England in 1957 and, as a passing comment, that the Soviet authorities have released a great deal more information in the aftermath than was ever released about Windscale or the Three Mile Island breakdown. The force and fallout from Chernobyl is estimated as being between 100 and 1000 times as bad as from the Three Mile Island generator breakdown in the United States in 1979. The deaths from the fallout have been estimated by Vladimir Chernousenko, the scientific director in charge of the 30km exclusion zone that was quickly established round the plant, as between 7000 and 10,000,[2] and this does not allow for later developments of cancer and genetic deformities[3] Nor is it possible to assess the damage to the environment – to lakes, rivers, fauna and flora. But it is indubitably substantial. Although, in 1986 and 1987, there was a slow-down in the building of nuclear power plants, particularly in the Soviet Union, construction seems to have resumed, even if at a slower pace. Whereas there were 417 known nuclear power plants in the Soviet Union in 1987, this grew to over 500 by 1991.

However, following disintegration of the Soviet Union, the Ukrainian Parliament voted in October 1991 to close down the whole site at Chernobyl within 2 years. There had been a further incident, though it did not result in any escape of radiation, and the vote was to eliminate all nuclear generators from the Ukraine. Popular feeling, at last able to make itself felt, had had its way.

Discussion. The focus in this chapter is on the rights, if any, we have to protection of the environment. As the Chernobyl story shows, many other rights are infringed when there is a major nuclear explosion. Many are killed immediately. Some have their lives painfully shortened, and some not yet born will suffer permanent impairments. The Lapps will suffer at least a period of shortage, and perhaps also illnesses. Cattle and sheep have had to be destroyed. So the right to life and to enjoyment of life, and rights to property have been affected. But we are concerned

---

2   Charles Oulton in London, reported by the *Canberra Times*, 15 April 1991, quoting *The Independent* of England.

3   Paul Brown in London, reported by the *Canberra Times* 26 April 1991, quoting *The Guardian* of England.

here with the degradation of the environment – the air, the soil and the living things.

Is there any remedy for this spoiling of the environment and, if so, on what basis? Do we have a right to protection of the environment, or to a sustainable environment? The short, hard answer is "no". But there have been moves in most countries for some time to punish those who pollute the air and the rivers and even the sea and the Antarctic area, and legislation about fumes emitted from internal combustion engines is gathering force. So there is something on the statute books of many countries. In the United States of America, for example, the federal law against pollution of air and rivers is quite tough and far-reaching.

At the international level there has also been activity. There are conventions against pollution of the sea, and the International Law Commission of the United Nations[4] is developing new codes to deal with those who pollute rivers shared by more than one country.[5] There was a UN Conference on Environment and Development (UNCED) in Brazil in 1992, and it managed to reach agreement on a series of draft agreements already being prepared. The central document is a Framework Convention on Climate Change which states that the signatory countries agree to take steps to protect the environment. The Convention provides for subsidiary agreements ("protocols") on specific pollution issues. A separate convention was also agreed on to deal with the protection of species (termed the Biodiversity Convention). The two conventions were signed by over 150 countries, and there is hope that they may soon come formally into operation.[6] In addition, there was general agreement on Agenda 21, which maps out the kind of action it is necessary to agree to and constitutes a program that will take into the 21st century to implement fully.

---

4   Currently chaired by an Australian, Professor James Crawford.

5   In international law a convention is a treaty or agreement between two or more countries. Usually, it only has legal effect in a country if there is legislation that puts it into effect ("implements it" is the technical phrase).

6   In international law, signing a convention is an indication of intent to "ratify". It is only when a country has made full arrangements, eg passing laws, setting up reporting mechanisms, that it will ratify. Only when the necessary number of countries has ratified (50 for the Climate and 30 for the Biodiversity Convention) will the treaty become operative in international law.

The only disappointment is that the need for the world community to set firm targets and timetables for limiting greenhouse gas emissions under the Climate Convention was not fully recognised, nor was the desired full commitment to North-South funding support achieved.

There are three conventions that deal with nuclear accidents. The International Atomic Energy Agency Convention 1957, which has 113 member states, provides safeguards all round the world for the sale and use of nuclear materials, and provides for inspection of nuclear plants. The Nuclear Agency Authority Convention 1957, established by the OECD countries[7] provides for cooperation between a limited number of countries on safety and regulatory aspects of nuclear energy and for the safety of workers in nuclear power plants in those countries. The 1960 Paris Convention on Third Party Liability in the Field of Nuclear Energy has 24 members (all European) and provides strict liability for the operators of nuclear power plants. It also requires member states to give individuals rights in domestic law to recover for damage caused by nuclear plants. It is currently being reviewed in the light of the Chernobyl disaster, but it is interesting that it was not used by the member countries when dealing with the aftermath of Chernobyl. Instead, all countries arranged for compensation for their own citizens, and none made claims on the Soviet Union. The reason is probably that they did not wish to pave the way for claims in the future based on any accidents that might occur in their own territories. A new agreement, the Convention on Early Notification of Nuclear Accidents 1987, is the only specific legal outcome of the Chernobyl disaster, but it clearly plugs a useful loophole in the earlier agreements.

Thus a start has been made at international level to deal with not only the consequences of nuclear accidents, but also with the apparently severe deterioration of the environment generally as a result of continuing development, depletion of the ozone layer by emission of fluorocarbons, and the destruction of forests. But there is a long way to go, and there is as yet no generally recognised right to protection of the environment in

---

7   The Organisation for Economic Cooperation and Development, which
     consists of the major Western European countries and the United States,
     Canada, Japan and Australia.

international law, although the industrialised nations, as just mentioned, are taking action in some areas to deal with some of the problems that can arise. The question of a general right is discussed further in Section III – Overview below.

II. THE FOREST-DWELLERS OF BRAZIL

The Story. The present century has been a tale of disaster for the peoples of the forests that cover much of the Amazon Basin of Brazil. A population estimated at perhaps 500,000-1 million in 1900 has dwindled to about 100,000-200,000, and the number of tribes has been reduced from over 200 to well under 100. Most of the peoples, though having in law a right to the land they and their ancestors have occupied for centuries, have been displaced and have no title. That tends to be vested in FUNAI (National Foundation for Indians)[8] – the agency set up in 1968 to supersede the old IPS (Indian Protection Service) and to protect Indian interests.

A current example of what is happening as the people get sucked into the ratrace of modern capitalist enterprise is at Acailandia. Acailandia is based on the mine at Carajas, 190km west of Maraba. Maraba is a relatively old town on the Tocantin River, that feeds into the great bay near Belem, where the Amazon itself also meets the sea. Acailandia is some 500km south of Belem and 2,500km north of Brasilia, and so is in the eastern Amazon.[9]

Acailandia services the vast mine opened up at Carajas in the late 1960s, and has proved to be the worst environmental disaster zone in the Amazon rainforest. Over 200,000 people live there, in muddy streets and poor housing, with no reticulation of water, open sewers and all the forests gone. Children work in the smelters and men work 14-hour days with much unpaid overtime.[10] So bad are the conditions that the European Court of Auditors has begun investigating the extent to which the

---

8   In Portuguese, the Fundacao Nacional do Indio
9   The Amazon basin itself occupies most of the north of Brazil and is some 3000km east to west and 200km north to south. It is bounded to the north by Columbia, Venezuela and Surinam, and to the west by Peru.
10 Most of these details have been taken from Jan Rocha, writing in Acailandia and reported under the title "Ecology, people pushed aside in forest plunder", *Canberra Times*, Sunday 2 April 1991.

demands of the European Community are responsible for what has happened. The forests are no more, having been burned up to satisfy the demands of the smelters. The ecologically balanced life of the forest people has gone, all of their culture and most of their family ties. They have become poor workers with poor health and no prospect of any kind of decent living conditions.

Discussion. Here again, the focus is on the effects of destroying the environment, this time of simple forest dwellers who had not managed to stake out specific proprietary rights to the land they used. The tragedy is that, as with the indigenous people whose stories are told in Chapter 1, they had achieved a balance with the natural habitat that left the environment stable. Now there are mud, treeless plains and palls of smoke. These people have been denied several basic rights: to live as a people or a minority, to fair and decent conditions of work, to an adequate standard of living and to family life.

Behind all this is the deprivation they have suffered of their age-old environment. It is no accident that they, like the Aborigines, the Penan and the Maori (see Chapter 1), have been denied enjoyment of their environment by the rapacious demands of Western economic enterprise. The consequence has been loss of their identity as people – first as a community and then as individual members of the community. The traditional western individual rights are necessary for the forest dwellers but, beyond those, rights of the whole community are also necessary. The classical individual rights are, to a degree, simplistic as they do not take into account the needs of the community, and are not appropriate to get to the base of the forest dwellers' problem. These people need a right *as a group* to enforce proper protection of their environment, either in its pristine state or else in an acceptable substitute form that does not destroy them as individuals nor their community as an entity in itself.

Group rights have been discussed in Part I. Here, we turn to consider the nature of a right to protection of the environment.

III. OVERVIEW

The peoples of Europe – and perhaps, as we do not yet know the full story, the people of the world as a whole – have suffered varying degrees of degradation of their environment through the Chernobyl accident. Although the Europeans as peoples affected by Chernobyl have survived, a few thousand unfortunate individuals have not. In contrast to their situation, the forest peoples of the Amazon have been destroyed as peoples or communities. In addition, although little publicity has been given to their fate, they have in individual terms suffered many more losses. Yet little protest has been made, and virtually no recompense given.

In each case, the environment of the peoples and of their individual members has been degraded. What, then, do we mean by "the environment"? Basically, we mean the things or conditions that surround human beings.[11] More specifically, we mean the climate, the state of the earth and the state of living beings (all animals, insects, trees, plants and so on). Sometimes we add the state of culture – the extent to which learning, the arts and community life generally are enjoyed by all. The environment can be good or bad and, if we want a right related to it, it must be to some kind of "good" or "enjoyable" environment. In legal terms, it might be appropriate to refer to a right to protection of the environment (the need for it to be good being assumed, as it is in say the right to life).[12] Nowadays, much of the discussion is about a "sustainable" environment. What that in effect means (though the phrase is grammatically clumsy) is that we want a right to an environment that is both *currently viable* and enjoyable, and that is being used in a way that will allow it to *remain* (sustain itself) in that state. Implementation of the right would occur through people being able to make claims that could be enforced to rectify deficiencies (make the environment viable) – as is necessary in the case of both Chernobyl and the Brazilian forest peoples. A satisfactorily formulated right would also enable claims to be made to prevent practices that do or could have the effect of spoiling it (so as to

---

11 Webster's Dictionary describes the conditions as being "climatic, edaphic [to do with the soil], biotic and sometimes cultural".
12 See Bailey, *Human Rights*, Ch 12.5.

remain sustainable) – as in the case of the action taken by the European countries in relation to nuclear power plants.

Often, the discussion of the need for a sustainable environment is linked with the right to development. That is an important component in the right: we do not want the environment to stay as it is and permit no improvement – development – for those whose environment or living standard is unsatisfactory. What we want is to be able to improve things *without* degrading (causing deterioration to) the environment. We want an environment in which growth and development is sustainable in the long term, for us and future generations of life. This does not·mean no change, but only no change that, taking all interests into account, is justifiable in terms of the local and the global future. With this further explanation, it may be suitable to adopt as a concept *a right to a sustainable environment*.

It could be argued that the idea of a right to a sustainable environment is too vague: that, like the argument for a general right to privacy, the law would be better to attack the problem of providing rights in a more piecemeal way. That is indeed what the law has to some extent done in the area of privacy, but without recognising a core right related to autonomy of person![13] Could it be that there is value both in attacking a series of particular issues such as water or air or sea pollution, and at the same time retaining a core concept that has some life of its own and influences, as well as is influenced by, the specific expressions of the right? If so, the core right *to a sustainable environment* would be related to the overall problems of a whole community, such as were experienced by the Brazilian forest people, where the whole of life is gravely affected. But in some cases, perhaps particularly those of less developed countries in Asia, Africa and South America, the core right might apply to a nation and, as at UNCED, to the world as a whole. The heart of it would be a *total* response to a unit, rather than a response to a particular problem, such as air or water pollution, or noise. The Chernobyl disaster, on the other hand, may in most cases – except perhaps those of the Lapps – be manageable within more specific environmental rules, such as those developed by the European Community and described briefly in Section I.

---

13 See the discussion of the right to privacy in Bailey, Ch 10, esp section 2.

It is very much in this general direction that the international conference in Brazil in June 1992 seems to have headed. The idea of having a "core" right could well be seen to be the significance of developing a "framework" convention, with a number of specific-issue protocols supporting particular aspects of the general right.

Another aspect of the concept of a right to sustainable development is caught up in the idea of calling the UNCED conference the UN conference on environment *and development*. The relatively new focus on the development issue is of extreme importance. It reveals the need to distinguish between the obligations of the "developed" and of the "less developed" countries. One of the questions that caused most difficulty in Brazil was what kind of obligations the developing countries would be prepared to undertake, having in mind that their development at present is often associated with severe degradation of the environment, too often in other parts of the world, as in the case of the Amazon forest. The degradation is inevitably exacerbated, if not caused, by the demands of the developed countries. The latter will have to pay more if environmentally sound practices are to be followed. That is the significance of the inquiry by the European Court of Auditors mentioned above.

If a right to a sustainable environment is to be effective, it will need to be implemented at both domestic and international levels. Here the Geneva Conventions on the protection of civilians and prisoners of war (the humanitarian conventions) establish an encouraging precedent. Each convention has 166 member states, ie virtually universal acceptance. Each country must, to be a member of the conventions, adopt into its own law a number of agreed provisions to enable those who break the conventions to be punished by domestic legal procedures. If the same could be done for the new range of environmental protection conventions, the world would be in a much better state to face the 21st century.

Finally, a note about indigenous peoples. They come at the bottom of all the pecking orders – legal, cultural, economic and welfare. Their needs must be recognised and enforced in the new environmental order that seems to be emerging. It should not be too much to hope that the new conventions would contain special clauses to protect the environment of indigenous peoples and so emphasise the historical and family links of all the peoples of the world.

For Further Reading

One of the most recent and also most interesting books about the Chernobyl disaster is by Professor Peter Gould of Pennsylvania State University. It is *Fire in the Rain*. It was published by Polity Press in 1990 and reviews some of the philosophical issues that arise. The legal aspects are well surveyed in Cameron C, Hancher L and Kuhn W (eds), *Nuclear Energy Law After Chernobyl*, Graham and Trotman, 1988. An account by a doctor well aware of the medical outcomes is *Chernobyl: The Real Story*, by Mould RF, Pergamon, 1988.

Current material on the situation in the Brazilian rain forests is almost all in newspapers. Two excellent books on the background are the report by Edwin Brooks and three others of a 1972 mission by the Aborigines Protection Society – *Tribes of the Amazon Basin*, Charles Knight & Co, London, 1973, which tells of a two month visit by a team from the Society; and a more historical assessment by Davis S, *Victims of the Miracle: Development and the Indians of Brazil*, 1977.

The various treaties on environmental matters being developed under the auspices of the United Nations are noted in environmental journals such as those produced by Greenpeace, and are published in the United Nations treaty series. They are sometimes referred to in journals of international or environmental law, such as the *American Journal of International Law* or the *Journal of Environmental Law*.

PART III

Achieving Equality – Discrimination and Affirmative Action

The claim to equality before the law is in a substantial sense the most fundamental of the rights of man. It occupies the first place in most written constitutions. It is the starting point of all other liberties.

Sir Hersch Lauterpacht,
An International Bill of the
Rights of Man, 1945.

... [T]he principle of equality before the law ... means ... to treat equally what are equal and unequally what are unequal. ... A different treatment is permitted when it can be justified by the criterion of justice [or the criterion of reasonableness].

Judge Tanaka of the International
Court of Justice in the South-West Africa case, 1966.

In this Part, the great modern move towards recognising the basic equality of all persons is considered, with a particular look at two bases for discrimination – race and sex – and at the newly emerging concept of rights for children. At the same time, questions are asked about how far members of the "majority" can be discriminated against, in the interests of the disadvantaged group. Sometimes the needs arising from the basic right to stay alive are so great that the "special" rights claimed for disadvantaged groups seem hardly relevant.

PART III

Chapter 8

Nelson Mandela and Martin Luther King

Combating Racial Discrimination

I. NELSON MANDELA

The Story. Millions of television viewers around the world on Sunday 11 February 1990 waited with growing impatience for Nelson Mandela to be released from the gaol a few kilometres from Johannesburg. He had been moved there not long before, after more than 25 years of mostly solitary style confinement at the remote maximum security Robben Island gaol for black political prisoners. In July 1964, convicted of high treason, he had been sent to Robben Island with five other leaders of the black movement, while the one white man convicted with him (Denis Goldberg) had been sent instead to Pretoria gaol.

Nelson Rolihlahla Mandela was born on 18 July 1918 at Qunu in the Transkei reserve area, not far from Umtata, and some 250km southwest of Durban. His was a branch of the royal family of the Thembu people, and he was brought up to assume tribal leadership in the traditional way, with an arranged marriage and preparation for participation in tribal functions. He was taught at a Methodist school and then at Fort Hare College. But before taking his BA at the latter he was suspended because of a boycott of members of the Students' Representative Council, which had been deprived of its functions by the authorities. Not wanting to merge back into tribal life, he left for Johannesburg 650km to the north. At the suggestion of Walter Sisulu, who became a lifetime friend and colleague, he began a law degree which was to provide him with his livelihood through the turbulent years before his long-term imprisonment in 1964.

However, his own inclinations, and his contacts with Sisulu and Oliver Tambo, with whom he was to set up an Attorneys' practice in Johannesburg in 1952, drew him into the mainstream of African nationalism. He joined the African National Congress (ANC) in 1944 and in 1950 assisted in founding its Youth League, of which he became President. He also became, a little later, General Secretary of the ANC. The ANC was the oldest established African society based on national rather than tribal loyalties. It began as the South African Natives National Congress in 1912, two years after South Africa was declared one of the Dominions and given its independence of Britain. Initially a moderate organisation, the ANC was beginning by the late 1940s to assume a more militant stance. The Prime Minister, Jan Smuts, of whom much had been hoped, abandoned the process of lowering racial barriers at the 1943 election and lost power in 1948 to the National Party, primarily representative of the Afrikans (Boer) interests.

From then on, the trend of the government was to ever-tightening control over the blacks. The Pass Laws, which had prevented blacks moving out of their residential area without a pass, were progressively tightened.[1] Other national legislation was introduced with surprising rapidity and a gruesome thoroughness. It covered every imaginable area of life – social, eg marriages; social security, eg most black workers were excluded; public amenities, eg railways; labour, eg refusal of skill certificates to Africans; property and residence; education; and political life. The titles of the Acts, mostly enacted in the early 1950s, indicate their purposes – the Group Areas Act 1950; the Reservation of Separate Amenities Act 1953; the Public Safety Act 1953 (Regulations under which allowed detention and ousted review by the courts); and the Suppression of Communism Act 1950 and its sequel the Subversive Organisations Act 1960 (under which the ANC was banned).

As if these were not enough, the South African Parliament also enacted the Internal Security Act and associated Emergency Regulations, by which individuals could be detained without

---

1   The Pass Laws had been in existence in some form or another since early in the 19th century. At least six forms of pass had been developed – for exemption, for "special" reasons, for seeking work, for night movements, for travelling and for tax.

charge, which were progressively tightened, and allowed detention for indefinite periods without trial and the Unlawful Organisations Act of 1960, which more or less completed the horrifying edifice of legal repression. In 1974 the Publications Act was passed, and in 1982 the Internal Security Act was further tightened although there was, paradoxically, some moderating of the system in 1981 with enactment of the Labour Relations Act that removed racially discriminatory provisions from labour law. In the political area, all black voting for and representation in the Union Parliament was abolished in 1960. (From 1936 there had been three representatives from the Cape Province in the Assembly of 153, and there had been four black Senators, chosen from four districts.)

These measures forced the ANC to ever-increasing militance, though tempered with the earlier tradition of moderation and a blend of non-violence that had been influential on Mahatma Gandhi. As the 1950 legislation was brought in, the ANC appointed Mandela national volunteer-in-chief of the Defiance Campaign. By 1952 the campaign was well under way. The objective was to inspire the black people with confidence in their ability to overcome oppression through non-violent challenge. An entrance to a suburban railway station in Port Elizabeth marked "Europeans Only" was entered, and arrests followed. Mandela and Sisulu were given suspended sentences on grounds of furthering the aims of communism. Later in the year, after his election as deputy to the President-General of the ANC, Chief Albert Luthuli, Mandela was placed under a ban order which prohibited him from attending gatherings and travelling outside Johannesburg. It was the beginning of long years of harassment, bans and charges, culminating in his discharge from the four-year Treason Trial in 1961 and his ultimate imprisonment in 1964, on grounds of sabotage and conspiracy that were laid in October 1963 (the Rivonia trial). Meanwhile, the massacre at Sharpeville had occurred in 1960. Notwithstanding all this, Mandela had met his wife to be, Winnie Nomzamo Madikizela in 1956, through his law partner Oliver Tambo. They married in 1958, after his divorce from his earlier wife had been granted, but the events of the following years did not allow them the time together they would have wished.

In real terms, the black population was by 1964 exposed to severe discrimination both in law and in practice. At the basic level, hundreds of thousands of black Africans had been forced to move to the segregated reserves. Hundreds of thousands worked in the gold mines at wages frequently less than one fifth those of whites doing similar jobs. Their landholdings were taken over, and there was much unemployment. Even more terrible, the system of education, already segregated, was designed by the "Bantu education" scheme initiated by Verwoerd in 1953 to fit African children only for menial tasks and not for further education or skills training. Resources were also skewed, so that government expenditure per capita in white schools was six times that in black schools. The Soweto uprising of June 1976, in which 200 were killed in the first week, and which led to the torture and death of Steve Biko in September at the hands of the police interrogators, was in protest over the government's education policies.

No wonder Mandela, in his statement of defence at the "Rivonia" trial[2] said –

> All lawful modes of expressing opposition to this principle [the principle of white supremacy – apartheid] had been closed by legislation, and we were placed in a position in which we had either to accept a permanent state of inferiority, or to defy the Government. We chose to defy the law. ... We first broke the law in a way which avoided any recourse to violence; when this form was legislated against and then the Government resorted to a show of force to crush opposition to its policies, only then did we decide to answer violence with violence ... the violence which we chose to adopt was not terrorism. ... We believe that South Africa belonged to all the people who lived in it, and not to one group, be it Black or White.[3]

The trial lasted for 11 months, and eight of the nine charged were found guilty and sentenced to life imprisonment – six blacks, one Indian and one white.

The multiple forms the discrimination against the blacks took are well summed up in the surprisingly moderately stated

---

2 Mandela and several other leaders including Walter Sisulu, and the white supporter Dennis Goldberg, were arrested at the underground headquarters of the ANC in Rivonia, a suburb of Johannesburg, on 11 June 1963.

3 Mandela N, *No Easy Walk to Freedom*, Heinemann, London, 1965, p 164.

leaflet circulated during the protests that followed the Sharpeville massacre of 1960 –

> People of South Africa
> The protest goes on
> Arrests cannot stop us
> Votes to all
> Decent wages for all
> End Pass Laws
> End Minority White domination
> We are not going to be frightened by Verwoerd. We stand firm by our decisions to stay at home ... forward to freedom in our own lifetime ...[4]

The rest of the story is quickly told. Mandela and his colleagues spent 25 years in prison. Mandela himself became a central figure – a "living legend"[5] – symbolising African resistance. His reputation not only managed to withstand the trauma of release from that cruel isolation but has grown both at home and abroad. He has also developed personally, according to "Mac" Maharaj –

> ... as a personality, Nelson is a very friendly and warm person to meet, but one also feels that he maintains a distance. To get to know him really well takes time ... when I did get to know him I realised that initially I hadn't really known him after all; his initial friendliness makes one think one knows him. ... Secondly, he has obviously cultivated a deliberate policy of concealing his anger. In his political line in the early years he gave vent to the anger he felt. In prison he has got his anger almost totally under control. ... In his manner he is kind, gentle and warm, but he has steeled and hardened himself. When he acts he wants to act in a cool and analytical way, and then follows through his decision with tremendous perseverance.[6]

As this is being written, the process of dragging South Africa towards a more equal society is fully engaged. The white leader, Prime Minister de Klerk, is having to deal with Mandela and the ANC while attempting to bring along his own stubborn white opponents and the equally stubborn Chief Buthelezi, leader of

---

4   Quoted in Benson, *Nelson Mandela*, referred to in Further Reading.
5   From a contribution by SR "Mac" Maharaj, sentenced for sabotage in December 1964, to "Memoirs of the Island", printed in Mandela N, *The Struggle is My Life*, noted in Further Reading at the end of the chapter, at p 200.
6   Ibid, 214-5.

the Imcata movement and of the Zulu people. Despite daily ebbs and flows, working relations do seem to be developing, and the government edging towards black participation in government. Incidents of violence and recrimination, such as in relation to the actions of the police and to the loss of life that occurred during the initially peaceful protest near Bisho, in September 1992 in the Ciskei homeland, can be expected to continue. But they should not be allowed to obscure the substantial movement that is occurring. One hopes for patience, particularly on the side of the black peoples. There are years of toil and bitterness ahead. Is it too optimistic to hope that the legal system can be rolled back relatively soon, and that progress, necessarily slow, can be made without major carnage in the building of genuine equality, sharing and social trust?

Discussion. South Africa has shown how a determined minority, even if reasonably democratic within itself, can progressively come to dominate the economic, legal and social system of a country and oppress the majority members. In this it has been uniquely successful in the world. But the days of oppression of the majority (rather than the minority) are clearly numbered. The tide that started with Mandela's release in 1990 will not now be stemmed. There are sufficient numbers of people of good will, and of others who simply count the crazy economic cost of maintaining a system of legalised suppression, to guarantee that.

All the human rights of the people seem to have been violated by the system of apartheid – and most notably the right to fair and decent conditions of work and to participate in the political process. The other violations of rights go with these – the torture, terror, poverty, dispossession and lack of decent education, the absence of fair trial and due process and the suppression of indigenous peoples as such. It is difficult to imagine a more terrible system, one more based on a determination to prevent equality in any area of endeavour. Indeed, it underlines, if there were need for that, the centrality in the human rights system of the doctrine of the equality of all human beings.

The international community has been well aware of the scandal of apartheid. It started by developing the International

Convention for the Elimination of All Forms of Racial Discrimination (ICERD). The convention, which followed the Declaration of 1963, was opened for signature in 1965, as the evils of apartheid were becoming more apparent, and became operative in 1969. The number of states that have accepted its obligations (now over 125) is exceeded only in the human rights field by the four humanitarian (Geneva) conventions on the treatment during war operations of the wounded, the sick, prisoners of war and civilians; and the conventions against Genocide and Torture.

Not surprisingly, the terms of ICERD include references, both implied and specific, to apartheid. In the preambular statements, it is asserted that "all human beings are equal before the law" and that "all practices of segregation and discrimination associated therewith" should be condemned. Later, alarm is expressed at the continuation of governmental policies "based on racial superiority or hatred, such as policies of *apartheid*, segregation or separation". The convention itself defines racial discrimination as including "any distinction, exclusion, restriction or preference based on race ... which has the purpose or effect of nullifying or impairing the ... enjoyment or exercise, on an equal footing, of human rights and fundamental freedoms".[7] The convention proceeds by requiring state parties to pursue policies designed to eliminate racial discrimination "in all its forms" and in particular by reference, in Article 4, to a long list of civil, political and economic, social and cultural rights[8] Even in prescribing the need for special measures to assist the victims of racial discrimination, *apartheid* was kept in mind. Articles 1.4 and 2.2 note that special measures to eliminate discrimination and barriers between races "shall in no case entail ... the maintenance of unequal or separate rights for different racial groups after the objectives for which they were taken have been achieved". It is not difficult to see how relevant ICERD was to circumstances in South Africa. It need hardly be added that South Africa has not ratified the convention.

---

7   Article 1.1 of the International Convention.
8   More than 22 rights are specified in Article 5, which was drawn up because at that time the two Covenants (on Civil and Political and on Economic, Social and Cultural Rights) were not yet ready for signature – they were only opened for signature in 1966.

II. MARTIN LUTHER KING

The Story. At about 6pm on Thursday 4 April 1968, Martin Luther King was waiting on the balcony of his motel in Memphis, Tennessee, for his colleague the Rev Ralph Abernathy to get ready before going out to dinner at the home of a Negro pastor friend. He asked the band below, which was to be at the meeting afterwards, to be sure to play "Precious Lord, take my hand". Almost as he stopped, a shot was fired. Less than an hour later he was pronounced dead at the emergency room of a nearby hospital. The nation was shocked, and its leaders attended his funeral service in Ebenezer Church, Atlanta. Black leaders called for protest, as a result of which some 46 people were killed, 3,500 were injured and 20,000 were arrested. The twelve hard years of non-violent struggle against racial discrimination and oppression were over. A more militant leadership sought to establish in the years ahead an equality for black Americans in the North that had eluded King and the Southern Christian Leadership Conference (SCLC) of which he was the leader.

Martin Luther King Jr was born on 15 January 1929 in his grandparents' house in Atlanta, Georgia. His parents were Negro. His mother, Alberta, was the daughter of Pastor Adam Williams, who had been born into a Negro slave family that was emancipated after the Civil War. His father, Martin Luther King Sr, was son of a Negro sharecropper who had a major alcohol problem that led to domestic violence. In breaking free from that, Martin Sr sought education and eventually became a Baptist pastor assisting Pastor Williams at Ebenezer Baptist church.

For Martin Jr, the pattern was somewhat the same. After completing high school in Atlanta, he went to Morehouse College at the age of 15 and graduated with distinction three years later. He felt a call to the pastorate of the church, and at the age of 18 was ordained and appointed as his father's assistant pastor. He went on to Crozer Theological Seminary – an "integrated" (racially) college – in Chester, Pennsylvania. Here, living with white as well as black student colleagues, he became aware of the prejudice against blacks. He felt he must avoid the typical stereotype of the Negro by never being late, loud, dirty, messy, or laughing too much. He found himself accused of misdemeanours he had not committed, and embarrassed by being refused service when taking a female friend to a restaurant. He had begun to sense, and to react to, the climate of racial prejudice still strong in the 1940s in the southern United States, and even in New England. The last stage of his career as a student opened in 1951 with the move, with a bachelor of divinity degree from Crozer and a scholarship, to Boston University, where he wrote his doctoral thesis and, perhaps more importantly, met his future wife Coretta Scott, a music student. They married in 1953 and both graduated in 1954. His doctorate (a PhD in Theology) was awarded in 1955.

It was not long before King, now back in Montgomery, Alabama, as pastor at the Dexter Avenue Baptist Church, became involved in the movement of black resistance and search for rights that was to be his life's work. His direct involvement in the protest movement began with the arrest of Mrs Rosa Parks, a 42-year-old seamstress, because she refused to give up her seat in a city bus to a white man. Under the Alabama segregation law, the front ten rows in buses were exclusively reserved for whites. Any seat behind that had to be given up by a black passenger to a white if the front ones were full. Black passengers were also required, having obtained their ticket from the driver at the front, to leave the bus and enter by the back door. It seems that it was not uncommon for the bus to drive off before they had managed to get in at the back.

In the previous year, the Supreme Court of the United States had handed down its landmark decision in *Brown v Board of Education of Topeka, Kansas*, 349 US 294 (1955). The court held that the "separate but equal" mode of public education was unconstitutional because in violation of the 14th Amendment that guarantees all citizens equal treatment[9] In early 1955, the Interstate Commission had issued a ruling that, for the same reason as adopted by the court, segregation on public buses was also unconstitutional.

---

9   The 14th Amendment, the last of the provisions in the US Bill of Rights (along with the first 10 Amendments made in 1791) was agreed to in 1868 and was the legal and constitutional sequel to the Civil War. By it, all persons born or naturalised in the United States are citizens (thus including Negroes, even if formerly slaves), their rights are not to be infringed, and they are all to enjoy "equal protection of the law".

The arrest of Mrs Parks occurred on 1 December 1955. King was elected president of the Montgomery Improvement Association (MIA), which was hastily formed following Mrs Parks' arrest. It was decided that the bus service, on which 70 percent of the passengers were black, should be boycotted on the following Monday, 5 December. The boycott was almost 100 percent effective. The consequence was that the white residents of Montgomery saw with amazement crowds of black people in the street making their protest manifest by walking to work or using taxis, which organised and offered cheap fares for groups during the months of protest. King set the tone with addresses in which the non-violence campaign was launched. That campaign was, over the next 7 years, to advance enormously the cause of equality for black citizens and brought King to great prominence both in the United States and abroad. It resulted in 1964 in his being both *Time Magazine* Man of the Year for 1963 and recipient of the Nobel Peace Prize.

Meanwhile, in Montgomery there were threats to King of assassination and violence, his home was bombed and in February 1956 he and 89 other leaders were indicted for breaching the 1921 segregation statute. The city refused to allow negroes equal access to the buses, or to be employed as drivers, and an alternative transport system organised by the negroes was challenged in the courts. As the challenge was being heard, news came through that the Federal District Court had, in *Browder v Gale* 142 Fed Supp 707 (1956), declared the 1921 state and municipal segregation laws invalid. The law was changed, but the Montgomery authorities declared that they would do all they could to neutralise it. In a comment typical of the attitude of those resisting the non-violence campaign, the City Commission said it –

> ... will do all in its power to oppose the integration of the Negro race with the white race in Montgomery, and will forever stand like a rock against social equality, intermarriage, and mixing of the races under God's creation and plan.[10]

Nevertheless, the victory of the MIA was real and the cause of non-violence was given a great impetus. It is often intransigeance, or even victories by those perpetrating injustice

---

10   Quoted in Colaiaco, referred to in Further Reading, at p 17.

and discrimination, that produce the greatest advances in the cause of the oppressed.

Over the next few years the campaign of non-violent protest extended widely through the South. The SCLC became the main organised force behind King. He was elected President and the Rev Ralph Abernathy Treasurer. Protests and resistance to discriminatory practices occurred all over the South, though there was a hiccup at Albany, Georgia, in late 1961, when there were widespread protests against segregation in transport and at lunch counters. The too-comprehensive aims of the protest, coupled with the non-violent tactics carefully adopted by the police, and the release three times of King following arrest, drew from the compelling nature, and the publicity value, of the protest.

Probably the greatest victory of all came in the city of Birmingham, Alabama. Although buses had been integrated in the 1950s, much remained to be done. Downtown stores refused to serve blacks (many displayed offensive Jim Crow signs[11]), lunch counters were segregated, blacks were confined mostly to menial jobs and there was discrimination in promotion. Blacks were also subjected to violence and intimidation, their churches and homes were attacked and accommodation was segregated. In May 1962, the SCLC decided to target the city by organising a boycott on downtown stores, including on lunch counters, and by repeated street demonstrations. The campaign got under way in early 1963, with the focus on the downtown stores.

The start of the Birmingham protest, originally timed for early March 1963, was deferred twice while local council elections were held. The Birmingham Manifesto was at last launched on 3 April. By Palm Sunday, 7 April, dogs were brought into play by the police and immediately there was wide media interest. Further demonstrations were banned on 10 April, and on Good Friday, after giving notice on the previous day of a defiance of the ban, King marched and was arrested along with other protesters. The process escalated, although King was

---

11   Jim Crow was a singing routine developed in the post-Civil-War era in the United States, and the name came to symbolise the segregation enforced by law on Negroes in the southern states. Jim Crow signs in effect implied that Negroes were not welcome. Strictly, they were illegal, but their social impact was strong, and the law was not enforced.

released on 20 April, and on 3 May dogs were turned on a large crowd including 1000 children. There was uproar across the nation. President Kennedy praised the actions of the demonstrators, and in early June announced a request to Congress to enact a new Civil Rights Bill.

King, in his famous "Letter from Birmingham Jail",[12] gave some of the deep down reasons why the blacks could no longer wait, but felt they must take matters into their own hands –

> ... when you have seen vicious mobs lynch your mothers and fathers ... when you have seen hate-filled policemen curse, kick and even kill your black brothers and sisters ... when you see the vast majority of your twenty million Negro brothers smothering in an airtight cage of poverty in the midst of an affluent society; when you suddenly find your tongue twisted and your speech stammering as you seek to explain to your six-year-old daughter why she can't go to the public amusement park that has just been advertised on television, and see tears welling up in her eyes when she is told that Funtown is closed to colored children, and see ominous clouds of inferiority beginning to form in her little mental sky, and see her beginning to distort her personality by developing an unconscious bitterness toward white people; when you have to concoct an answer for a five-year-old son who is asking: "Daddy, why do white people treat coloured people so mean?"; ... – then you will understand why we find it difficult to wait.[13]

After Birmingham, the SCLC continued with its efforts in the South. With the virtual defeat of *de jure* segregation there, the aims of the movement gradually broadened, though they did not formally do so until 1966. The aspirations of the gradually broadening aims are movingly encapsulated in King's famous speech "I have a Dream" –

> I have a dream that one day this nation will rise up, live out the true meaning of its creed: We hold these truths to be self-evident, that all men are created equal.
>
> I have a dream that one day on the red hills of Georgia the sons of former slaves and the sons of former slave-owners will be able to sit down together at the table of brotherhood ... .

---

12 Reproduced in King ML, *Why We Can't Wait*, Signet, New York, 1963, as Chapter 5.
13 Ibid, p 82.

> I have a dream that my four little children one day will live in a nation where they will not be judged by the colour of their skin, but by the content of their character ... .
>
> This will be the day when all of God's people will be able to sing with new meaning, "Let freedom ring" ... .[14]

This, probably his greatest speech, was given at the end of a long hot afternoon of speeches near the Lincoln Memorial in the centre of Washington. Some quarter of a million people were present on that day, 28 August 1963, at the culmination of the "March on Washington for Jobs and Freedom". The title given to the march itself symbolises the new, broader emphasis of the movement that was beginning to appear and that culminated in the protest at Chicago in 1966.

In that year, symbolising the focusing of attention on the North, King moved to Chicago. Efforts were made to rouse the urbanised refugee Negroes living in the northern industrial cities to join the non-violent movement, with a focus on the need for the city's "slumlords" to improve their properties. But the Northern Negroes were more dispirited, more hopeless, less rousable than the Southerners, and there was not such instant and effective support. Further, important sections of the black movement felt more direct and violent action was necessary. It was against this background of internal dissension and lack of support that the campaign finally switched from being a protest movement to being a social movement – a movement with broader and increasingly national aims, including the alleviation of the poverty so movingly referred to in the Birmingham Jail letter.

Stiffening resistance to the move for black equality, and the cross-currents of the Vietnam war which King opposed, led to growing difficulties in maintaining momentum through 1967 and 1968. King alluded to this, and to the possibility of his death, in a sermon at Ebenezer Baptist Church in Atlanta, in February 1968. In March he was called to assist with a strike and protest in Memphis, Tennessee and addressed a meeting of 15,000 in a Masonic temple. Increasing concern was being felt about the effectiveness of the non-violent mode. Following the issue on 3 April of an injunction against further marching at the request of the Mayor and a better-than-expected evening meeting, it was

---

14   Quoted in Slack, mentioned in Further Reading below, pp 85-6.

agreed that King would address a rallying meeting the next day, 4 April. The rest has been told ...

Discussion. The struggle against racial discrimination is written across the whole of the political and legal history of the United States. The status of serfdom was recognised in the United States Constitution (it still is).[15] Those central events in its history, the civil war in 1856 and the movement led by King a century later, were about racial discrimination. Many of the major decisions of the United States Supreme Court have been about racial discrimination. Its doctrines about discrimination have been developed round race rather than sex, in contrast to the greater concentration on sex discrimination in Australia and other Western countries. The battle has been for real recognition of the equality of blacks and whites. That day has not yet come, and King's dream still stands unfulfilled. Although there has been progress, the sequence of conservative Administrations and the tragic riots in Los Angeles following the unnecessary beating by police of a black man in mid-1992, underline that the transition to equality is far from complete. Discrimination on grounds of race bites deep into a civilisation, and takes much time, effort and sacrifice to eliminate. Changing the law does not necessarily achieve this, but it does at least give the oppressed group a means of fighting against the discrimination.

The second clear conclusion from the United States experience is that at the heart of racial discrimination lie the pursuit of power, the exploitation of social dominance and the practice of oppression. Even in an apparently democratic society, inequality can remain. Enfranchisement of the racial minority does not necessarily lead to improvement. Full and equal participation in the political processes is necessary, as is so perceptively required by Article 25 of the International Covenant on Civil and Political Rights.[16] But for full participation, some degree of equality of education, and of social standing, is necessary. And for these, some degree of economic equality. It is this gradually broadening perception of the magnitude and

---

15   See Articles I ss 2.3 and 9.1 and Article IV s 2.3

16   Article 25 of the Covenant states in part that "Every citizen shall have the right and the opportunity, without ... any distinction ... to take part in the conduct of public affairs ..."

depth of the task involved in eliminating racial discrimination that lies behind the decision in Chicago in 1966 to broaden the aims of the non-violence movement.

Finally, the story shows that the dominant white group, with its control of the cities and the police and the law, is able to break a movement based on non-violence, unless there is a change of heart in the majority. The non-violence movement went a considerable way with this, but failed to maintain the momentum or impact for long enough. Those fighting for racial equality probably have to change methods continually as the effectiveness of the current mode wanes. It is not a happy story.

III. OVERVIEW

The stories of Mandela and King have been told because they illustrate just what a scourge the practice of racial discrimination is. Cruelties and denials of rights can be associated with racial discrimination in a way that is hardly possible in the area of sex discrimination. On the other hand, the evil of sex discrimination has caused half the population of the world to be placed in an inferior situation – mostly not so inferior as in the case of oppressed racial groups, but even more entrenched in the fabric of a society than racial discrimination. The issues associated with sex discrimination are discussed further in Chapter 9. Here, the point being made is that racial discrimination must rate as one of the two forms of discrimination most damaging to peoples and individuals.

It is not possible, either, for countries like Australia or the United Kingdom – or Malaysia or China or Russia or Ethiopia – to escape on the ground that they have not perpetrated discrimination as pervasive or destructive in its effects, as have South Africa and even the United States. The fact is that almost every country practises its own form of racial discrimination. Normally, the majority group oppresses the racial minority through law, culture and employment practices. But that need not be the case, as South Africa shows. Nor need the racial minority be as substantial as in the United States. The stories about indigenous peoples in Chapter 1 show how even tiny minorities can be cruelly discriminated against on account of their race. Thus every country in the world, it can safely be said, needs to consider its own record in the area of racial discrimination and to act to eliminate it.

The second interesting issue that emerges from the cases of the United States and South Africa is that the oppressed race needs strong and competent leadership. It is no accident that both Mandela and King were members of leading or privileged groups in their own race. Without that confidence in their individual integrity and capacity, it is almost impossible for a member of an oppressed group to emerge as a leader. Whether the leader is essentially a political or a religious figure does not seem to matter, though in the end the political leader probably has less chance of taking a secondary role. It was easier for Archbishop Tutu, and the other leaders of the South African Council of Churches, to stand aside and adopt a role supporting the ANC than it may have been for King, who was essentially a political leader, to find an accommodation with the thrusting political leaders of the black movement in the United States. It is also not without significance that the ANC structure is based on the United States model. The ANC has a legislative-style Congress, a "military" wing,[17] an executive, and clear perceptions of being a kind of shadow state. To some degree, it was also able to keep its "peaceful" arm separate from its "military" arm. In these ways, it was better organised than the SCLC both for its ongoing protest activities and for ultimate negotiation with the government.

Another message that emerges clearly both from the two cases here used, and from many other situations, is the importance of international support for the cause of the group against which discrimination has been directed. It is worth noting that ICERD carefully defines racial discrimination to include both activities consciously designed to oppress on ground of race and also situations that have that effect regardless of intent or motive (the definition talks of discriminations that

---

17 This, the Umkhonto we Sizwe (Spear of the Nation), was greatly strengthened in 1961, when Mandela was given the task by the ANC of preparing it as the separate arm of the ANC that would, when necessary, undertake sabotage operations. Many of its members were located progressively, and as occasion and the attainment of independence permitted, outside South Africa in the neighbouring states of Angola, Zambia, Zimbabwe, Tanzania and Mozambique.

have "the purpose *or effect*" (emphasis added)). Thus the convention proscribes what is often termed "indirect" discrimination (the law or practice has the *effect* of discriminating) as well as deliberate (or "direct") discrimination. There is no doubt that the gathering force of the sanctions imposed on South Africa in the 1980s, and the criticisms of the United States treatment of its Negro population, have had a significant effect in causing governments and legislatures to moderate their positions. In the case of Australia, where the main difficulty has been the oppression of the Aboriginal people, the threat of Aboriginal action overseas, and criticism by overseas visitors, has been powerfully influential on local politicians.

The reader will have noticed the importance attached to education by both Mandela and King. It is often not realised how important the educational system can be in creating and reinforcing a sense of inferiority in the oppressed group. Even if members of the group are able to attend "integrated" schools, their home background may lead to poor results and to consequential feelings of inferiority and later inability to move beyond the lower levels of employment, thus perpetuating the cycle. If "Bantustan" style schools are established, the effect is much worse. On the other hand, if the school system specifically addresses in a constructive way the needs of the oppressed group, the educational process can be one of the most powerful means of eliminating discrimination.

It remains to reflect briefly on the role the law plays in the matter of racial discrimination. The Marxist thesis that the law is the instrument of the ruling class, and that it can be used as an instrument of oppression, is well borne out in both cases. However, that that is not law's only function is illustrated by the way in which the changes in the bussing and educational segregation laws in the United States worked. They both signalled, and in themselves brought about, change. The new laws gave the Negro people a means of asserting their rights for themselves. In this way, the very existence of the new law helped them to become more united in their struggle. Instead of the law being a means of keeping them down, it became a means of focusing their efforts to assert their rights. They became as it were, full members of the society. So in these two ways – as instrument and as empowerer – and also as educator and setter of standards, the law can make an important contribution to the elimination of racial discrimination. It should be added that a number of countries have enacted laws making discrimination on grounds of race unlawful.[18] This legislation has in each case established an executive agency to handle complaints and to promote the cause of good race relations through education, publicity and intervention in particular issues. Such legislation is a valuable and empowering mechanism for furthering the cause of racial equality.

The South-West Africa cases,[19] brought in the International Court of Justice by Liberia and Ethiopia against South Africa, mark an important stage in the emergence of international legal challenges to racial discrimination. The outcome of the cases, commenced in 1962 and completed in 1966, is disappointing. By a majority the ICJ held the two countries did not have standing to bring a challenge to the legality of applying apartheid to the former League of Nations Mandated Territory of South-West Africa. However, the minority dissenting judgment of Judge Tanaka produced a statement of the basis of discrimination that has become a classic.[20] He noted that different treatment can be justifiable, because –

> ... the principle of equality before the law does not mean the absolute equality, namely equal treatment of men without regard to individual concrete circumstances, but it means the relative equality, namely the principle *to treat equally what are equal and unequally what are unequal.* (Emphasis added.)

He said that one has to determine when not to treat people equally by reference to the criteria of justice or reasonableness, and that these criteria exclude the notion of arbitrariness.

---

18 For example, in Australia the *Racial Discrimination Act* 1975, in the United Kingdom the *Race Relations Act* 1976 (repealing earlier legislation of 1965 and 1968), in Canada the *Human Rights Act* 1976-77 (and the Ontario legislation dating back to 1962), and in New Zealand the *Race Relations Act* 1971. In the United States, the Supreme Court has developed case law based on the Bill of Rights and the *Civil Rights Act* 1964 that achieves much the same effect – see the discussion on King in Section II above.

19 The two cases are really two phases of the one challenge. The relevant documents are set out in (1968) 37 *International Law Reports* (both phases) and in ICJRep 1962 318 and ICJRep 1966 4.

20 See especially the book by McKean, *Equality and Discrimination Under International law*, noted in Further Reading below.

Selecting race as a basis for special treatment was, he argued, wrong because it was not analogous to the special treatment of minorities. Race is too indeterminate a criterion, compared with say sex, language or disability. So the apartheid system was arbitrary in its application, that is it did not treat equals equally and unequals unequally in a just way, and therefore it was unlawful. Although Judge Tanaka's opinion was not endorsed by the court, it has had a powerful influence on thinking about discrimination all round the world, and particularly about the inconsistency of racial discrimination with human rights principles.

For Further Reading

For Nelson Mandela, a good short biography is that by Mary Benson, *Nelson Mandela*, Penguin, England, 1986. An account of the work of the ANC and other black groups in South Africa is given in Davis SM, *Apartheid's Rebels: South Africa's Hidden War*, Yale, New Haven, 1987. Two books containing material written by Mandela himself were published during his imprisonment. The first is *No Easy Walk to Freedom*, with a foreword by Ahmed Ben Bella and an introduction by Oliver Tambo, Heinemann, London, 1965. The second is *The Struggle is My Life*, and contains speeches, writings and some historical documents as well as comments by some of Mandela's fellow-prisoners. It was published by International Defence and Aid Fund for Southern Africa, Canon Collins House, London, 1986.

The most comprehensive book available about Martin Luther King is Oates SB, *Let the Trumpet Sound: The Life of Martin Luther King Jr*, Harper and Row, New York, 1982. His religious significance is assessed in Slack K, *Martin Luther King*, SCM Press, London, 1970 and there is an account of the movement as a whole in Colaiaco JA, *Martin Luther King Jr: Apostle of Militant Nonviolence*, St Martin's Press, New York, 1988. A more critical account appears in Williams JA, *The King God Didn't Save: Reflections on the Life and Death of Martin Luther King Jr*, Eyre & Spottiswoode, London, 1971. King's own book, *Why We Can't Wait* was published by Signet, New York, in 1964.

An interesting account of the South-West Africa case and of the international law relating to equality and discrimination is contained in McKean W, *Equality and Discrimination Under International Law*, Clarendon, England, 1983. An excellent account of the development of the international law on racial discrimination appears in Lauren PG,

"First Principles of Racial Equality: History and the Politics and Diplomacy of Human Rights Provisions in the United Nations Charter", (1983) 5 *Human Rights Quarterly*, 1.

Chapter 9

The Cases of Donka Najdovska, Lynette Aldridge and Johnson Controls

Sex Discrimination and Affirmative Action

I. THE CASE OF DONKA NAJDOVSKA

The Story. During the six months from April 1980, Donka Najdovska and 33 other women made a series of complaints against Australian Iron and Steel Pty Ltd (AIS). They complained under the New South Wales Anti-Discrimination Act 1977 that they had been discriminated against on grounds of their sex because their applications for work at AIS had either been delayed much longer than similarly dated applications from men, or had not been accepted.

AIS is a large steel-producing enterprise associated with Broken Hill Pty Ltd, one of Australia's largest companies. Its workforce at the time was about 8000, of whom about 500, or 6 percent, were women. AIS is located at Port Kembla, a few kilometres beyond Wollongong which is an hour and a half's comfortable drive from Sydney. Wollongong is situated in picturesque surroundings on the undulating strip of land wedged between attractive mountains to the west and the sea to the east. Port Kembla itself is flatter and opener, and from its smokestacks heavy clouds of smoke and steam issue from time to time, though pollution controls have reduced the threatening pall that used to hang permanently around the city and harbour.

127

The AIS works are the single most important source of employment in the Wollongong area, which houses somewhat less than a quarter of a million people, many of them migrants from Europe. Its main industry in the past was coal mining, but the mines have gradually been phased out as they became uneconomic to work, and the city has been plagued with continuing high levels of unemployment.

Following the complaint from the 34 women, the Counsellor for Equal Opportunity instituted extensive investigations. It emerged that AIS' employment practice in the iron working areas was very heavily oriented towards recruiting male workers. Although the complainants had sought employment from dates in 1977 onwards, it was discovered that of the 4289 ironworkers taken on during the three years to April 1980, only 58 (1.3 percent) were women.

While the complex background to this complaint of direct discrimination was being investigated during the early 1980s, there was an encouraging change in AIS' recruitment pattern. For example, between 1 July and 22 August 1980, 468 employees were hired, of whom 71, or just over 15 percent, were women. The trend continued, but then there was a downturn in the economy. AIS ceased recruiting in 1981, and towards the end of 1982 decided that it would have to retrench some of its workers. It decided to adopt the policy of "last on first off", thereby giving preference to the more senior employees. That is generally accepted as a fair way of handling a difficult situation, but in this case the effect was almost immediately to cause retrenchment of the women who had lodged the complaint of discrimination and had subsequently been employed by AIS. So in late 1982, and during the first half of 1983, the women lodged a second round of complaints. These were of indirect discrimination, and were directed against both the policy and, as it occurred, the actual retrenchment.

By May 1984 the Counsellor for Equal Opportunity[1] had reached the conclusion that the issues needed legal resolution and that further conciliation was unlikely to be effective. Accordingly, all the complaints were assembled and referred to

---

1   By 1982, the Counsellor's position had been abolished, and a new position of President of the Anti-Discrimination Board substituted, but the functions were, in relation to the handling of complaints, the same.

the Equal Opportunity Tribunal. The Tribunal held a series of hearings which culminated in decisions against AIS on both the major grounds of complaint – of direct discrimination relating to the recruitment procedures and of indirect discrimination relating to the retrenchment policy. The precise amount of the compensation awarded to each woman varied, but it is said that overall the compensation was in excess of $2 million and that the individual payments on both the direct and indirect grounds of discrimination ranged from about $5000 to about $75,000.

However, the battle was not over when the Tribunal handed down its judgment in 1985. AIS appealed first to the Court of Appeal of New South Wales,[2] which found against it in May 1988, and then to the High Court of Australia, which found against it in late 1989.[3] In both the appeal cases, AIS decided not to contest the Tribunal's *direct* discrimination decision (on the delays in recruiting) but only the *indirect* discrimination decision (on the retrenchment policy). The three New South Wales judges and the five High Court judges all applied the complicated definition of indirect discrimination in different ways (except for Justices Deane and Gaudron in the High Court, who wrote a joint judgment).

The unchallenged decision of the Tribunal on the "direct" discrimination complaint was based on section 24(1) of the Anti-Discrimination Act, which provides that –

> A person discriminates against another person on the ground of his [sic] sex if, on the ground of –
> (a) his sex;
> (b) a characteristic that appertains generally to persons of his sex; or
> (c) a characteristic that is generally imputed to persons of his sex,
> he treats him less favourably than in the same circumstances, or in circumstances which are not materially different, he treats or would treat a person of the opposite sex.[4]

The Tribunal found that the discrimination was clearly within paragraph (1)(a) of section 24. Both the statistics of

---

2   See (1988) EOC 92-223.
3   (1989) 168 CLR 165.
4   This provision is virtually identical to the one contained in other Commonwealth and State legislation in Australia, and in the legislation of other countries such as the United Kingdom, Canada and New Zealand.

recruitment mentioned – before and after the complaints were lodged in 1980 – and what was said to the women when they applied, supported that. So also did the attitude of most of the men working at AIS. The investigative study mentioned above that took place during the early 1980s revealed that many of the men resented the presence of women; that many thought women could not do the heavy labour required; and that the attitude of some members of the management group was distinctly sexist. The Tribunal quoted one superintendent to the effect that "over my dead body do women ever work here, and I don't care what the law says or anything about the law, I'm not interested"[5]

The *indirect* discrimination claim, which was appealed to the two higher courts, was also complex. Under section 24(3) of the Anti-Discrimination Act –

> A person discriminates against another person on the ground of his sex if he [sic] requires the other person to comply with a requirement or condition –
>
> (a) with which a substantially higher proportion of persons of the opposite sex to the sex of the other person comply or are able to comply;
>
> (b) which is not reasonable having regard to the circumstances of the case; and
>
> (c) with which the other person does not or is not able to comply.

It needs to be emphasised that the three elements of the requirement or condition (paragraphs (a) to (c) above) all have to be complied with if the discrimination is to be unlawful. This contrasts with the definition of direct discrimination in sub-section (1), quoted above, where the discrimination exists if any one of the three conditions applies.

There are several points to note about indirect discrimination. First, it is not referred to in this way in any legislation. The name comes from the fact that the discrimination

---

5   See (1985) EOC 92-140 at 76,387. The three hearings in the Equal Opportunity Tribunal all go under the name *Najdovska v Australian Iron and Steel Pty Ltd* and are reported in the CCH Equal Opportunity Law and Practice series in –

(1985) EOC 92-120 – admissibility of conciliation proceedings;

(1985) EOC 92-140 – whether complaints justified, ie whether AIS' actions were unlawful; and

(1986) EOC 92-176 – determination of compensation payable.

caught by the provision is usually not imposed on particular individuals, but comes by way of a general rule or requirement. In our case, the requirement was the "last on first off" rule which, as the Tribunal observed, is "facially neutral". That is, it does not appear discriminatory, but turns out to be so when applied (in our case, because an unfair number of women were retrenched). Second, the courts have not been technical in applying the concept of a "requirement" – it does not have to be under a law or a contract but can, as with AIS, be in effect a management decision or policy.

Third, the requirement has to be one with which, in our case, more men than women can comply. A greater proportion of men were "senior" in our case, and so less were retrenched. The discussion in the High Court in *Australian Iron & Steel Pty Ltd v Banovic* (1989) 168 CLR[6] is complicated, and revolves round how the "pools" of complainants and of respondents (the women and the men in our story) are to be determined.[7] Although a variety of "pools" were chosen, an important element in them was the recruitment figures mentioned above. In both the High Court (by the majority) and the Court of Appeal (unanimous) the outcome was the same – that a higher proportion of the men was able to escape retrenchment, and thus that indirect discrimination was involved. The High Court dissentients, Brennan and McHugh JJ, considered the "pool" to be the total workforce, in which the proportions of men and women before and after the retrenchments were very much the same.[8]

Finally, the requirement is one with which, in our case, the women "do not or are not able to comply". Clearly, the women were not able to have been in the workforce earlier, and there was no way they could have avoided joining relatively late in the recruitment phase. So there was no difficulty in finding that they complied with the third of the criteria that go to make up a discriminatory requirement.

6   This was the name under which the case went during the appeal, because Ms Najsdovska had retired and Ms Banovic became the representative complainant.

7   The "pools", or numbers in the group, are necessary so that the *proportion* (see s 24(3)(a)) affected can be determined for the purposes of s 24(3).

8   Indeed, as McHugh J pointed out, the women came off slightly better, with the proportion of female ironworkers retrenched being 6.27 percent compared with 6.77 percent for male ironworkers.

Discussion. There was great rejoicing in the women's movement when the successful outcome to Najdovska's case was announced. It was felt that the tide must be turning, and that the wall of discrimination was being broken down. There were good grounds for the rejoicing, but the tightening economic conditions of the late 1980s and the early 1990s seem to have slowed the process, though it is continuing. That is the first conclusion that has to be drawn from the enforcement of anti-discrimination legislation: its implementation is often slow and painful.

One of the reasons for the slowness is that a major change is being made in the attitudes and practices of the whole community. Such changes do not come about quickly. But in addition, earlier legislation is often found to impede progress, both in itself and in the way those opposed to change use it. So in the AIS case the company itself sheltered behind the "safety" or "protective" legislation which has been the subject of much discussion all over the world. Originally introduced to protect women and children from unsafe work practices, it has in more recent times often been used for, or has had the effect of, preventing women obtaining jobs they were well able to do. It is mostly based on the now outmoded stereotype that all women are weaker than all men.

In the AIS instance, the Factories Shops and Industries Act 1962 of New South Wales prohibited women lifting weights of more than 16 kilos. But the investigative studies found that there were many jobs, eg cranedriver, which were weight-barred but in which women were working; and that there were enough positions not weight-barred, even taking into account that some progression jobs beyond the entry point were barred even if the entry job was not, to warrant rejecting AIS' major claim that the weight restrictions justified its refusal to recruit women in more equal numbers. Several years later, so deeply entrenched are these "protective" laws, discussions are still going on about their removal, and the third story below will show another aspect of them.

Third, the definitions of discrimination, particularly for indirect discrimination, are very complicated. They were built up from United States decisions and, as will be shown in Section IV below, are now somewhat outdated. However, neither the present, nor the new, definitions can avoid giving the courts the task of interpreting what is reasonable in the circumstances of the particular case. The "reasonableness" criterion proves particularly difficult in the case of indirect discrimination. The criterion is often criticised, particularly by feminist thinkers, because it is administered largely by male judges, and tends to be male in its orientation, as the traditional test – "the man [sic] on the Clapham omnibus" – suggests. However, given particularly the earlier direct discrimination in recruitment, none of the majority judges (all but one male) felt the "last on first off" test could be regarded as reasonable.

While it is not easy to see how the legislation could do other than use the "reasonableness" criterion, it is important that its application be carefully watched to ensure that it itself does not become a form of indirect discrimination. The assessment of discriminatoriness is often made by examining statistics, as in our story. These show how the system adopted actually works in practice. For this reason, indirect discrimination is often called "systemic" discrimination. As discrimination becomes less direct and more subtle, not being apparent in a particular case but appearing as a result of the way the system works – whether it be in retrenchment, or in the provision of life policy benefits or home loans – there will be increasing need for the kind of investigations carried out so successfully by Ms Chloe Refshauge for the Counsellor of Equal Opportunity.

II. The Case of Lynette Aldridge

The Story. In January 1985, Lynette Aldridge got her first full-time job. She had been unemployed for a year when the Commonwealth Employment Service put her in touch with Mr Grant Booth. She was delighted to get the job, a few weeks before her birthday in April, when she was to be 20. Mr Booth ran "Tasty Morsel Cakes" on behalf of the four owners, his wife, her parents and himself. The job was to assist him in selling cakes, and in preparing cakes for sale by icing them and so on. The shop was in an arcade in the Brisbane suburb of Stafford. In total it was about 4 metres wide and 13 metres deep, with rather less than half being the public area, including a front counter and a refrigerator. The section behind was where the baking, and the icing and other preparatory work, were done and the benches and storage bins were kept. So there was not much space in either the baking area or behind the counter. Apart from Mr Booth, Miss Aldridge was normally the only person who worked there.

From the beginning, things were not altogether easy for Miss Aldridge. When she saw Mr Booth at his home before deciding to employ her, he asked her "What would you do if I slapped your bum?" While she was at work she was subjected to repeated actions of a sexual nature that she found objectionable, but which she ignored or only mildly objected to because she so much wanted to keep the job. She believed she would almost certainly lose it if she proved too difficult, because on some occasions Mr Booth would ask her, when she was resisting, if she wanted "a holiday on the government", which she interpreted as meaning that she would lose her job.

The repeated events of this kind weighed on Miss Aldridge and, after talking the matter over on more than one occasion with her friends, she decided to leave, much as she wanted to stay in employment. On 20 January 1986, just a day less than the first anniversary of her appointment, she gave a week's notice. On 24 January, Mrs Booth (one of the four owners) terminated Miss Aldridge's employment. In February, Miss Aldridge complained to the Brisbane office of the Commonwealth's Human Rights Commission that she had been the victim of sexual harassment. The Commission's conciliators in Brisbane made efforts to reach a conciliated settlement, but that proved impossible, so the case was brought to the Commission itself in Canberra. The Commission arranged a two-day hearing in Brisbane in November, and awarded Miss Aldridge damages of $7000 for loss of wages and for humiliation, injury to her feelings, and pain, suffering and discomfort.

Regrettably, the defendants did not pay the amount awarded by the Commission. So Miss Aldridge had to seek a further hearing and determination of her complaint by the Federal Court. The hearings, which lasted in all for six days and covered many legal issues including the validity of the sexual harassment provisions of the federal Sex Discrimination Act 1984, took place in Brisbane. In May 1988 Spender J handed down his judgment. In general, he endorsed the findings of the Commission. He ordered that Mr Booth pay Miss Aldridge the sum of $7000.

During the course of his judgment he summarised the key facts leading to his finding of sexual harassment –

> The applicant claims that during the year of her employment Mr Booth made repeated unwelcome sexual advances by touching her on the bottom, on the breasts, both inside and outside her clothing, rubbing his hand up and down her leg and kissing her on the neck and lips, by pulling her hair, by requesting sexual intercourse and threatening the termination of her employment ... and by engaging in acts of sexual intercourse at the cake shop. ... She says that the first act of intercourse occurred after trading on Saturday, 27 April 1985. On that occasion, Miss Aldridge said that, after the shop had closed ... she was icing a cake and Mr Booth came behind her and was trying to kiss her: "he started mucking around and I started to push him away. ... And I ended up falling on the floor, and he got on top of me, and got his penis out of his shorts, and I said, 'OK, OK I'll do it with you then'. And then he got off me and he went to the chemist. ... " After [he] had purchased some condoms, intercourse occurred on the floor of the baking section.[9]

The facts are not pleasant, and it is in many ways a pity to have to recount them. But this kind of incident is so common, and the effect on the victim so great, that it is important that people know just what kinds of harassment take place. Sometimes the harassments are much less than those experienced by Miss Aldridge.

Whether more or less serious, acts of sexual harassment occur with considerable frequency. Something like one quarter of all complaints under the Sex Discrimination Act, and the parallel state legislation,[10] involve sexual harassment. What can be said with certainty is that these insensitive acts take the form almost exclusively of harassment of females by males. Feminist thinkers on the whole welcome the provisions that make sexual harassment unlawful, both because they empower women to make complaints and because they have the effect of bringing a

---

9   *Aldridge v Booth* (1988) 80 ALR 1 at 18-9.
10   Five of the six States, and one of the two self-governing Territories, now have legislation that directly, or in effect proscribes sexual harassment. The exceptions are Tasmania and the Northern Territory.

"private" activity into the "public" arena. The purpose of making actions part of the public arena is that they become the subject of law, and therefore can be regulated or prevented by law. Feminist thinkers also tend to assert that sexual harassment is discrimination, not simply an act analogous to the tort of trespass to the person. That is because it is so nearly universally related to the gender of the person (the object of harassment is almost invariably a woman, not a man) that it becomes a form of gender discrimination and so a form of gender or sex discrimination, not just a gender-neutral wrong, as is a tort. Says Catherine MacKinnon, a leading thinker in this area –

> Sexual harassment as experienced during sexual harassment seems less an ordinary act of sexual desire directed towards the wrong person than *an expression of dominance laced with impersonal contempt*, the habit of getting what one wants, and the perception (usually accurate) that the situation can be safely exploited in this way – all expressed sexually. It is dominance eroticised. ... Sexual harassment ... is not merely a parade of interconnected consequences with the potential for discrete repetition by other individuals. ... Rather, it is a group-defined injury which occurs to many different individuals regardless of unique qualities or circumstances, in ways that connect with other deprivations of the same individuals, among all of whom a single characteristic – female sex – is shared.[11] (Emphasis added)

Using that analysis, Spender J said in Aldridge that legislation without specific provision for sexual harassment can cover most cases –

> It seems to me that sexual harassment is a form of discrimination, as a matter of analysis. ... In jurisdictions where sexual harassment in employment is not proscribed as such, courts and tribunals have held that sexual harassment in employment, of the kind formulated in section 28 [of the Commonwealth Sex Discrimination Act], constituted discrimination against women within the field of employment on the ground of sex. ... [He then cited a number of Canadian, United States and Scottish cases, as well as some Australian cases and in particular *O'Callaghan v Loder* [1983] NSWLR 89.] In my opinion, when a woman is subjected to sexual harassment as defined in section 28 she is subjected to that

---

11 From *Sexual Harassment of Working Women*, and quoted in Graycar and Morgan, *The Hidden Gender of Law*, pp 354 and 355, and discussed in Further Reading.

conduct because she is a woman, and a male employee would not be so harassed: the discrimination is on the basis of sex.[12]

It should be noted that Spender J was careful to confine his analysis to conduct of the kind specified in section 28 of the Commonwealth legislation. That legislation requires a person to be subjected to "unwelcome conduct of a sexual nature" in the course of her employment, and to have a reasonable basis for fearing that rejection of the conduct would prejudice her in her employment. In the employment situation, there is no doubt that Spender J is correct in his analysis. There is strictly no need for special legislation. But there are two other sets of situations that the basic provisions against discrimination on grounds of sex do not cover and for which, in the view of the author, specific anti-harassment provisions are necessary.

For example, imagine the case of a man who is not a regular harasser, but who is genuinely attracted to a particular woman; and that the woman is simply not interested. He may press his claims even more strongly if she tries to keep him away. Indeed, her refusals may not so much reduce as increase his ardour. She naturally begins to feel harassed, particularly if "he won't take 'no' for an answer". He is clearly harassing her, but is he discriminating against her on grounds of her sex? The author doubts it. The man is harassing her because she is a *particular* woman, not just because she is *a* woman. It could be argued that the woman in this case is not able to get rid of him because of the long tradition of male pursuit and of female subordination to the sexual desires of men. But the argument may be difficult to sustain in court-type proceedings, particularly if the judges are male.

In the view of the author it is safest to include specific provisions in anti-discrimination legislation to cover sexual harassment as such. If the man in the example just quoted were to be a fellow-employee of the woman, it is unlikely that she would be able to get a remedy under section 28. Even if rejected, he would be unlikely to try to prejudice her in her employment, and indeed he might not have any power to do so. But he would still have harassed her. The more recent legislation in Australia, South Australia, the Australian Capital Territory and

---

12   (1988) 80 ALR 18.

Queensland has included provisions that eliminate the need for fear of detriment in employment, one difficult hurdle for a complainant to jump. It has improved the earlier legislation in three other ways. First, it has broadened the definition of harassment so that it covers an act of a sexual kind that results in the woman feeling "offended, humiliated or intimidated ... and it is reasonable in all the circumstances" that she should feel that way. This is better than section 28, which requires an "unwelcome" approach and fear of "disadvantage" in employment. Second, the description of the effect on the harassed person is made more objective, and is separated from the need to show justified fear of disadvantage. It would cover the hypothetical case described in the previous paragraph. But there is still the added requirement of "reasonable" that, as discussed earlier, has its drawbacks.

Third, the South Australian and ACT legislation has extended the area of harassment to the provision of goods and services and accommodation and the ACT also to harassment between students. If, in the example above, the harassment was purely "social", ie is not within the employment or the goods, services and accommodation fields, then no unlawful act occurs. The public/private distinction is maintained. In the interests of protecting free social contact and relationships, and of people's privacy (a very important right – see Chapter 6) it may be that this is as far as the law should go. However, experience may show that there are still areas where the law should protect women if equality is to be attained between the sexes. If so, then, as the area of need is identified, new legislation should be framed and enacted. In this connection, it is to be noted that the Queensland Anti-Discrimination Act 1991 has extended sexual harassment into a free-standing concept by making it an unlawful action that applies provided the person harassed is reasonably humiliated, offended or intimidated by the conduct. It may be that it is paving the way for a more generalised concept of harassment, that could later be extended to other grounds such as race, disability and opinion.

III. The Case of Johnson Controls

The Story. Johnson Controls is a United States company that makes batteries. It has a manufacturing plant in the central State of Wisconsin. For many years, it refused to employ women because of health hazards associated with the lead inevitably used in the manufacturing process. The hazards apply to all workers, but particularly to pregnant women, when the foetus can be affected. However, with the enactment of the United States Civil Rights Act 1964 and the broadening offer of employment for women, Johnson Controls began to employ females, and in 1977 adopted a policy relating to women. It noted that protection of the health of the unborn child "is the immediate and direct responsibility of the prospective parents". The conclusion of the 1977 policy statement was that it was not appropriate for the company to take specific measures to prevent women capable of bearing children from working in the plant: that might be illegal discrimination. Instead, it adopted a policy of warning women of the dangers to the foetus of exposure to lead and of advising them that they should not seek a job that carried lead exposure risks. It asked them, at the time of applying for any job, to sign a statement that the company had warned them of the risks.

However, in 1982 Johnson Controls decided that this was not enough. It moved from a policy of warning women to a policy of exclusion. It indicated that it would not place women "who are pregnant or who are capable of bearing children" in jobs that would or could result in exposure to lead. This meant substantial exclusion of women from the firm, because the jobs excluded were not only those in which there was direct exposure to lead, but also those from which promotion, transfer or other processes could lead them to exposed jobs. The only way a woman could avoid the exclusion was to produce a medical certificate to the effect that she was not capable of bearing children.

In April 1984 a group of employees, and also several unions, brought an action in the Federal District Court of East Wisconsin challenging the policy on the basis that it amounted to sex discrimination under Title VII of the Civil Rights Act 1964. The court found in favour of the company. It said that the doctrine of business necessity applied to exonerate the company. Under that rubric, the courts had developed a view that if a serious hazard to a foetus could be shown; that the only risk occurs through the employment of women; and that there is no alternative reasonable way of protecting the foetus, then the policy of refusing to employ women capable of becoming pregnant is justifiable. On appeal, the Court of Appeals for the Seventh Circuit in September 1989 upheld the District Court by a majority of 7-4. Applying the business necessity test, the majority found first, that all the parties agreed that there are substantial risks to the unborn child if its mother is exposed to lead, and that the damage if caused can be permanent. Second, it recorded that Johnson Controls had found the voluntary exclusion program did not work, and that none of the parties had been able to propose an alternative way of avoiding the problem for the unborn child. Indeed, observed the majority –

> The union has failed to present even one specific alternative to the manufacturer's foetal protection policy, much less a demonstration of how any particular economically and technologically feasible alternative would effectively achieve the manufacturer's purpose of preventing the risk of foetal harm associated with the exposure to lead of fertile female employees.[13]

The appeal, under the name the *International Union, United Automobile, Aerospace and Agricultural Implement Workers of America, UAW v Johnson Controls, Inc* (1991) 59 Law Week 4209, was heard by the Supreme Court in October 1990. In its judgment, delivered in March 1991, the Supreme Court overruled the earlier decisions. Writing for the court, Justice Blackmun[14] said that the question at issue was whether the affirmative action policy in favour of the unborn child taken by Johnson Controls was valid, or whether it infringed the sex discrimination provisions of the Civil Rights Act. He noted that the Court of Appeals had felt its decision represented a nice balancing of the rights of the employer, the employees and the unborn child. But he also noted that there was a minority in the court that had dissented. His opinion in effect built on the dissent. In essence, he said, there was a clear sex bias in the Johnson Controls policy. Fertile men, but not fertile women,

---

13   *Auto Workers v Johnson Controls Inc* (1989) 58 Law Week 2193, at 2194.
14   The same Justice who wrote the majority opinion in *Roe v Wade*, and the powerful dissent in *Webster* – see Chapter 6.

were given a choice whether to risk the side effects of exposure to lead. The policy was not facially neutral, as the Court of Appeals had asserted. It did not protect the children of men, and it was based on gender and childbearing capacity rather than on fertility alone. Further, "the absence of a malevolent motive does not convert a facially discriminatory policy into a neutral policy with discriminatory effect" (p 4212). Accordingly, the principle of business necessity was not applicable. The policy was unlawful because it was sex discriminatory.

Discussion. The story is not easy to understand because the kernel of it is the dilemma of affirmative action being taken to benefit one group (pregnant women and their babies) at the expense of a larger group (all women, or at least all women capable of bearing children). So how do you reconcile the two – the benefit for the pregnant woman and her unborn child against the benefit for women generally (ie increased employment opportunities)?

The first point of interest is that the affirmative action was taken by a company, and not by the government. Affirmative action can be taken by any person, and particularly by any employer, to assist disadvantaged members of the workforce. One aspect of the case not specifically discussed by the Supreme Court on this occasion was whether the unborn child is in fact properly treated as a person. In *Webster v Reproductive Services*, discussed in Chapter 6, the court said that its decision on privacy would not have been different whatever status is given to the unborn child. In *Johnson Controls* one suspects that the same view might prevail: the court was deciding whether the policy was sex discriminatory and not about the status of the unborn child. It was clearly of the view that the 1964 Act should apply according to its terms, and that a discriminatory act, however well-intentioned and beneficial to its target group, was not lawful.

The second point of interest that emerges follows from this. It is that any form of affirmative action will harm someone. In this case, the action in favour of the unborn child would harm the employment interests of women (and not men). This is the difficulty with affirmative action programs. Affirmative action is sometimes called "reverse" discrimination. That name focuses on the persons, usually the majority, who form the group by reference to which the disadvantage is measured. In *Johnson Controls* the disadvantaged persons, that is the "victims" of reverse discrimination, are the women of child-bearing age. They had to suffer employment disadvantage in favour of the potentially unborn child. In other cases, it is the man who "suffers" compared with the female employee, because he does not get the appointment or the promotion.

In the leading and famous United States case of *Regents of the University of California v Bakke* 438 US 265 (1978), Mr Bakke, a man of European descent, did not get admitted to the medical school though his marks were better than those of a black man who was admitted under a quota. The Supreme Court held that a firm quota that had no regard for merit (Mr Bakke could show his marks were better than those of several blacks) was not acceptable. What the court has done in that and a series of later cases is to limit the extent to which the "majority" group suffers in the interests of remedying past injustice and achieving fairer rules. On the other hand, the people who have suffered the disadvantage are able to get preference, even if that does sometimes mean a marginal member of the "majority" group fails to get the job, the promotion, or admission to the training course. Essentially, what is allowed is preferential treatment of a "soft" kind that takes into account the merits of claimants from both groups and then decides in favour of the disadvantaged group member. What is not allowed is the absolute preference that comes from the enforcement of quotas, regardless of the merits of individuals in the two groups.

In Australia and some other countries, there is now legislation that institutes affirmative action plans. So far the legislative measures have only protected women in employment, and not elsewhere, so they are less comprehensive than the measures allowed in the United States as permissible discrimination. In the United States, at least race and sex are the subject of affirmative action decisions, although the action has not extended beyond employment and education. It does not extend, for example, to the provision of goods and services[15] Nonetheless, particularly in education, special programs, often called "remedial", are in operation to assist children with

---

15 However, it is extended to federal government employment and those who
    contract to supply services to the government.

learning difficulties or handicaps and there are special housing programs for disadvantaged individuals and families, though here the basis is more poverty as such than race, sex or disability. The practice of assisting disadvantaged individuals and groups is common in countries with welfare programs, and the issues have simply been sharpened where there is anti-discrimination legislation. There, perceptions are sharpened because the legislation *forbids* discrimination on certain grounds, such as sex or race. The question is how far the legislation will allow *preference*, as distinct from *equal treatment*, for members of the disadvantaged groups.

It is this kind of issue that Justice Blackmun was referring to when he commented that the *Johnson Controls* measures to protect unborn children did not turn a "facially discriminatory policy into a neutral policy with a discriminatory effect". What he had in mind was that when there is an unlawful discrimination (in this case against women), the mere fact that there is a legitimate purpose in mind – to protect unborn children – does not also legitimate the discrimination. In the strict sense, "affirmative action" should only be applied to situations in which there is an unlawful ground of discrimination (race, sex etc) and reverse discrimination occurs in assisting the members of the disadvantaged group.

In most anti-discrimination legislation, there is a specific clause that allows action to bring the members of the disadvantaged group to equality. Thus section 33 of the Australian Sex Discrimination Act 1984 provides –

> Nothing in [the provisions defining unlawfully discriminatory acts] renders it unlawful to do an act a purpose of which is to ensure that persons of a particular sex or marital status or persons who are pregnant have equal opportunities with other persons in circumstances in relation to which provision is made by this Act.

The purpose will, of course, extend to allow "positive" or "affirmative" measures to be taken on behalf of all the individuals or groups for whose benefit the legislation has been enacted. In Australia, the attributes other than sex, marital status and pregnancy that have been targeted include age, race, impairment, religion, political belief or activity, lawful sexual activity and association with persons having those attributes. So a widening group of persons is being protected, and allowed also to be the target of affirmative action.

III. Overview

The three stories have shown various aspects of the attempts made in modern Western democracies to bring about greater equality between the sexes. The Najdovska story shows how the disadvantages suffered by women in employment – and in other areas of life – can be both direct and immediate, in this case as a result of specific recruitment and promotion policies. It has also shown how the disadvantage can be indirect or systemic, and so bear unequally on women even though facially neutral. It is this kind of systemic discrimination that affirmative action programs are designed to avoid. It would have been possible for AIS to decide, in advance of any case brought by the women, that in its lay-off policies it would adopt a practice the result of which was more favourable to women than the last-on-first-off practice. That could have been shown to mean more men laid off, and so to be reverse discrimination. In this situation the criteria are not altogether clear, except that "quotas" that apply mechanically, no matter what the particular merits of the people involved are not acceptable. In Mr Bakke's case, apart from the quota principle in itself, which made the "system" unlawful, ie unacceptably discriminatory, an important question not asked was how much better his results were than those of the lower graded blacks.

In the Johnson Controls case, the Supreme Court suggested some criteria that can be used to assess the legitimacy of affirmative action programs. First, the affirmative action cannot be permitted to affect adversely a group – in this case potentially child-bearing women – whose members are protected by anti-discrimination legislation. The policy could only be lawful if, on first examination, it were shown not to be discriminatory on grounds of sex (because this is unlawful). Second, the discriminatory policy (in its effect on the potentially child-bearing women) would have to be shown to be basically reasonable. That is, its effect on them would have to be proportionate to the evil being avoided. In this case, said Justice Blackmun, the number of women who might become pregnant would be very small and "Concerns about a tiny minority of women cannot set the standard by which all are judged" (p 4211). Third, the policy would have to "effectively and equally protect the offspring of all employees" (p 4211). In other words, it could not generate a further kind of unacceptable discrimination in achieving the desired end. Affirmative action programs must themselves be non-discriminatory except in relation to the whole of the target group

Thus the cases of Najdovska and Johnson Controls illustrate just how closely sex discrimination and affirmative action are related. The objects of the two programs are similar. The methods of implementation in the United States are much the same as in the United Kingdom, Canada and Australia – both need enforcement by the courts. But in countries such as Australia, while the anti-discrimination legislation is ultimately enforced by courts, affirmative action legislation is implemented by administrative action and by legislative definition of the contents of acceptable programs. Although it is sometimes said that anti-discrimination is retrospective in its effect, and affirmative action prospective, that is not an altogether accurate distinction. Anti-discrimination does have important prospective effects. Most employers, once found to have acted unlawfully, will avoid further discrimination. In cases such as that of AIS, the effects can be expected to be lasting, and even to spread to other firms. It would be more accurate to say that anti-discrimination deals with past discrimination, has some effect in preventing future discrimination, and also is available if an affirmative action program fails to remove the discrimination to which it is addressed.

Sexual harassment is in one sense the epitome of sex discrimination. It can occur by itself, as perhaps happened in the case of Lynette Aldridge. Even then, it is simply a particular example of the pervasive exercise of male power in the employment situation. It is a manifestation of the power inequality of women in the workforce – Grant Booth was the employer, she the employee.

But even if, as noted above, sexual harassment is made unlawful in other areas such as in the provision of goods and services, one may want to ask whether a good deal more is necessary than just cleaning up particular facets of community life. If male dominance comes ultimately from the crude fact of greater physical power, then new and more fundamental ways will have to be found of dealing with the problem of harassment. Our society will have to become one in which each individual – male or female – is respected for her or his inherent dignity as a human being. Males will have to learn new roles in which ultimate resort to physical force is not acceptable, and in which they can retain their self-respect without, as Catherine McKinnon so perceptively said, resorting to the "expression of dominance laced with personal contempt". Women will have to avoid using their generally greater skills in breaking down self-respect that have the effect of provoking men to acts of physical violence on them or surrogates.

All this means concentrating on the achievement of substantive rather than formal equality. It means, applying Judge Tanaka's dictum in the South-West Africa case quoted in Chapter 8, that equals have to be treated equally, but unequals unequally in accordance with justice, reasonableness, and respect for the inherent dignity and worth of each human person. This is an endeavour that the law cannot achieve because it relates to people's perceptions and motives rather than to their actions as such. But it is one the law can positively support, as this chapter has shown. It can do this by the application of increasingly refined rules designed to avoid action by stereotype rather than by reference to the particular person and her or his maximum enjoyment of rights.

As part of this continuing refinement of the applicable legal concepts, two examples may usefully be mentioned. The first relates to the definition of discrimination. The definition of the two aspects of discrimination – direct and indirect – quoted in the story of Najdovska above shows the end product of an effort to encapsulate, in legislation, principles that the United States Supreme Court in particular has evolved through the hearing of many cases. But in the process, the definitions, have become very convoluted. In an Act passed by the Legislative Assembly of the Australian Capital Territory in December 1991 a new definition was adopted that, in the words of the Chief Minister, Ms Rosemary Follett, "is a clear statement of what we mean by discrimination without the unnecessary tests and conditions which unduly complicate the matter in other jurisdictions."

Section 8 of the Discrimination Act 1991 of the ACT reads in part –

> For the purposes of this Act, a person discriminates against another person if –
> (a) the person treats or proposes to treat the other person unfavourably because the other person has an attribute referred to in section 7 [such as sex, race, sexuality, impairment or religious or political opinion]; or
> (b) the person imposes or proposes to impose a condition or requirement that has, or is likely to have, the effect of disadvantaging persons because they have an attribute referred to in section 7.

Direct discrimination is covered by paragraph (a). It covers both acts that have happened and actions that are proposed. It may, for example, occur as a result of the adoption of a policy or the taking of a decision. This could be a valuable protection for someone seeking to prevent the implementation of a discriminatory decision. The earlier legislation may not cover decisions, as distinct from actions.

Indirect discrimination is covered by paragraph (b). It avoids the reference to "proportions" that has caused so much trouble in Banovic and other cases. It goes back to the early formulation in the Australian Racial Discrimination Act 1975 that an action based on race is unlawful if it has "the purpose *or effect*" of violating a human right. The coupling of the imposition of a requirement or condition with its "effect" is the way the "indirect" or "systemic" notion has been built into the ACT Act.

Use of the concept of "effect" has been the occasion of a good deal of criticism, because it is said that it is not fair to look at "results". All one should do is look at the action itself. But of course, if that is done, the second aspect of the Najdovska case would have failed. Those who oppose the "effect" or "results" notion also tend to oppose reverse discrimination, because they say the consequence is to disadvantage the "majority" group – the women in both Najdovska's and the Johnson Controls cases.[16] A provision along the lines of the ACT legislation should

---

16   Brennan J made a similar point in his (dissenting) judgment in Banovic, the sequel to Najdovska, when he said –
    ... the Act does not provide for "reverse discrimination" ... in order to undo the effect of prior unlawful discrimination. ... If an employer were to dismiss men simply on the grounds of their sex ... [he] would

make it easier for courts not to get caught in the dilemma of one (positive) form of discrimination not being allowed because it would result in another (negative) form, as did Brennan J in Banovic (see footnote 16). The criterion is simply whether the requirement or condition has the effect of disadvantaging the targeted group and is reasonable in the circumstances. If it does, it is unlawful: the consequence for others is not relevant, providing the disadvantage caused to them is "reasonable" in the circumstances.

There may come a time when women, or racial minorities, or the Aboriginal people are effectively equal in their enjoyment of rights with the rest of the population. Usually, that point will come as a result of deliberately adopted affirmative action programs, such as providing for education for the target group, or redefining merit so that women have an equal opportunity for jobs or promotion in a particular enterprise. At that point of time, all anti-discrimination legislation ceases to operate to the advantage of the target group. That is, it requires strict neutrality among equals. The reason is that the legislation states that when a situation of equality has been reached, special measures that are designed to achieve it but are necessarily discriminatory as they do so, are no longer exempt but are to be struck down as discriminatory. If, for example, the AIS workforce became reasonably evenly balanced as a result of modified retrenchment rules and of fairer recruitment practices, then the lay-off order might permissibly be strict order of seniority.

This is what the international conventions against discrimination have specifically provided for through their doctrine of "special measures". Both the Racial Discrimination Convention 1969 and the Women's Discrimination Convention 1981 contain "special measures" provisions. Articles 3 and 4 in the latter Convention read –

> Article 3
> States Parties shall take in all fields, in particular in the political, social, economic and cultural fields, all appropriate measures, including legislation, to ensure the full development and advancement of women, for the purpose of guaranteeing them the

---

be guilty of unlawfully discriminating. ... Why should employees bear the burden of rectifying the consequences of past discrimination? (168 CLR pp 172-3).

exercise and enjoyment of human rights and fundamental freedoms on a basis of equality with men.

Article 4

1. Adoption by States Parties of temporary special measures aimed at accelerating *de facto* equality between men and women shall not be considered discrimination as defined in the present Convention, but shall in no way entail as a consequence the maintenance of unequal or separate standards: these measures shall be discontinued when the objectives of equality of opportunity and treatment have been achieved.[17]

In formulating these articles, the international community has, in the area of discrimination, as in the area of general human rights, thought through the issues and drafted pioneering provisions that have stood the test of time. It should nevertheless be added that, although Australia and many other countries have legislated to put the conventions into effect, there are still major difficulties, particularly in the area of sex discrimination. There are major reservations in parts of the Islamic world, for instance, about the achievement of full equality. There are also, as mentioned earlier, major difficulties across the world as a whole because of the need to move away from the ultimate power derived from physical strength that is probably the primary reason for male dominance. That dominance begins in the "private" area of the home and childhood, and flows over into the more "public" areas of domestic and international life. The problem of male dominance over women is probably one of the greatest hurdles to be overcome in achieving full enjoyment of human rights for all human beings and not just men. There is yet more challenge to come to current modes of thinking and acting as those who develop feminist thinking (not necessarily always women) push back the barriers to analysis, thought and action that have grown up around the age-old practice of discrimination on grounds of sex, which really means the exercise of excessive power, in both the public and the private spheres, by males over females.

---

17 Convention on the Elimination of All Forms of Discrimination Against Women, which is a primary basis for the Australian Sex Discrimination Act. The parallel clauses in the Convention for the Elimination of All Forms of Racial Discrimination are Articles 1.4 and 2.2.

For Further Reading

On the matter of sex discrimination generally, including indirect discrimination and affirmative action, a really excellent recent book is by Graycar R and Morgan J, *The Hidden Gender of Law*, Federation Press, Sydney, 1990. It is a combination of materials and of script written by the two authors, and achieves a nice balance between the two. It contains excellent references and quotations from texts and cases, and is the best and most current book available. There is a review of Australian law, and of the situation in other countries, in Bailey PH, *Human Rights: Australia in an International Context*, Butterworths, 1991, ch 6. Also good are Bacchi C, *Same Difference: Feminism and Sexual Difference*, 1989 and, in more legal vein, being analyses of English and Australian experience respectively, Pannick D, *Sex Discrimination Law*, Clarendon, 1985 and Thornton M, *The Liberal Promise: Anti-Discrimination Legislation in Australia*, OUP, Melbourne, 1990. A provocative collection of materials and commentary is Scutt J, *Women and the Law*, Law Book Co, Sydney, 1990.

The topic of sexual harassment is covered in most of the books mentioned in the previous paragraph. The leading book, a highly regarded expression of the feminist viewpoint, is MacKinnon CA, *Sexual Harassment of Working Women*, Yale, New Haven, 1979.

Affirmative action is the subject of very widely different views. Supportive views are put forward by Graycar and Morgan, referred to above, in Chapter 5 on Work, and in the book edited by Sawer M, *Program for Change: Affirmative Action in Australia*, Allen & Unwin, Sydney, 1985. A cautious view, thoroughly argued and basically supportive, is put by Goldman AH, *Justice and Reverse Discrimination*, Princeton University, Princeton, 1979. Most of the books mentioned above also have sections on affirmative action, as does Bailey PH, *Human Rights: Australia in an International Context*, Butterworths, Sydney, 1990, Chapter 6, which also recounts the Australian experience, as does Scutt, referred to above, in Chapter 3. There is an excellent analysis of the concept of merit in Burton C, *Redefining Merit*, Monograph 2, Affirmative Action Agency, Ambassador Press, 1988, ISBN 0 644 069222 8.

Chapter 10

The Cases of Awet Josef of Eritrea

and the Gillick Children

The Rights of Children

I. AWET JOSEF OF ERITREA

The Story. Awet Josef was born on 2 January 1980, in a camp for orphans and refugees in Eritrea, formally a northern district of Ethiopia. Solomuna Camp, where Awet was born, was "formally" in the north of Ethiopia because, in 1952, the United Nations had declared Eritrea to be "an autonomous unit federated with Ethiopia under the sovereignty of the Ethiopian crown". The federal arrangements were not respected by the government of Emperor Haile Selassie. For a decade, the Eritrean people attempted, but failed, to establish and maintain a measure of freedom from the control of Addis Ababa.[1] One measure after another – the displacement of Tigrinya, language of the majority, by an Ethiopian language (Amharic); the banning of political parties and of trade unions; and the closure of newspapers – led to the commencement of armed revolt in 1961.

By 1980, when Awet Josef was born, there had been two decades of fighting. The Eritrean People's Liberation Front (EPLF) had become the major organ of resistance, and with other national groups had established a "liberated" area in the north of Eritrea. But two decades of war and intermittent famine had begun to take their toll. More than 50,000 Eritreans had been

---

1   Capital of Ethiopia, and some 800km south of Solomuna Camp.

killed in the fighting, and more had died of starvation and the illnesses that often came with it.

Special camps were established in various parts of liberated Eritrea to care for the orphans and women in particular. By being located together they were accessible to the trickle of international relief that was to become substantial by the late 1980s. Continuous bombing of roads, villages, fields and other places of congregation resulted in heavy casualties and a resort to moving only by night or when cloud cover was low. The economy, fragile at any time and in large part subsistence, was being systematically broken down and the morale of the people undermined.

Little Awet was reasonably healthy when born in January – he weighed 3250 grams (7lb 4oz) and his after-birth examination revealed no problems. But at two months, the first of the illnesses that were to dog his short life struck. Like so many other Eritrean babies, denied a home and normal conditions, he contracted gastroenteritis. His mother took him to the camp hospital, where he was treated for a week and then allowed to leave in good condition. In May, he had another bout of illness – diarrhoea and fever – and was returned to hospital. Malaria was diagnosed, and he was given chloroquin. Being strong, he recovered quickly. However, his mother, believing her milk was not proving suitable for him, asked for milk powder. After much time explaining by the health workers that she and Awet were both doing well, and that supplement would only be needed later, she left, only to return in late June with her baby sick again. This time it was an amoebic infection (amebiasis). Five days later he left, with his mother instructed how to complete the treatment at "home". She was also shown how to prepare home-improvised weaning food for him.

No further contact was made with Awet and his mother, who disappeared until February 1981, when he weighed 7.4 kilos (16lb 4oz), about 2.5 kilos or 20 percent underweight. He had continued to be fed at the breast, and had not been given the weaning food. It seemed he had not liked it. He was emaciated, and there were other signs of wasting (marasmus).

In June, an epidemic of measles swept the camp. Awet caught the measles, and his condition was complicated by further episodes of diarrhoea and vomiting. After a few more days, on 12 July 1981, he died, aged 18 months. A week before his death his weight had gone down to only 6.2 kilos (it should have been about 11 kilos), so he was not quite double his birth weight.

This tragic story could be repeated thousands of times each year for the mothers and fathers of Eritrea over the past three decades. Indeed, the story got worse as the 1980s proceeded, with a new onslaught by the Ethiopian army, this time supplied with Russian guns, equipment and armament. During the 1960s and 1970s, the suppliers had been the United States, aided by Israel. Ethiopia had been a pawn in the power game, being seen as useful to give European powers a strategic hold on the Horn of Africa, where the Soviet Union already had established links with Somalia. This outside "aid" was provided to Ethiopia with the particular object of helping to subdue the Eritreans. Without the Eritrean province, Ethiopia had no Red Sea coast, and thus no powerful strategic advantage in terms of controlling the use of the Suez Canal. So the destruction wrought on Eritrea was not simply from Ethiopia, but was also brought about by successive great powers interested not at all in the Eritreans but only in broad Middle East and Northern African affairs. Nor did the other African countries want to see Eritrea's bid for independence succeed. If it did, they saw possible implications for their own dissident groups. One is reminded of the position of Indonesia and East Timor, discussed in Chapter 2, and of the "floodgates" argument.

We do not know anything of Awet's father. The balance of probabilities was that he was away fighting the Ethiopians. Alternatively, he may have been dead – killed in the fighting, or possibly of starvation and associated illness. He is unlikely to have been one of the few left on the coffee or vegetable-growing farms, because if that had been so his wife and Awet could have been with him. Whether Awet's father were alive or dead, Awet's life would have been neither easy nor particularly happy, and certainly not what it would have been had there not been two decades of war.

On 24 May 1991, the incredible happened. A new era opened for Eritrea. A significant portion (possibly 150,000 men) of the largest standing army in Africa, that of Ethiopia, was defeated south of Asmara. Only 60,000 escaped, and some 70,000 were repatriated to Ethiopia. Dispirited and fed up with fighting a purposeless and losing war, the mainly youthful and conscript army surrendered to the Eritrean forces who had been using largely captured Soviet weapons. Asmara, a city of about 250,000, is the capital of Eritrea and lies only 100km or so south of Solomuna Camp. Eritrea, with its population of some 3.5 million, is now setting about the task of rehabilitating itself and becoming a member of the United Nations. That task is daunting. Some half a million refugees can be expected to return to Eritrea from the neighbouring countries to which they fled during the years of war and famine. The ports will have to be opened again, the homes and roads rebuilt, the farms brought back to productivity and the people re-nourished. The EPLF forces have shown a lead, as they did during the years of war, this time by volunteering to help with reconstruction by working in the fields without pay. Around the world, relief funds and supplies are being sought and a desperate battle against disease, famine and starvation is currently being fought, as it is in so much of northern Africa. Will this courageous young nation survive beyond its early infancy, as little Awet and so many others did not?

Discussion. Awet Josef has not thousands but millions of counterparts in virtually every part of the world except Western Europe, North America, Australia and New Zealand. The question must be asked: is there any point in talking about special rights of the child (such as for juvenile justice or sound education or autonomy) for him or those who have perhaps just managed to survive the many threats their environment contains? Is it not better simply to regard them as having basic human rights, along with the rest of humankind? Are special rights for children really only appropriate for those lucky enough to be born into the affluent countries of the world?

The surprisingly universal support being given to the International Convention on the Rights of the Child suggests that many countries, especially in Africa and Asia, think the rights of children should be given special recognition. The convention, which was opened for signature in January 1990, had been signed or ratified by no less than 140 countries by September 1991 – little more than 18 months later. With that number of signatures and ratifications, it is likely very soon to be more widely supported than any other international human rights instruments except the humanitarian conventions, which have virtually universal support, and the genocide and torture conventions. Perhaps, aided by the tireless work of the United Nations International Children's Emergency Fund (UNICEF) and many other organisations and individuals, the Awets of many generations are not suffering altogether in vain.

The question still remains, whether a special convention is a useful measure for most of the world. The author believes it is. It is a substantial statement of the rights of children, and many of its Articles avoid simply reproducing provisions already contained in the two International Covenants. For example, Articles 12 and 13 make specific claims for the rights of children to have their views heard and to receive and impart information and ideas. Those rights are not well observed in most countries. Then again, Article 17 provides that the mass media are to be obliged "to disseminate information and material of social and cultural benefit to the child" and Article 22 draws special attention to the needs of the child refugee. He or she must receive appropriate protection and be assisted in tracing parents or other family members. Articles 28 and 29, on education, require equal opportunity; accessibility of higher education; exercise of discipline at school "in a manner consistent with the child's human dignity"; the development of respect for human rights; and the development of "respect for the environment". Thus important special needs of children are enshrined in the convention. They can become the subject of special domestic programs and of international review through the reports countries must make under Article 43 to the independent expert Committee on the Rights of the Child.

The story of Awet shows, however, the weakness and the dependence of every child. Even if he or she is born into a society in which civil/political and economic/social rights are well observed, dependence is a primary mode for many years. During that time, it is of vital importance that the child is nurtured so that a fully competent adulthood can be achieved. Malnourishment, particularly at Awet's stage, may result in permanent under-performance, both physically and intellectually. And so, if unchecked, the cycle of poverty and disadvantage will be carried forward for another generation, through no fault or action of the child. Indeed, the importance of economic/social rights is perhaps particularly great for the child. It may be possible later to overcome racial, sex or linguistic disadvantages. But the consequences of deprivation of vital foods, particularly proteins, and of vital salts, such as iodine, can never be made good. The child will never be able to obtain these for him or herself – they are most needed at an age of virtually total dependence. So here, the attainment of basic human rights for the population as a whole is essential. If they are not implemented, the cycle of disadvantage will continue.

II. The Gillick Children

The Story. Mrs Gillick, with her husband and four children, lived north of London, England, within the West Norfolk and Wisbech Health Authority area. She was a Roman Catholic and took exception to a circular issued in December 1980 by the West Norfolk and Wisbech Area Health Authority. The circular, which replaced an earlier one of May 1974, and originated in the Department of Health and Social Security (DHSS), allowed doctors of the Authority to give advice about contraception to "a person under the age of 16" without parental consent. The circular made it clear that the doctor or other professional, if approached by such a person, should "always seek to persuade the child to involve the parent or guardian ... at the earliest stage of consultation, and will proceed from the assumption that it would be most unusual to provide advice about contraception without parental consent".

Mrs Gillick was not satisfied with the terms of this guidance to the health professionals. She wished to reserve exclusively to herself and her husband the right to decide about contraceptive advice while the children were under 16. In January 1981 she wrote to the Authority –

Concerning the new DHSS guidelines on the contraceptive and abortion treatment of children under both the legal and medical age of consent, without the knowledge or consent of the parents, can I please ask you for a written assurance that in no circumstances whatsoever will any of my daughters (Beatrice, Hannah, Jessie and Sarah) be given contraceptive or abortion treatment whilst they are under 16 in any of the family planning clinics under your control, without my prior knowledge, and irrefutable evidence of my consent?

The Authority replied within a week emphasising that it would be most unusual for the advice to be given without parental consent, but that in the last resort it was for the relevant professional to decide, as a matter of "clinical judgment". This did not satisfy Mrs Gillick. She wrote in March forbidding any contraception or abortion advice to her children while under 16, without her consent. As the Authority did not change its position, she commenced proceedings through the Cambridge Registry of the Supreme Court in August 1982. The proceedings were heard successively by a single Judge of the Court of Queen's Bench in 1983, by the Court of Appeal in 1984 and by the House of Lords in 1985. In the end, Mrs Gillick lost her case. The initial decision of Woolf J, against her, was reversed by a unanimous decision of the Court of Appeal (three Justices), but was finally accepted by a majority of the House of Lords (3-2). The path-breaking majority judgment of the House of Lords was therefore supported by only four of the nine Judges hearing the case.

The case, which is a landmark decision in favour of the rights of children, is known as *Gillick v West Norfolk Area Health Authority and the Department of Health and Social Security.*[2] What Mrs Gillick sought was two declarations by the courts. The first was to the effect that neither the DHSS nor the Authority had legal power to issue a circular in the terms mentioned above. If she had succeeded in this request, the offending part of the circular would have had to be withdrawn. Second, she sought a declaration that it would be illegal for any health professional employed by the Authority to give contraceptive or abortion advice or treatment without her consent.

Mrs Gillick's first request raises interesting but complex questions of administrative law – how far the circular could be reviewed by the courts because it was not a "decision" but only guidelines. All the judges agreed that the circular was in itself expressing a matter of public policy. Since the current law is that

---

2   The Queen's Bench proceedings (with Woolf J) are reported in [1984] 1 QB 581 and the Court of Appeal and House of Lords proceedings in [1986] AC 112 at 116 (Court of Appeal) and 150 (House of Lords).

policy decisions are not reviewable (only actions carrying out policy are), the courts all held that the issue and contents of the circular were not reviewable. However, it would be unlawful if that expression of policy led doctors to commit a crime. The crime would occur if, by giving unauthorised contraceptive advice or treatment to persons under the age of 16, the offence under the United Kingdom Sexual Offences Act 1956, of encouraging unlawful sexual intercourse with a girl under 16, had been committed.

On this latter point, the judges did not agree. The Court of Appeal, and the minority in the House of Lords, considered that the guidelines would lead to a breach of the Act because doctors were in effect being counselled to give advice that would condone, and perhaps even encourage, intercourse by a girl under the age of 16. As such, these judges held that the advice given by DHSS was not sound because of potential illegality, and the declaration sought by Mrs Gillick should be given. The majority of the House of Lords (and Woolf J) considered there were many circumstances in which the guidelines need not necessarily lead to the commission of a criminal offence under the Sexual Offences Act, and that accordingly the guidelines were valid and no declaration requiring their withdrawal or revision should be given. If an offence were to be committed under them, then an appropriate prosecution could follow, but the whole statement of public policy should not be struck out.

However, the House of Lords majority view went beyond concluding that the guidelines did not necessarily encourage criminal actions. The three judges addressed also the underlying question of the power of parents over their children aged less than 16 that was addressed directly by Mrs Gillick's second request. This was that the courts declare that her under-16 children should not be allowed to have contraceptive advice or treatment without parental consent. It raised directly the power parents have over their children, and the rights of children to make their own decisions. It also raised the question whether the circular was contrary to section 8 of the United Kingdom Family Law Reform Act 1969.[3] On these matters, the division of the

---

3 Section 8 provides that a minor aged 16 may consent to medical treatment as if of full age, but that this provision does not make ineffective "any consent which would have been effective" if the Act had not been passed.

courts was as described above. The Court of Appeal and the minority in the House of Lords considered that the parents had the right to determine what advice, if any, their children received outside the home, and that section 8 of the Family Law Act confirmed this position.

The majority of the House of Lords, however, which finally decided what the law is, took a different view. The three judges said that there were two lines of cases. One line emphasised the developing right of a person less than the age of majority (a minor) to make decisions for her or himself. The other line pointed to the fact that minors are not in law fully competent to decide for themselves, and to the need to leave final authority for making decisions with the parents or, failing them, the courts. The courts' jurisdiction in such cases is known as the *parens patriae* jurisdiction.[4]

Essentially, the division in the British courts on the question of children's rights was along the lines mentioned in the previous paragraph. The majority of the House of Lords preferred the first – the children's rights or autonomy – approach. They made it clear that the autonomy rights of children exist, and will be enforced, even at the expense of loss of parental power to control them, and even if the child may not necessarily make a decision that is in his or her best interests. However, the larger number judges noted that the right of the child to make his or her own decision is not absolute. A statute may (as the Family Law Act did not) impose a limit on a child's capacity, eg that he or she is only competent at age 16; and there may be situations where a court or welfare authorities will be able to intervene, using statutory or common law powers.

More broadly, as Lord Fraser (a member of the majority in the House of Lords) noted –

> ... the view that the child's intellectual ability is irrelevant cannot, in my opinion, now be accepted. It is a question of fact for the judge (or jury) to decide whether a particular child can give effective consent to contraceptive treatment. (p 172)

4　This is an ancient jurisdiction inherited by the courts from the Crown. It stems from the concept that the monarch, and the courts on his/her behalf are, in the absence of suitable care from elsewhere, responsible for the welfare of all within the state, including particularly those unable to care for themselves, such as people with intellectual disability or deserted children.

Lord Scarman (a member of the majority in the House of Lords) commented that it was up to the House of Lords to make clear what principles should be followed in dealing with particular situations involving the autonomy of the child –

> Parental rights clearly do exist, and they do not wholly disappear until the age of majority. (p 184) ... But [as expounded by Blackstone] parental right yields to the child's right to make his own decisions when he reaches a sufficient understanding and intelligence to be capable of making up his own mind on the matter requiring decision. Lord Denning MR captured the spirit and principle of the law when he said in *Hewer v Bryant* [1970] 1 QB 357] ... "the legal right of a parent to the custody of a child ends at the 18th birthday; and even up till then, it is a dwindling right which the courts will hesitate to enforce against the wishes of the child, and the more so the older he is. *It starts with a right of control and ends with little more than advice.*" (p 186 – emphasis added) ... It will be a question of fact whether a child seeking advice has sufficient understanding of what is involved to give a consent valid in law. Until the child achieves the capacity to consent, the parental right to make the decision continues, save only in exceptional circumstances. Emergency, parental neglect, abandonment of the child, or inability to find the parent are examples of exceptional situations. ... (p 189)

Discussion. The Gillick case has been heralded as an important advance in the recognition of the rights of the child to autonomy, as against the "right" of the parents to control the child. In many ways, it seems more helpful to think of the issue as raising the question to what extent the parents have *power* over their children. In human rights discussions, many of the rights claimed represent some qualification of the way a power – usually of the state – may be exercised in relation to the person, eg in terms of false imprisonment (power of police); or freedom of expression (power of the press to defame); or right to a fair trial (power of the court). One does not usually talk in terms of the state having a "right" to imprison people, impose curbs on freedom of speech etc, but rather of its having a power that can be abused. So it is with parents. They have *powers* over their children, and *rights* against the state relating to the extent to which a government can interfere with the autonomy of the family. It is useful to keep the two concepts clear, while noting that the Gillick case raises both issues. As Lord Templeman said, the case "involves consideration of the independence of a teenager, the powers of a parent and the duties of a doctor" (p 199).

At the heart of the discussion is the extent to which a child can have autonomy. Clearly a babe in arms can have very little, as is illustrated by the story of Awet Josef. Nevertheless, remembering that the child is in the process of becoming an adult, parents need to consider how they should treat the child. Some of these issues are considered further in Chapter 14, where corporal punishment is discussed. In the past, the law has tended to back to the full all manifestations of parental authority. But the times are changing, as the Gillick and Hewer cases show. Parents now must recognise the developing autonomy of their children, and the law will now protect, and if necessary insist on, that autonomy.

Despite the bold assertion by the House of Lords, people still think in terms of the dependent status of children. They do not consult them about many matters, such as the governance of schools or the running of the home, on which they might have important contributions to make. Genuine listening to what children want might in many cases save later revolt, and the traumas that always go along with that, as well as promoting the development of the children and increasing their happiness. For awareness of autonomy rights to develop, there is a need for talk about the issue at home, in school and elsewhere. As Bishop Michael Challen said –

> "Rights-talk" fundamentally is to be conducted by example, practice and words, within the context of family life. Parents, for good or ill, are the models of "rights-talk" – as they are for other aspects of human responsibilities and practices. ... The school has the similar responsibility of treating all children as persons of inherent and infinite worth notwithstanding their personal characteristics. This principle is to be lived out both in the classroom and the schoolground. In particular the school's use of authority needs to be consistent with the rights of the pupil. ...[5]

---

5   In "How Can 'Rights-talk' Help Children: A Practical Perspective", reproduced in Alston P and Brennan G (eds) *The UN Children's Convention and Australia*, Australian National University Centre for International and Public Law, Canberra, 1991, p 14.

However, as Lord Scarman pointed out, there is a risk in giving children greater autonomy. They may make mistakes. But that is their right as young persons. This does not remove the obligation of parents and others in authority, such as the doctors at the Norfolk Health Authority centres, to make every effort to give them wide and perceptive advice and counselling. But it does mean that, in the end, the child should be empowered to make his or her own decisions. His or her right and power should not be gainsaid, even if the older (more powerful) person disagrees with the conclusion the child reaches.

In many respects the International Convention on the Rights of the Child, although it took a decade to complete and was only opened for signature in 1990, is more concerned with the limitation of the power of existing authority figures such as parents, welfare authorities and courts, than with positively conferring rights on the child. However, that is in a sense the other side of the same point, and in any case the convention is not all couched in that way. In terms of recognising the autonomy of the child, Article 5 of the convention is probably the most significant –

> States Parties shall respect the responsibilities, rights and duties of parents or, where applicable, the members of the extended family or community as provided for by local custom, legal guardians or other persons legally responsible for the child, *to provide, in a manner consistent with the evolving capacities of the child*, appropriate direction and guidance *in the exercise by the child* of the rights recognized in the present Convention. (Emphasis supplied)

Although Article 5 is couched in terms of the authority of the state and of the parents, it does specifically recognise that the child him or herself can *exercise* rights. This is an important breakthrough, given that legal systems do not recognise children as full legal persons until they reach a stated age, usually 18 years. By Article 5, a *child* can exercise rights. Further, both the state and parents are required to recognise "the evolving capacities" of the child. This, of course, is just what the House of Lords did in Gillick. One difficult question is how these evolving capacities are to be determined. On this, the two major judgment-writers in the House of Lords majority took a slightly different position, as shown by the quotations above of Lord Fraser and Lord Scarman. Lord Fraser took the view that it was the judge's own (subjective) view of the child's capacity that was determinative. Lord Scarman considered it was the capacity (objectively determined) of the child that was the key.

Whether the subjective or the objective test is preferred (the author prefers the latter), the Gillick case does at least show that the courts are capable of reaching a conclusion as to capacity, and then of applying it. The further question then arises: can the courts be expected to do this in every case, or should some general rule be determined? The rule establishing when a minor becomes an adult is of the latter kind, and it has given rise to the problems discussed above. But is it satisfactory to leave the matter for determination in each individual case? Clearly not. The best course seems to be to lay down particular ages for particular purposes, such as signing contracts, agreeing to medical treatment or being capable or receiving service of notices (the reason for many statutory provisions), while providing in a general provision applying to all such particular ages that the courts have power in a particular case to decide whether a child under the specified age has the capacity to do the act in question (sign a contract, agree to medical treatment, etc).

In the area of consenting to medical treatment, the United States courts have gone a long way towards clarifying the position. They have distinguished the emergency case from the general run of medical treatment, and in that area have allowed a child, if capable of consenting, to do so. They have also, for the general run of cases, distinguished between the "unemancipated" child (who has no power to consent) and the "emancipated" and "mature emancipated" child. The latter is always regarded as having capacity, including to override parental wishes, while in the case of the "emancipated" child a "best interests of the child" (as interpreted by the courts) tends to be the basis for the decision.

Another difficult area is that of religion. How far may parents bring up their children according to their own religion, and when does the child have the right to refuse to participate? All persons have the right, according to Article 18 of the International Covenant on Civil and Political Rights, to freedom of religion. That right includes "freedom to have or adopt a religion or belief of his choice" and to manifest that religion in "worship, observance, practice and teaching". Article 18 also provides that parents are to have a right (power) to bring up their children in accordance with their own convictions. There is the possibility here of a clear conflict between the power of the parents and the right of their child. But is it appropriate for the state to intervene in this kind of matter, where the issues are so delicate and so much a matter of private life? The sensible outcome that seems to be emerging in the United States that the parents have the primary power and responsibility of watching over, and indeed directing, the child's religious upbringing, at least until the child becomes "emancipated". The state will only intervene if the physical or mental well-being of the child is seriously threatened, or there is some other compelling type of interest. There is further discussion of this issue in connection with the Mennonite children – see Chapter 3.

III. OVERVIEW

The stories of Awet Josef and of Mrs Gillick illustrate the two extremities of children's rights. The one shows the total dependence of the infant child on its mother, the other the need of the child increasingly to be able to assert its own independence. The Convention on the Rights of the Child has, as shown above, attempted to grapple with both these extremes. Perhaps understandably, it has handled less effectively the consequences of recognising the autonomy rights of the child, and it may not have emphasised sufficiently the peculiarly acute need for special feeding during infancy. It nevertheless provides an important base for domestic and international action. The case of Awet shows how much the majority of the world's children are dependent upon international aid if they are to escape from the vicious cycle of deprivation. The Gillick case shows how domestic action is needed – through the machinery of government – to ensure adequate recognition and enforcement of children's rights against the power exercised by so many in the community – parents, schools, courts, police, welfare authorities and the medical profession, to mention but a few. A child's eye view of the world must see it as peopled with a huge number of "authorities"! Now that the Convention has set some standards, each country must try to build them into detailed legal protections in all areas of the child's life.

Some have asked whether it is really possible for children to have rights. For many centuries in Western countries, and still today in many parts of the world, children are regarded as property, and as under the full control of their parents. If one bases one's view of rights on a contractual theory, like Locke or Rousseau, it is hard to see how children can be repositories of "rights". Broadly, these theories assume that rights come from (invisible) contracts between members of the adult world. Children, not being part of that world, could not make contracts on their own behalf, and at best could only have derivative rights. On the other hand, if one bases one's theory on the Christian view that all people (children included) are children of God, then it is not so difficult. The duties of love, care and respect inherent in that belief should (even if for two millenia they have not) include children as having a right to care, and to act when capable of so doing, just as much as adults.

Another way of avoiding the contractarian dilemma that it may not suit the contracting parties to provide well for all children has been suggested by Dr Eekelaar.[6] He suggests that the duty of parents to care for their children – or the rights of children against their parents and others – may be based in two sources. One is the assumed and basic obligation to promote human flourishing, which exists in any human society. The other, which derives from the particular society into which the child is born, is based on the moral obligation to conform to social practice in that society. Some will find one of these theories, or a modification of it, satisfying. Others will not, and then will need to pursue the question further if they wish. For the author, obligations to the child, based on the Christian concept of equality as illuminated by modern thinking about human rights, suffices, as outlined in the previous paragraph.

The involvement of the great powers in the plight of Awet suggests one further reflection. If the resources poured into Ethiopia by first one and then the other side in the East-West rivalries of the four decades after World War II could instead have been harnessed to developing the productivity of both

---

6   Eekelaar J, "Are Parents Morally Obliged to Care for Their Children?", (1991) 11 *Oxford Journal of Legal Studies* 340.

Ethiopia and Eritrea, not only would there have been greater happiness in those areas, but the present dire need for aid in both countries might well have been avoided. Awet might indeed have lived to benefit from the kinds of decisions made by the House of Lords in Gillick.

For Further Reading

There is not a great deal of material on Ethiopia. However, a good short coverage is given in Pool D, *Eritrea: Africa's Longest War*, Anti-Slavery Society, London, 1982 (note our indebtedness again, as in Chapter 7, to the publications supported by this splendid Society). Another useful book, in which a number of authors survey different aspects of Eritrea's problems, is *The Eritrean Case: Proceedings of the Permanent Peoples' Tribunal of the International League for the Rights and Liberation of Peoples*, Research and Information Centre on Eritrea, Rome, 1982. Davidson B, Cliffe L and Selassie BH (eds) *Behind the War in Eritrea*, Spokesman, Nottingham, England, 1980 gives a good account of Eritrea's historical claims to nationhood, the liberation struggle, and the social revolution that has accompanied the struggle.

The Gillick case sequence is found in the 1984 Queen's Bench and 1986 Appeal Cases series of United Kingdom Law Reports, with details as in the text. There are numerous articles about it, the best being by John Eekelaar, "The Emergence of Children's Rights", (1986) 6 *Oxford Journal of Legal Studies*, 161. He has also written a complementary article on the duties of parents – "Are Parents Morally Obliged to Care for Their Children?" in (1991) 11 *Oxford Journal of Legal Studies*, 340. Both articles explain the history of the issues and so provide a valuable context for the discussion of the rights, powers and obligations of all those involved.

On the more general question of the human rights of the child, there is a brief account in Bailey, *Human Rights: Australia in an International Context*, Butterworths, Sydney, 1990 and there are good longer discussions in Wringe CA, *Children's Rights: A Philosophical Study*, Routledge, London 1981 and in Franklin B (ed), *The Rights of Children*, Blackwell, Oxford, 1986. Wringe is not too heavy, and Franklin includes chapters by different authors on children in care, sexual rights, girls' rights and black children's rights.

PART IV

Liberty and Security for Individuals

O the mind, mind has mountains; cliffs of fall
Frightful, sheer, no-man-fathomed. Hold them cheap
May who ne'er hung there.

"No Worst, there is None",
Gerard Manley Hopkins.

The condition upon which God hath given liberty to man is eternal vigilance; which condition if he break, servitude is at once the consequence of his crime, and the punishment of his guilt.

John Philpot Curran,
Speech on the right of election of Lord Mayor of Dublin,
10 July 1790.

The power of the state can work so well for good and ill. In this Part, we see it trying to deal with difficult situations in times of public and private emergency. These may be times when people are unemployed, or when they get across the regime in one form or another. In Ireland, the regime was the security services; in Scotland it was the education authorities. In all these situations, claims are made by often well-meaning individuals in the employ of the state that they know better what is good for citizens than do those citizens themselves.

Chapter 11

The Cases of Monica Mignone and Patient Vera

Personal Rights to Liberty and Security of the Person in Times of Emergency

I. THE STORY OF MONICA MIGNONE

The Story. Monica Mignone was born in Buenos Aires in 1952![1]
She was still living there in early May 1976, when she was taken
away at 5 in the morning by five men who appeared to be
wearing some military clothing and were carrying military
equipment. Her father, a lawyer and the rector of a university in
Buenos Aires, had opened the door in response to a ring and the
men had pushed past to get his daughter. She was told to dress.
After a rough and peremptory search of her bedroom, and
particularly of the books and papers in it, she was taken off.
Forty minutes later, the Mignone home was quiet again, but
without Monica, the second of the Mignone's five children.

Monica was an educational psychologist at a nearby hospital
and she was also a teaching assistant at the university of which
her father was rector. She was an active-minded and socially
concerned young woman. In her spare time, she had worked as a
volunteer assistant in one of the slum areas of the city along with
other friends, including two priests. It turned out that they too

---

1   For this story I am indebted to, and gratefully acknowledge, the book by
Iain Guest, *Behind the Disappearances*, published in 1990 and discussed in
Further Reading at the end of the Chapter.

had been taken away – five of them during the night and another later in the day.

As Monica was being taken away, one of the captors had suggested she take with her enough money for a return taxi fare, leaving some hope that she might soon come home. But when, after some hours, she had not returned or been heard of, her parents went down to the Palermo army barracks to see whether she was there. No, she was not there, they were told. When they inquired of the local police, the response was that they had received instructions not to patrol, that night, the area in which the Mignone home was situated.

Argentina had been going through a difficult period politically. A century-and-a-half earlier, in 1810, it had thrown off Spanish rule. In 1853 it had adopted the first, and one of the most democratic, of the post-colonial constitutions in South America. There were provisions for a democratic franchise and, although there were arrangements for the state to assume additional powers and suspend some individual liberties in case of national emergency, these were carefully hedged round. The rights of the citizens were protected by, for example, the continued availability of the writ of *habeas corpus*. Even though the President was able to order the arrest and detention of a person as a matter of emergency administrative power, the power did not allow for punishment. For that, the courts would have to be approached and a proper prosecution launched and conviction obtained.

Until the mid-20th century, Argentina slowly developed, and became known as a reasonably stable democracy with a good record of beef production and a sound balance of payments. But in 1930, and then again no less than five times during the next half-century, the military seized power, later reinstating civilian rule. In 1972, only three and a half years before Monica was taken away, President Juan Peron had triumphantly returned from the exile to which the army had sent him in 1966.[2] However, he was ill, and died in 1974, to be succeeded by his second and much less popular wife Isobel. She

---

2   President Peron had been elected in 1947 and, with his revered wife Evita, had strongly supported the workers of Argentina. Unionism had flourished and he had been highly popular, but he was deposed in 1966 as a consequence of the first military coup.

was unable to draw the threads of government together, and in March 1976, the month before Monica's disappearance, she was deposed by a new kind of dictatorship – that of a military Junta consisting of three generals drawn from the army, navy and air force. Although it was to turn out to be one of the most terrible governments of modern times, it was given a cautious welcome by world leaders generally. They were taken in by the seemingly civilised appearance of the prime leader, Lieutenant General Jorge Videla, and were relieved by the removal of Isobel Peron.

The Junta promptly set about locating and destroying any possible resistance to its rule. It in effect waged war on a large part of the population, by trying to weed out all the "subversive" elements. An indication of the attitude of the authorities is gained from their view that people like Monica were dangerous because they worked in the slums. One of the two priests with whom Monica had been working, Father Yorio, was suddenly released from detention in October. He said one of his interrogators had commented that although he was known not to be violent, he had gone to live with the poor: "living with the poor unites them. Uniting the poor is subversion".[3]

The prime engine of detention, torture and destruction for the regime was the large and handsome Navy Mechanics' School (the ESMA).[4] Located near the centre of Buenos Aires, it provided adequate space and facilities in normal times for some 5000 students. It was turned over immediately by the navy authorities under Admiral Massera, who had been promoted by Peron for his work in security and who assumed responsibility for all security matters in the new regime. All over the country other smaller, though less elaborate, detention centres were established, but this was the central and pivotal one. It is simply not known how many Argentine citizens "disappeared" into these centres, but a careful estimate suggests that some 10,000 disappeared over the years 1976-83, when the Junta was finally brought down. About half that number – 5000 people – were dealt with in the ESMA, and probably most of the 700 foreign citizens who also "disappeared". As Iain Guest puts it in *Behind the Disappearances* –

---

3   Guest, *Behind the Disappearances*, p 36 (see Further Reading).
4   Standing for "Escuela Superior de Mecanica de la Armada".

The Junta turned disappearances into a government policy and in
so doing gave a new meaning to the concept of state terror. It was
as deliberate, methodical, and calculated as collecting tax ...[5]

The practices meted out to the detainees in the ESMA
buildings are too horrific to detail. They included long periods of
imprisonment, often in chains. They continued so long as it
seemed the individuals might be able to provide information
about other suspects. The detention was interspersed with
periods of torture that included hooding, being driven blindfold
to unknown destinations for interrogation, and other practices
similar to those adopted in Northern Ireland in the early 1970s
(see Chapter 14). There was also a dreaded and infernal machine
known as Caroline, which consisted of a broom handle with two
long, electrically charged wires on the end. These waved and
weaved as they were applied to the detainee's naked body
(especially to the sexual areas, head and tongue) and spat,
shocked or burned as the contact was made. Very few escaped
from ESMA: the regime could not afford to have escapees if the
terrible secrets of the torture were not to become public
knowledge.[6] The dead were disposed of in many ways – one
being by dropping the bodies from service helicopters into the
nearby estuary of the great River Plate, heavily infested with
sharks.

The disappearance of Monica and so many others as a result
of the practices of the new regime led to gathering and
ultimately effective action within the community. In April 1977,
a year after her disappearance, Monica's father made the first of
three applications for *habeas corpus*, to order the authorities to
produce her and 1540 other persons who had disappeared and
whose names he and others had laboriously collected over the
year since her disappearance. Although one of the essences of
the application for *habeas corpus* is that it be acted on promptly,
the applications took a very long time to be heard. It was only in
December 1978 that the Supreme Court declared it had no

---

5   Guest, p 32.
6   It should, however, be added that the Argentine practices make those
    adopted by the British and Northern Ireland authorities pale into
    insignificance in terms both of the numbers involved and of the nature of
    the acts of torture practised.

jurisdiction because the authorities had responded by denying any knowledge of the persons named –

> This court considers it its unavoidable duty to bring this situation to the attention of the executive, and to urge it to employ the measures within its power to create the conditions to enable the judiciary to rule on the cases brought before the courts.[7]

Other steps were being taken. About the same time as Monica's father, Emilio Mingnone, was approaching the Supreme Court for the first time, the mothers of many of the disappeared persons began to organise. Fourteen women, feeling they had little to lose, and that some form of direct protest was appropriate since the public authorities had entered their private domain by causing their children to disappear, met in the Plaza del Mayo, a square onto which the President's residence fronts. That was early in May 1977. They became known as "The Mothers of the Plaza del Mayo" and for years they pressed forward with enquiries, asking questions of the authorities, and gathering ever more support. In October they were joined by a like organisation, the Grandmothers of the Plaza del Mayo. The grandmothers were searching for children whose parents also had often "disappeared", leaving only the troubled, sorrowing, angry grandparents. The story of the Mothers and Grandmothers of the Plaza is still being told, and has been filmed. It is a story of heroism, love and careful gathering and sifting of the evidence. Many have eventually found the graves of their children or grandchildren.

The mothers and grandmothers also played a part in assisting the bringing to trial in 1985 of nine former military leaders. They were charged with murder and other forms of homicide, illegal detention, torture, kidnapping and falsification of documents. After a five month trial, they were found guilty of a range of offences. Of the nine, who stood for many more, only five were imprisoned – for periods ranging from life to four-and-a-half years. The other four went free. It was hardly a fitting sequel to the years of horror. However, the new President of Argentina, President Alfonsin, then made a difficult political decision. He decided that no further human rights prosecutions were to be made: the continued operation of the state was at risk,

---

7   Quoted in Guest, p 51.

and now that some had been punished, the country should seek to reunite and put behind it the horrors that had occurred.

And what of Monica Mignone? As late as mid-1979, three years after her "disappearance" her father, Emilio, met Admiral Massera, the security chief, lured on by the suggestion that he had news of Monica. Massera gave no news of Monica, but told of the death of two of her associates. As with so many of the other individuals that were taken away, Monica was never found. Nor was her grave, if there was one, ever identified. What she suffered before she died is unlikely ever to be known. Her captors and torturers – it is inconceivable there were none – will carry the guilty secrets with them until they die, unpunished by the law. The awful power of the state, in the hands of cruel and callous individuals, is probably the very worst of the evils a citizen has to fear.

Meanwhile, Monica's brave father Emilio did not rest at seeking a writ of *habeas corpus* in the courts. In 1976, prompted partly by the campaign of Mr Jimmy Carter for the Presidency of the United States, and his emphasis on human rights, a team from Amnesty International visited Argentina. The team of three was led by an English peer, Lord Avebury. The United States member, Congressman and Jesuit priest Robert Drinan, made good contact with Emilio, and subsequently took up his case internationally. It was the beginning of the mobilisation of international information and opinion about the situation in Argentina, and led to strong counter-measures by the government. In 1979, the Centre for Legal and Social Studies was established with USAID assistance and Emilio Mignone was made its director. It provided a focus for resistance to the regime, both for people inside Argentina and for international contacts. Partly because of his involvement with the centre, and partly because of his appearance in Geneva in 1981 before the Working Group on Disappearances appointed by the United Nations Commission on Human Rights,[8] Mignone was again

---

8   The Working Group was established under the auspices of the Commission on Human Rights (CHR), the most significant semi-independent agency of the United Nations. The CHR itself, originally composed of 35 members and envisaged in the United Nations Charter itself, now has 43 members, but is about to increase to 53. It consists of representatives of the governments whose countries have been elected each three years to serve on it. It meets in Geneva, for about 6 weeks in January and February of each year.

detained. On this occasion, he was released following United States intervention, despite the coolness of President Reagan's administration to the cause of international human rights.[9]

In Argentina itself, the deep-seated unpopularity of the Junta, and the failure of the effort to regain the Malvinas (Falkland Islands) in the war with Britain in 1982, led to the appointment as interim President of a steady and respected former General, Major General Reynaldo Bignone. He was charged with preparing the country for new elections and a return to democracy. The elections were held in 1985 and the Radical President Raoul Alfonsin was elected. Under President Alfonsin the trials already mentioned were arranged, though a special Commission was appointed to carry the process forward, thereby enabling the government to distance itself a little and perform the difficult balancing act of restoring democracy while not provoking another military takeover. Although some unity and self-respect were restored under President Alfonsin, economic conditions deteriorated and in July 1989 President Carlos Menem, a Peronist, was elected. Because of the unpopularity of President Alfonsin, he took office immediately rather than in December. The country experienced disastrous inflation (700 percent) in 1990-91, a military coup was defeated in December 1990 and the state of siege was lifted after only three days. The battle for democracy continues, as the aftermath of the terror is tidied up, a more orderly system of government is painfully rebuilt, the painful memories of the past heal somewhat, and the fate of friends and relatives, even if often at least as bad as feared, is determined with some measure of certainty.

---

9   The work of the Argentine Ambassador to the United Nations, Gabriel Martinez, receives considerable attention in *Behind the Disappearances*. It seems that he managed to deflect attention and criticism from Argentina, and even to ensure that the outspoken, scholarly, courageous and highly articulate Theo van Boven, Director of the then United Nations Centre for Human Rights in Geneva, was not reappointed in 1982. The author, who has spent some time with, and has a great regard for Mr van Boven, had been unable to unravel the mystery surrounding the failure to reappoint him, and is greatly indebted to Iain Guest for his research, and the extensive and damning documentation he provides in his book about the intrigue at the United Nations and the downgrading of the human rights effort at that time.

Discussion. The story of Monica Mignone shows just how far the rulers of a country may be willing to go if they feel their grip on power threatened. It also shows, more hopefully, that in the longer term such rulers are unlikely to be able to maintain their position.

It was only as the 1970s drew on that the international community became aware of the monstrosity of the behaviour of the Argentine Junta. The first decisive step was taken in 1980, with the appointment of the Working Group on Disappearances. It was different to the Commission on Human Rights (CHR)[10] itself, because it consisted of people appointed for their expertise in the area, and not of representatives of the member governments, as was the CHR.

When the word "representatives" appears in international jargon, it serves notice that the people attending are doing so as representatives of their governments. This means that they are under the direction of their governments, even if some latitude is left to them. So one cannot expect the CHR to be a free agent: its work and conclusions will usually reflect the current state of international power and balance. However, it has appointed a Sub-Commission on Discrimination and the Rights of Minorities which has a more continuing existence and a good deal more freedom of action than the CHR itself. Although the Sub-Commission is responsible to the CHR, it is not responsible to the individual governments. The Working Groups of the Sub-Commission are even more independent, and tend to work more continuously. Being less directly responsible to governments, they usually operate more independently and with less responsiveness to the imperatives of governments.[11] It was before the Working Group on Disappearances that Emilio Mignone appeared in 1980 (see p 172).

---

10 See footnote 8.
11 In addition to the working group on disappearances, the working groups appointed by the CHR include groups on the rights of minorities, on gross violations of human rights, on the right to development and on human rights in South Africa. The Sub-Commission on Minorities also appoints working groups, including groups on indigenous populations and on slavery; and special rapporteurs, who are experts in a particular field and are usually charged with making a report on a particular subject such as the abolition of the death penalty, the state of human rights in particular countries, or states of emergency.

Three important questions arise from Monica's story. First, there is the meaning of "disappearance". Second, there is the meaning of liberty and security of person. Linked to that is the role of the writ of *habeas corpus*. First, then, the meaning of disappearance. Disappearance was accurately described in 1980 in a despatch from Buenos Aires by a United States diplomat at the US Embassy there –

> Disappearance is a euphemism for the unacknowledged detention of any individual by security forces. Based on everything we know we believe that detainees are usually tortured as part of interrogation and eventually executed without any semblance of due process.[12]

There are two tragic aspects of this definition: the emphasis on the misuse by the state, which should be there to serve the needs of all the people, and the awful consequences for mostly innocent individuals of the inevitable conclusion of this kind of abuse of power.

Second, there is the meaning of liberty and security of person. The concept and its setting in the context of a framework of law is one of the significant achievements of Western democracy. Action of the kind described in Monica's story clearly violates the right to liberty and security of person, however that might be defined. The international community, in Article 9 of the International Covenant on Civil and Political Rights (ICCPR), defined the right as in essence being that –

> Everyone has the right to liberty and security of person. No one shall be subjected to arbitrary arrest or detention. No one shall be deprived of his (sic) liberty except on such grounds and in accordance with such procedure as are established by law.

If we are correct in assuming that Monica was in some way tortured or subjected to cruel or inhuman treatment, the captors would also have violated Article 7 of the ICCPR, which proscribes actions of that kind. Article 7 encapsulates another aspect of the right to liberty and security of person, and a more detailed account of it and its significance is contained in the stories about the Irish detainees and Jeffrey Cosans in Chapter

---

12   This is from a cable dated 26 September 1980, the text of which was extracted from the US Department of State under the Freedom of Information Act 1967. It is quoted in *Behind the Disappearances* at p 32 and the text appears in Appendix 3, pp 430-2.

14. If Article 9 were insufficient, then Article 10 would also apply. It provides that "All persons deprived of their liberty shall be treated with humanity and with respect for the inherent dignity of the human person". If these were not enough, the Argentine government and its officers would also have been guilty of violating that final right – the right to life which, provides Article 6 of the ICCPR, "shall be protected by law". Article 6 continues by stipulating that "No one shall be arbitrarily deprived of his (sic) life".

It emerges from this brief review of the international human rights provisions that it is totally impermissible to treat people in the way the detainees in Argentina and other countries have been treated. It is to the great credit of Amnesty International and those who support it that a large and growing number of people is now actively exposing governments who violate the rights of individuals to liberty and security of person. Yet, unfortunately, governments still do persist with such practices, hoping perhaps that they will "get away" with it.

The exposure of the violations in Argentina gave impetus to agreement in 1986, after many years of obstruction by representatives of the Argentine and other like-thinking and practising governments, to an international convention against torture. The Torture Convention[13] was opened for signature in 1987 and is now in force. Australia and other countries have ratified (become bound by) it. It has two main requirements. First, each signatory country has to ensure that its laws provide offences for the punishment of torture and other inhuman treatment done by anyone, whether within or outside its borders. Second, to ensure individual responsibility, the law must provide that it is not a defence to claim the torture was perpetrated under "superior orders" or as a matter of "necessity" arising from conditions of war, internal political instability or public emergency.[14]

For the purposes of the Torture Convention, torture is defined with an emphasis, largely resulting from the Argentine

---

13 Its full name is the International Convention against Torture and Other Cruel, Inhuman or Degrading Treatment or Punishment.

14 The Australian legislation implementing the convention is the Crimes (Torture) Act 1988, and the relevant sections are sections 6 and 11.

experience, on actions by the state and its officials, whether direct or indirect –

> "Torture" means any act by which severe pain or suffering, whether physical or mental, is intentionally inflicted on a person for such purposes as obtaining from him or a third person information or a confession, punishing him for an act he or a third person has committed or is suspected of having committed, or intimidating or coercing him or a third person, or for a reason based on discrimination of any kind, when such pain or suffering is inflicted by or at the instigation of or with the consent or acquiescence of a public official or other person acting in an official capacity. (Article 1 of the Convention)

The definition is deliberately designed to target public officials or those acting at their behest, because of the importance of dealing with what is definitely the major instrument of torture – the state. There would be much to be said for broadening it to cover a wider group of powerholders, such as those involved in drug-trafficking and other international crime. Notice how well the kind of actions involved in the Argentine horror are covered by the definition.

The other matter of importance to personal liberty needing mention is the constitutional guarantee of *habeas corpus*. As mentioned earlier, the protection of the writ was built into Argentina's 1853 Constitution. Although the guarantee continued to exist in Argentina, it became ineffective because the government authorities refused to comply with the order of the court to produce the named person or justify his or her continued detention. Great significance has been attached in countries with British-related legal systems to the *habeas corpus* remedy. Invented by the British courts in the 13th century, it was the ultimate protection of individual liberty and security of person. *Habeas corpus* required the person holding a body to produce it, and it was designed to ensure that the King or his agents did not wrongfully detain people without bringing them to trial. It was progressively refined and extended in its ambit to cover people not technically in prison. In Sommersett's case, decided in 1772, a negro slave was ordered to be released from a ship on the River Thames where he was held. It has been applied to obtain the release of people in mental institutions, of persons detained by immigration officials and of minors in custody. It works by a person asking a court to order (through issuing the *habeas corpus* writ) the custodian to produce the detained person and to show on what authority he or she was detained. If no authority is shown, the court orders the person to be released, and a heavy fine can be imposed on the gaoler. The remedy has been seen all over the world as an important protection of civil and political rights. Hence it was, as mentioned in Monica Mignone's story, included in Argentina's first democratic constitution. It was included in the United States Constitution (Article I section 9) and it is incorporated in many legal systems. In Australia and other common law countries, it exists as a common law remedy. This means that the courts have inherent power to issue it without any enabling legislation (although there is legislation that does strengthen it). But, in the end, as a remedy made available by judges, it cannot prevail against a rights-disregarding and ruthless junta or ruler, or where courts have been forced into subservience by dismissing judges who decide against the policies or interests of the government.

II. THE STORY OF PATIENT VERA

The Story. Patient Vera lives in Australia and has suffered from severe depressions that come on unpredictably and make it difficult for her to cope with her life.[15] When depressed, she feels she is no good for anything, is unable to work or even to care properly for herself, and just has the sense that the world does not want her. When she is not depressed, she often feels resentful, guilty, angry with the world generally, and sometimes with those who try to help her most, including her doctors or psychiatrists and her family. In addition, Vera suffers bouts of fairly severe epilepsy. If the medication is working, the fits don't occur very often, but if it has been missed or is not rightly adjusted, she can suffer severe fits and often damage to herself. She can be, when not suffering from either the bouts of depression or the epilepsy or the anger, an attractive person who can just about cope with life, and can make friends. But her recurrent disabilities make it difficult for her to keep her friends

---

15   We do not know her real name, and it is right that, to protect her privacy in her local community, neither it nor other personal and identifying details should be published.

and to sustain any kind of normal, purposive life, either alone or with her family.

Towards the end of April of 1992 she was hospitalised by her doctor because of a severe bout of depression, and in the hope that there might be some way of at least stabilising that and also her epilepsy. There are drugs that can help with both conditions, but they are not always compatible, and of course a person's own body rhythms can affect any finely tuned balance that may be arrived at. The hospitalisation was arranged under the compulsory treatment provisions of the Mental Health Act 1983 of the Australian Capital Territory (ACT) because Vera herself did not want to be treated. She was feeling bad, and that there was no point in it at all. She preferred to be at home, and to avoid the hospital and the psychiatric ward, which she feared. Initial compulsory treatment orders last only for 28 days. In late May, the court was approached for an extension, and also for approval to administer electro-convulsive therapy (ECT). The approval is required under the Mental Health Act to protect patients from consenting under the influence of others, and to ensure they make up their own minds, aware of the risks. The court approved the extension of the order, but not the administration of ECT.

Under the terms of the ACT legislation, doctors may give patients in compulsory care most normal kinds of treatment, such as drugs, counselling, tests and so on. But if they consider electro-convulsive therapy (ECT) or brain surgery to be necessary, they have to get the specific approval of a court. Because ECT is regarded as less risky than psycho-surgery, which often involves the removal of the frontal lobes of the brain and thus of important perceptor and conduct-controlling functions, the Magistrates' Court is authorised to consent to it. If psycho-surgery is needed, the Supreme Court has to approve.

Many experienced doctors use ECT in conditions of severe and continuing depression, such as Vera suffered. It can be, but is not necessarily, painful. There are times when it is not only immediately unsuccessful but leaves the patient with continuing damage to his or her thinking and emotional capacity. Vera was asked whether, having in mind that she was very run down and that her condition was not showing any improvement, despite all the efforts of herself and her doctors, she would be willing to try ECT. She said she would not, partly because she was afraid of it – there were so many awful stories she had heard – and partly because she feared that it might bring on her epilepsy, which was more or less under control through the administration of drugs. (It is fairly well substantiated that epilepsy, involving as it does disturbances in the electric patterns of the brain, can be brought on or exacerbated by ECT.) On the two occasions on which Vera attended the court, she asked coherently that the approval not be given, repeating the reasons just mentioned.

Her doctors believed that perhaps Vera's only hope was to have a session or two of ECT. Although the court had refused to authorise ECT at the time of the extension of the treatment order, the doctors decided that they would again seek the approval of the court. They arranged a special hearing that, in the interests of the patient, was conducted in private as are most hearings related to mental health. The Magistrate was not convinced that the case made out by the doctors, which was necessarily an "on balance" proposition, was strong enough to outweigh the patient's objections, and so refused the order. Vera nonetheless remained in the hospital under the compulsory treatment order because it was felt she was not able to look after herself if released.

In the days that followed, her psychiatrists talked with Vera, and attempted to persuade her that she should try the ECT. They pointed out that if well administered it need not be painful, and that it was about the only measure left to them after years of effort. In the end, Vera said she would agree, and signed a consent form.

On 15 June, ECT treatment was administered. It was not obviously successful. Then the worst happened, and Vera began to suffer from severe epileptic fits. As the days went by and there was no improvement in her condition, she was transferred first to a medical rather than a psychiatric ward in the Canberra hospital, and then to a hospital in Sydney, from which she was discharged early one morning without ceremony and without any available friends or family to support her, or funds to enable her to return to Canberra. Although initially not readmitted to a hospital, she has since been given further treatment. An informant contacted the newly appointed Community Advocate of the Australian Capital Territory, who has a special duty of care for young persons and people with forms of disability, including mental illness. She followed the matter up, and also made a report to the ACT Government.

Towards the end of June, the discussions that had been taking place in the Canberra hospital about the ECT administered to Vera became public. It seems there was very little questioning in hospital circles of the medical correctness of the decision to administer the ECT. However, there were serious questions about whether a patient under a compulsory treatment order is able to give a valid consent to ECT, or whether it is ethical to try to get consent in such circumstances. What section 45 of the Mental Health Act provides is that a person under a treatment order may not be given ECT without the consent of a magistrate. The question is whether, if the doctors had a consent from Vera, that consent would override section 45 because it is there to prevent treatment of an unwilling patient and not one who, even if under a treatment order, has consented.

During the public discussion there were strong attacks on the effectiveness and hence use of ECT from both individuals and non-government organisations who seek to protect the rights of mentally ill patients. They also attacked the administration of ECT to a patient under a compulsory order, on the basis that section 45 precludes a person under compulsory treatment from giving an effective consent unless that is endorsed by a court, a view with which the author agrees. The hospital authorities expressed concern, and have indicated that they may not support the doctors if they are charged with an offence. The two psychiatrists have in fact been charged, but the result of the care is not yet known.

Discussion. We cannot forecast what the final outcome will be for Vera. But we do know that what happened to her raises one of the most critical issues in the area of civil liberties. It is about the invasion of personal privacy by the state. If Vera had come into the hospital seeking ECT, and her request had been supported by a doctor as seems almost certain, she could have received it. But if she is in hospital under a compulsory treatment order, and then consents, is that consent valid, or does the Act protected her from treatment except with the consent of the court?

Vera's case raises dilemmas that it is almost impossible to resolve in a way that will be right for everyone. In such circumstances, the human-rights-favouring option is to err on the side of being absolutely sure that the treating authorities are not in some way obtaining a consent under duress. This is what the ACT law seems to do. Duress does not only mean *force*: it is sufficient, in law, that undue *influence* is exerted. Having in mind the essential dignity of the human person, it should be demonstrably clear that a person has consented before there is any invasion of his or her liberty or personal autonomy. If s 45 of the Mental Health Act is read that way, it would be extremely difficult, if not impossible, to treat a compulsory patient without an order of the court. On the other side are the carers, probably taxed to the limit of their patience by a difficult and fearful patient, and feeling that if they have to go back to a court she will probably renege on the consent they have tried so hard and for so long to obtain. She had at last, they would feel, agreed to what they were certain was her only remaining hope for at least a measure of continuing autonomy.

All of us have to make difficult decisions like that for ourselves. The author's view is that in the end, even if the strong tenor of medical advice is towards treatment, the consent of the patient is vital. For too long, mental health legislation has treated mentally ill persons as having no rights, and as being permanently disabled and totally incompetent. True consent can only come if there is equality between the parties. The circumstances of a compulsory order; the desire to leave the confines of the hospital sooner rather than later; fear that the doctor or psychiatrist may withdraw their help or listening ear; or that refusal to agree may annoy them, even if no bad consequences are feared – all these make genuine consent of the patient difficult to obtain. If she is in compulsory treatment, genuine consent is even more difficult to ensure. It is time the benefit of the doubt went to the patient, even if that results in more personal suffering than would have followed adopting the medically preferred option. In Vera's case, we seem to have the worst of both worlds – she has unlawfully, and probably against her better judgment, been given ECT, and has suffered severe illness and rejection by the hospital system as a result.

Behind all this is the long battle the supporters of the rights of mentally ill people have waged to protect their freedom from unreasonable invasion by medical and other caring authorities. The Australian Human Rights and Equal Opportunity Commission (HREOC) has recently taken up the cause of people with mental illness. Through the activities of the Human Rights Commissioner since 1990, community awareness of the discrimination suffered by people with mental illness has been raised. The point is made, with accuracy, that more often than not they are treated as having some kind of "disease" that is shameful and should be hidden. Note, incidentally, that Vera suffers here from a double dose of discrimination: she has the "hidden" disability of epilepsy; and she has the stigma of severe mental illness in the form of depression. Although Vera's case is rather more extreme than most, people with mental disabilities find their civil and political rights are curtailed by detention for treatment, by the possibility that it will be difficult to get out once in, and by being given often invasive forms of treatment in their interest, whether they like it or not. Sometimes, indeed, their capacity to re-establish themselves in the community, both by having been confined and as a result of that experience, is diminished. Their economic, social and cultural rights also are curtailed in many cases, by their not being able to obtain income support through pensions or subsidised medical treatment through the hospital system they are curtailed also, through discrimination in the job field, and socially.

The feeling of "shamefulness" is attested to by Michelle Leslie, another sufferer from depression. She experienced it acutely when given a series of ECT treatments under compulsory order, and still regrets the whole affair. She felt her requests for cessation of the treatment were simply ignored. Even a clear wish not to have more therapy can be overridden. Her case underlines the importance of never allowing a person in compulsory treatment to consent. Even if they do not, they may still receive the treatment, and often with great fearfulness.

In 1983 the Human Rights Commission, the predecessor of HREOC, investigated the then operative arrangements for the treatment of people with mental illness. It found that they were treated partly under the greatly outdated Lunacy Act 1898 of New South Wales, and partly under the 1938 Lunacy Ordinance and Inebriates Ordinance of the ACT. The New South Wales legislation was conceived in what has become known as the "legal" model, and the ACT legislation in the "medical model". The "legal" model was an advance on the situation before the end of the 19th century, when lunatics were in effect rightless. It gave lawyers and the courts the primary say in determining the fate of the "lunatic". The "medical" model made the law less legalistic by giving the primary say to the doctors, under court supervision. In either case, wide and virtually unregulated powers were available to decide when and how to treat persons with mental illness, which included the power to have them detained.

The commission concluded that although the arrangements were better than they had been before the 1938 legislation modified the Lunacy Act, they were still heavily biased against the rights of a person suffering from mental illness. Accordingly, the commission recommended provisions that were much more respectful of the rights of the sufferer and which, broadly speaking, might be termed a "rights-based" model. One advantage of a rights-based model is that it might both suggest, and to some extent compel, a more respectful review of, and then treatment for, mental illness. It might lead to a wider range of treatment options – to include, for example, counselling, or removal of such exogenous causes as domestic violence.

The commission's recommendations were largely incorporated in the ACT Mental Health Act 1983. Three main protections were built into the Act. First, the condition of the people who would be potentially subject to the wide powers conferred by the Act was carefully defined. Second, the more invasive powers, such as to administer ECT, were only to be exercised after the need for their use had been reviewed by a court. Third, only a short period of compulsory detention (three days) was permitted before a court had to authorise detention, and the initial order only lasted 28 days, after which regular review was to be undertaken.

It was under that "rights-based" legislation that Vera was taken in for compulsory treatment. It was by the exercise of a medical discretion, after what was almost certainly an invalid consent, that she was given ECT. In a welcome stand in support of the rights of patients, the hospital has said it will not meet the legal costs of doctors who disregard the law. Calls are now being made to allow doctors to administer ECT without consent to patients being detained under compulsory treatment orders!

Nevertheless, the 1983 legislation was felt by some, and especially by the families of persons with schizophrenia, to give too much weight to the protection of the sufferer. A Committee of review was appointed. It reported in 1990[16] and made three important contributions to the development of the legislation. First, it drew attention to the need of carers, particularly families, to have some relief (respite) from the burden of looking after family members with schizophrenia and other disabling but not continuously and totally disabling conditions. It made a number of recommendations for improved emergency and respite care. Second, it usefully refined the categories of care and treatment for mental illness. Third, it suggested that there be power in a court to order individuals who are considered a danger to themselves or others to refrain from engaging in violent or harassing behaviour. In this latter aspect, the Committee drew on the provisions now included in legislation giving remedies against domestic violence.

However, two aspects of the Committee's report give rise to possible concern. First, it proposed a revised definition for "mental dysfunction", which is the principal test to be met before a person can be compulsorily detained for treatment. Second, it suggested a way of taking a person into compulsory care that gives the patient less protection than under the 1983 legislation. On the matter of mental dysfunction, the Human Rights Commission considered people should only come within the ambit of the powers conferred by the legislation on doctors and mental health authorities if their mental functioning is *severely* impaired by their illness. The 1990 committee believed the legislation should be operative provided the person's capacity is *substantially* impaired, a lower threshold.

On the matter of involuntary detention, the commission considered a person should only be subject to the compulsory

---

16   ACT Mental Health Review Committee, *Balancing Rights: A Review of Mental Health Legislation in the ACT*, published by the Public Affairs Branch of the ACT Department of Health, Education and the Arts, 1990.

provisions if suffering either from *severe* mental dysfunction or from social breakdown. To suffer from social breakdown, a person would have to be at risk of suffering lasting and *serious* harm through being incapable of obtaining goods and services or making decisions or taking actions to support an autonomous life. The ACT review committee proposed, on the other hand, that a person should be able to be admitted involuntarily to treatment if he or she is *believed* by a doctor to be suffering from "substantial" mental dysfunction and as a consequence requires immediate care and detention for the protection of self or others; and refuses treatment and cannot receive it unless detained. This, it seems to the author, amounts in effect to reversion to the pre-1983 "medical model".[17] It makes it too easy for a person's liberty to be drastically restricted simply because a doctor thinks it would be a good idea. The threshold for invasion of liberty and privacy is too low. There is too little emphasis on objective assessment of the actual condition of the person, against defined standards, and on review of that condition by a court or other independent tribunal aware of the rights of the patient. There is also too little willingness on the part of governments to provide adequate, or even minimum, rehabilitative facilities, as the Human Rights Commissioner has found in his inquiry.

One other aspect of the difficulties of people suffering mental illness seems worth drawing to attention. It is that there has been relatively little interest, at international level, in their plight. Whereas those suffering from gross political abuses of state authority, such as through torture and illegal administrative-political detention have been well provided with a number of law-based statements of their rights, this has not been the case with mentally ill people. They have been put out of sight, and with that their rights have been overlooked![18] There are Declarations on the rights of mentally retarded persons and of disabled persons, but they have not led to conventions or

---

17 It should be noted that New South Wales has in effect reverted to the "medical model" by amendments to the Mental Health Act made in 1990, which removed the greater emphasis on rights-based provisions included in the legislation some years earlier.

18 One only needs to reflect on the conscienceless use of the "mentally ill" powers in the former Soviet Union, which has been recorded in, for example, Ken Kesey's *One Flew Over the Cuckoo's Nest*, to realise that the apprehension is real.

Covenants, as was the case for the Declaration on Torture and the earlier Universal Declaration of Human Rights. It is not that one wants to discredit the medical profession or health carers, or to overlook the needs of caring families, but the time has come to ensure that the individual whose life and liberty is involved has available remedies against the few members of those professions who are excessively authoritarian and repressive in outlook or who in other ways exploit the weakness of those already suffering as a result of mental illness. Indeed, it might be hoped that the carers could be brought to see that a rights-based system is indeed in their interests as well as those of their patients, because it sets clear principles by which to operate, and will protect those who abide by them.

III. OVERVIEW

The story of Monica Mignone illustrates how the state, by declaring a situation of *public* emergency related to the internal affairs of the country, and then finding that it cannot quickly remedy the position, can move into terrible acts of oppression and cruelty that violate the human rights of citizens and often result in a situation far worse than the one that justified the declaration of emergency. The resort by states to declarations of emergency is of major concern around the world. The Philippines, for example, were ruled for many years by President Marcos under emergency powers; there have been states of emergency declared for longer or shorter periods in Malaysia, Indonesia, Burma, Guatemala, Chile, Argentina, Lebanon, Israel, Ethiopia, Somalia and South Africa. It is for this reason that many nowadays are calling for removal of "emergency" provisions that allow derogation from the normal protection of rights such as personal liberty and freedom of speech. If, notwithstanding this, emergency situations are to be provided for, then they should be provided for by law. But the providing law should ensure that the state of emergency must terminate within a short period unless renewed, again for a short period, and with some form of popular consent, such as by a supporting resolution of the Parliament.

Vera's story shows how people's rights can be violated when a *private* rather than a public emergency occurs. Vera was held a virtual prisoner because of the development of a situation of personal crisis, and because the doctors used the mental health legislation to place her in temporary custody for compulsory treatment. She too was felt to be a "danger" to herself and others, and she had to be "put away", as the saying used to be when we spoke of lunatics and asylums. All was done for her with the best of intentions, but the next stage was an extension of the order and then the administration of the dreaded ECT, and finally temporary expulsion from the hospital system. Better than being dropped into the River Plate, perhaps, but hardly humane. It may have been Vera's intransigence that brought the situation about, but behind it was her illness and the frustrating position of the doctors. How hard it is for both! Once again, the point seems to come through: it is better for the carers to allow a person autonomy than to risk the assertion of rights-infringing powers, even if the result may be suicide. One should not be forced to remain alive – an issue further discussed in Chapters 4 and 5.

Both stories show how the power of the state can be abused by people either working directly for the government, such as public servants, or upon whom the state has conferred special power, such as doctors or welfare officers. In either case the effect is the same: the power the state has assumed as protector of society has been used to reduce the capacity of the individual to control his or her own life. It is because of this element of power that the state is so often said to be the prime abuser of rights. It doesn't sit easily, does it, with the concept of the welfare state? Not so often recognised is that, in the more complex society of the 20th century, private persons also may abuse that power. The history of the slow deprivation of rights in Argentina shows that it may be a long time before a situation is reached where the deprivation of rights becomes a matter of systematically implemented policy. But that is often the inevitable conclusion of the slide.

The history of mental health legislation shows that in some cases strong pressures may develop, not necessarily from the professionals but perhaps from those such as family members and friends who have had by default to exert powers of control over the unfortunate person with a disability. Characteristically, the pressures are usually backwards towards more power for the carers – towards a more repressive regime. All too rarely are the pressures from the powerholders towards a more refined regime, in which the recent advances are retained, but are then refined to produce arrangements that more fully recognise the rights of all parties. In the case of the ACT, "all parties" would include not only the sufferers, but also the carers outside the hospital system, and of course doctors and nursing staff. It is indeed ironic that, just as the excess of the doctors in Vera's case came to light, a committee reported that doctors should have the power of detention more readily available to them, and entitled its report "Balancing Rights"!

More fundamentally, both cases raise the important issue of how the basic rights of people to life, liberty and security of person should be protected. Many have advocated bills of rights that would give citizens a means of invoking the assistance of the courts when their rights are threatened. But what good are the courts, if a regime like that of the Junta in Argentina gets into office; or if doctors treating mental illness have easier access to detaining powers, as proposed in the ACT; or simply disobey the law? Others mention as the best protections an independent judiciary and the "rule of law". One difficulty with this is that the appointment of judges is in the hands of government. What guarantee is there that governments will appoint strong, fair judges? One remedy that has been suggested is to have special Judicial Commissions at least to make recommendations to governments about eligible persons, even if they could not make final decisions. So far, governments have resisted that proposal, but it may be a desirable safeguard, even if the requirement is that the Judicial Commission must submit several names rather than only one, and that the government must choose from the names submitted.

In discussions of personal rights and freedoms, the concept of the rule of law is one that is often referred to in common law countries such as Australia, Britain and Canada. It has been developed largely by British judges, who have not had a comprehensive bill of rights to draw on. It means that, in the exercise of their power to adjudicate between individual litigants, and between individuals and the state, the courts have developed the doctrine that all persons are to be subject to the same law, and that no-one exercising the power of the state may infringe the rights of others unless in accordance with the law. Assuming the laws are just, that is a great protection. But of course it depends on the good sense of the judges, and on their independence and fortitude when under pressure from governments frustrated by their decisions to protect individuals, as in the 17th and 18th century cases of *Semayne v Gresham*[19] and *Entick v Carrington*.[20]

In Semayne's case, Richard Gresham found his house had been cleared of contents to satisfy the debts of the friend (George Berisford) with whom he had jointly rented the house. Berisford had died, and the creditors moved in to secure their debts. Gresham went to the courts, and his right to sole possession of the property was upheld as against the private suitors of Berisford. As reported by Lord Coke, later Lord Chief Justice of England, "the house of every one is to him as his castle and fortress" – often cited as "an Englishman's home is his castle". The case was built upon a century and a half later, in Entick's case, when the then secretary of state ordered that John Entick's home in London be searched for suspected seditious documents. The search went on for four hours, many private documents were looked at, and many taken away. Lord Camden, Chief Justice of the Court of Common Pleas, resoundingly supported Entick, saying that –

> ... the power ... claimed by the secretary of state is not supported by one single citation from any law book. ... By the laws of England, every invasion of private property, be it ever so minute, is a trespass. ... there has been a submission of guilt and poverty to power and the terror of punishment.

So, under the concept of the rule of law, the privacy of the person and his or her home is strongly protected against the agents of the law, whether acting at the behest of private persons or of agents of the state. No-one is above the law. That is the essence of the concept. It is obvious that the writ of *habeas corpus*, which enables the courts to check whether a person is lawfully detained, is a related and vital part of the concept.

---

19 (1604) Smith's Leading Cases Vol 1, p 85 and 77 English Reports at p 195.
20 (1766) 19 State Trials 1030.

One difficulty with the doctrine of the rule of law is that it is applied primarily by the judges – that is, it is what is often called judge-made law. Judge-made law cannot prevail against legislation. Even if the judges are fearless and just, they can be frustrated by bad laws – and in many cases states of emergency are proclaimed under law. The answer has been well given by the European Court of Human Rights. It has emphasised that even if the law itself contravenes the human rights to life, to privacy, to liberty and security of person, it does not negate the human right itself, and the law should be struck down. If there is no incorporation of human rights in a Bill of Rights, or in a binding international agreement such as the European Convention on Human Rights, then the individual is left without a remedy against the invasion of the state. This aspect is further discussed in Chapter 6, in relation to the action taken against James Malone by the police authorities.

What the stories of Monica and Vera have shown is how important full protection of the basic right to liberty and security of person is to individuals everywhere. They have also shown how easy it is for those rights to be eroded, and how they can never be regarded as fully secure. They have also shown how potentially threatening the power of the state is to enjoyment of that right, and how easily even good motives can lead to oppression. Ideally, what is needed is a democratic system that works well; a strong and independent judiciary; and good laws. Failing all those, one needs individuals and non-government organisations who are aware of rights and of when they are being violated, and of the need to stand up for them even when, as almost always, that means risks to personal comfort and security. It is not an easy message, but it is a truth that has to be spoken and acted on, if we are to continue to enjoy the precious gift of freedom that is the right of all persons. It was never more truly said than that the price of liberty is eternal vigilance.

For Further Reading

The story of Monica Mignone is to be found as a thread running through the fascinating and disturbing book *Behind the Disappearances: Argentina's Dirty War Against Human Rights and the United Nations*, by Iain Guest, published in 1990 by University of Pennsylvania Press, Pennsylvania. It gives an insight not only into the internal affairs of Argentina, but also into the international machinations that take place in the United Nations and elsewhere in the interests of sovereign states and their rulers. For an account of more recent developments in Argentina, *Latin America: Transition to Democracy*, by Ronald Munck, published by Zed Books, London, in 1989, is good. More recent material on Argentina has been contributed to *Current History* in 1991, 1990 and 1983 by Gary Wynia, who has also written a major book *The Politics of Latin American Development*, Cambridge University Press, New York, 1990.

The story of Vera appears in a couple of dozen entries in the *Canberra Times* between June 15 and 20 August 1992. The report by the Human Rights Commission, *The Proposed ACT Mental Health Ordinance 1981*, (Report No 2), AGPS, Canberra, 1982 describes well the law as it then was and the need for change. The Human Rights and Equal Opportunity Commission has just completed a major two year examination of the human rights of people in Australia who suffer from mental illness, and published its report in December 1992. It will provide excellent and up to date information, comment and proposals on mental illness.

More generally, the concept of the rule of law is discussed briefly in Bailey, *Human Rights: Australia in an International Context*, Butterworths, 1990 in Chapter 3, esp pp 63-6 and 76-7. An interesting but conservatively-oriented defence is contained in Geoffrey deQ Walker, *The Rule of Law: Foundation of Constitutional Democracy*, Melbourne University Press, 1988. A rather different view, that takes a somewhat sceptical look at the role of judges as occasional law-makers, and at how they might use a Bill of Rights, is given in Lord McCluskey's *Law, Justice and Democracy*, the Reith Lectures 1986, Sweet and Maxwell, 1987. A critical legal studies approach is contained in AC Hutchinson and P Monahan (eds), *The Rule of Law: Ideal or Ideology*, Carswell, 1987.

The rights of people with mental illness are discussed in the Report (No 2) of the Human Rights Commission, *Proposed ACT Mental Health Ordinance 1981*, AGPS, Canberra 1982 and in the excellent and comprehensive report of a committee of inquiry in Victoria : Report of the *Minister's Committee on Rights and Protective Legislation for Intellectually Handicapped Persons*, December 1992. It surveys the issues broadly, rather than with a narrow focus on intellectual handicap.

Chapter 12

The Cases of Karen Green and Joseph Brodsky

The Right to Work

I. THE CASE OF KAREN GREEN

The Story. Karen Green lived in Hobart, the capital city of the Australian State of Tasmania. Her mother was a widow and was receiving a pension which included a supplement to assist her to support Karen while she was in full-time education. As she was nearing the end of her fourth year of secondary schooling, Karen, then aged 16, made the decision to leave school and look for a job. On 25 November 1976, the day before school ended, she visited the Commonwealth Employment Service (CES) and put in train the process of becoming registered as seeking employment. She was told that there was no work currently available and that she should call again when she had the results of her exams. In the early part of December, she started looking for a job on her own account, but again had no success. She made further efforts in January and February, but was unsuccessful on each occasion. At that time in Australia, there was something of a recession, and young people were finding it particularly difficult to get jobs.

When she returned to the CES shortly before Christmas, Karen was given a proper interview, but the earlier advice was repeated – that it was unlikely there would be a job for her for some time.[1] However, the office told her that she could not get unemployment benefit until late February, when the school year

---

1   In Australia, January is a particularly bad time for job-seekers, because it is a holiday period. The unemployment figures always rise, and are usually higher than at any other time of the year.

began. At that stage, if she still had not been able to get work, she could start receiving the benefit.

On 22 February, the day school went back, Karen called again at the CES. She took with her the forms she had been asked to complete, and the certificate showing her school results. She was told there were still no jobs available. She filled in another form, and not long afterwards began receiving unemployment benefit cheques.

Karen felt she had been cheated by the office in that she had been unemployed since the end of November, and had genuinely tried to get work. Normally, it is only necessary to wait for a maximum of two weeks before benefit payments start, but Karen had had to wait three months. From February on, she received the benefit, and so received some income support (simultaneously, her mother lost the supplement she had been receiving for maintaining Karen). Advised and supported by the local welfare groups, and in particular by Ms Pat Truman of the Australian Council of Social Service, Karen's case was taken to the courts. She sought a direction to the Department of Social Security that she should be paid her benefit from the end of November rather than the end of February, and an order for payment of the amount due.

The case, *Green v Daniels* (1977) 51 ALJR 463, was quickly moved to the High Court because of the importance of the issues for school-leavers all round Australia, and because of the severe budgetary implications of having to pay benefit for three months to many thousands of unemployed recent school-leavers.

It emerged in the case, which was heard by Stephen J in Melbourne in March 1977, that the Department of Social Security had issued an instruction to its officers handling unemployment benefit that they were not to pay benefit to school-leavers until the new school year had started. The Department took the view that it was too difficult to determine whether a particular individual was actually returning to school (or going on to tertiary education), or was just looking for some income over the vacation.

Karen Green and her supporter Pat Truman asked Stephen J to make declarations to the effect that Karen should be paid unemployment benefit for the three months and also be awarded damages for the wrongful denial of the benefit. Their main argument was that the Director-General of Social Security, or the delegate in Tasmania acting on his behalf, had not followed the requirements of s 107 of the Australian Social Services Act 1947 when refusing to pay her the benefit. Section 107 requires the Director-General to be satisfied of three matters: that the person is unemployed; is capable of and willing to undertake work; and has taken reasonable steps to find work. They claimed that Karen had complied with the requirements and that the circular was not in accordance with the Act because it directed that no benefit be paid to school-leavers until it was clear that they were not returning when the next year started. It amounted to the adoption of a general instruction that had to be followed in all cases. What the Act required was, they claimed, that the Director-General or his delegate should make a specific decision about the first and third of the criteria laid down by s 107, not just apply a general rule about the school summer vacation. In short, he should specifically consider the facts of her case and, in particular, whether or not Karen was unemployed and had taken reasonable steps to obtain work.

Stephen J agreed with Karen Green's argument. He found that the circular did not accord with the requirement that in each particular case the Director-General (or his delegate) be "satisfied" that the applicant was unemployed and had taken reasonable steps to obtain work. He directed that the Director-General make a decision according to law, ie specific to Karen's case, and not simply apply the general rule laid down in the Manual issued to guide officers. But he refused to give Karen the declaration she sought that the Department should pay the benefits back to November 1976. He in effect agreed with the proposition put on behalf of the Director-General –

> ... that no duty owed to the plaintiff [Karen Green] was imposed on the Director-General by the Act. ... [A]n unemployment benefit [is] no more than a gratuity which, once granted, might be cancelled by the Director-General in his uncontrolled discretion – s 131. The absence of any obligation imposed by the Act upon anyone to make payments of unemployment benefits was also relied upon ... . (p 469) (Emphasis supplied)

In Karen's case, a further decision was made by the Director-General in late May, in accordance with the law as interpreted by Stephen J. He determined that she was unemployed and capable of undertaking work, but that she had not taken "reasonable steps to obtain work suitable to be obtained by her". The issue was taken up in Parliament on no less than 12 occasions, first by the Leader of the Opposition and former Prime Minister, Mr Gough Whitlam, and later by Mr Beazley and Mr Bowen and others. But the government stood firm. It said it had announced on 23 March 1976 that benefits would not be paid to school-leavers before the expiry of 6 weeks from the end of school. The purpose of the decision was to avoid the difficulty of determining the intention of the school-leavers. It also took account of the fact that it would be difficult for the school-leaver to take "reasonable steps" to find employment in the short time between end of school and Christmas.

On the other hand, the Opposition Labor Party alleged that the government had stood over the Director-General, Mr Daniels, and that it was depriving some 35,000 school-leavers of their right to a benefit. It claimed that the government had acknowledged its acceptance of defeat in the courts by not appealing Stephen J's decision, and that it was flouting the law. Said Mr Bowen, Deputy Leader of the Opposition, in commenting on the decision to refuse Karen Green a benefit –

> ... she had no chance. She was prejudged. It was an issue of the economic policy of this Government. The Government was going to do 2 things: keep the unemployment statistics down and keep its financial liability down.[2]

In October 1977 the government introduced a series of amendments to the Social Services Act 1947. One of them was to add section 120A. Its effect was to declare a person leaving school ineligible for unemployment benefit for six weeks after the end of the school year. It became operative on the date of the Royal Assent – 10 November 1977. The result is that no school-leaver, including people in similar situations in relation to tertiary education, is able to claim unemployment benefit for six weeks from the end of the academic year.

Discussion. It may well be asked what relevance Karen Green's story has to the right to work. The answer is that it illustrates

---

2   See *Hansard*, House of Representatives, 31 May 1977 at p 2183. It was estimated that the government may have saved $10-12 million by the decision.

very clearly the absence, for unemployed persons in the Western world, of anything approaching a right to work. It also emphasises that, by providing only an unenforceable entitlement to a benefit, Australia is not fully implementing Article 9 of the International Covenant on Economic, Social and Cultural Rights, which provides that member states are to "recognise the right of everyone to social security, including social insurance". An enforceable right to work would mean that an unemployed person would be able to claim some compensation in the absence of a job. What Karen's case shows is that unemployed people do not have a *right* to enforce the payment of an income benefit while out of work involuntarily, let alone to enforce the provision of a job. What they have is a *process* right – to have the Director-General decide the case according to law. The trouble is that the government can then change the law, if it does not like the way it works, as it did in Karen's case. In the meantime, even if it appears that there is intended to be an independent power in a senior officer to determine whether or not the unemployed person is capable of, and wanting to work, and the person seems by any ordinary criteria to comply with the conditions for receiving a benefit, the government may be able to prevent the benefit being paid, either by a policy decision or by legislation.

Looking at the problem from the point of view of the government, it can be said that the period of six weeks is not long. It is often not easy to get jobs over Christmas, and it is sensible to leave a little longer than the usual time for a person to look for a job. Further, a person may not actually decide whether to return to school until he or she has had a chance to explore the availability of jobs. It would be costly, and perhaps intrusive, to ask enough questions to be sure of a person's decision during the six weeks of the summer vacation, and equally costly and difficult to take action later to recover the benefit paid if the person does decide to go back to school, or to proceed to tertiary education.

So it is really a question of judgment whether the decision of the government in the Karen Green case did amount to infringing her right to work. The right to work is not easy to define. In the International Covenant on Economic, Social and Cultural Rights, which more than 90 countries, including Australia, have ratified, Article 6 provides for the right to work and Article 7 for a right to proper conditions of work. The Articles in part are –

Article 6

1. The States Parties to the present Covenant recognise the right to work, which includes the right of everyone to the opportunity to gain his living by work which he freely chooses or accepts, and will take appropriate steps to safeguard this right.

2. The steps to be taken ... to achieve the full realisation of this right shall include technical and vocational guidance and training programmes, policies and techniques to achieve ... full and productive employment under conditions safeguarding fundamental political and economic freedoms. ...

Article 7

The States Parties ... recognize the right of everyone to the enjoyment of just and favourable conditions of work which ensure, in particular –

    a) Remuneration which provides all workers, as a minimum, with:
       i) Fair wages and equal remuneration for work of equal value ..., in particular women being guaranteed conditions not inferior to those enjoyed by men, with equal pay for equal work;
       ii) A decent living for themselves and their families ... ;
    b) Safe and healthy working conditions;
    c) Equal opportunity for everyone ... ;
    d) Rest, leisure and reasonable limitation of working hours. ...

It is clear that what has been prescribed in the International Covenant is not so much a general right to work, which would entail work being available, as details of particular aspects of that right. So there are to be free choice of work, adequate training, proper pay and conditions for workers, equal opportunity for men and women and paid leave. In this, the right is somewhat like the right to a fair trial provided for in Article 14 of the International Covenant on Civil and Political Rights. Article 14 provides that everyone is "entitled to a fair and public hearing" and then mentions many important elements such as a right to appeal, to be presumed innocent until proved guilty, to be tried without undue delay, to have the assistance of an interpreter and so on. The concept of "work" is in the area of employment somewhat analogous to the concept of a "fair trial" in the legal process world. You cannot compel "work" to be there any more than you can compel "fair trial". But you could give a remedy if it was judged that "work" or "a fair trial" was not available. However, this has not been done. What has been done is to lay on governments the obligation to do what they can on the general issue, and prescribe many of the particular features of what is desired – good pay, equal opportunity and choice of job in the work area, presumption of innocence, minimum delay, trial in one's presence and so on in the fair trial area.

Some have described this kind of right as "programmatic" rather than specifically enforceable. That is a good, technical, lawyer's way of describing it. Perhaps the point would be easier to understand if it were said simply that these are rights laying down a general aspiration in a very complex area. One knows broadly what is wanted, and can mention all sorts of specifics that are necessary. But the legal obligation on Western governments has stopped short of guaranteeing "work" or "fair trial" as such. Instead, international law requires them to ensure particular incidents of the right – to pay, to an interpreter and so on. We have here reached the limit of what the law can do, and have found an area where the "moral" (or political, in activist terms) aspects inherent in all human rights take over.

Some have claimed that this aspect of human rights means that economic rights are not really rights at all. It is the author's view that this is to target the wrong issue. All human rights involve value judgments – whether civil and political or economic and social. The value, whether it be an economic right such as work, or a civil right such as fair trial or liberty of person, cannot be embodied in specifically enforceable legislation. But there is point in stating the general objective or right (work, fair trial etc).[3] The point is that the general statement of the right then exists as a way of assessing how well the specific provisions in place – relating to conditions of work, provision of legal assistance, or regulation of police powers of arrest – are achieving the broad purpose (right to work, fair trial etc). As the community's perception of what a right to work entails changes, so the details can be changed. To some extent

---

3   The High court has recently done just this in relation to a fair trial – see *Dietrich v The Queen* (as yet not in a published report), 13 November 1992.

the basic concept also changes – how far, for instance, coercion to do a particular job is appropriate. At that point, other rights may come into play, such as the right to freedom of movement, or to freedom of religion. In all of that, however, the general concept of a right to work etc remains valid as an objective, as a guide to the courts, and as a measure of the acceptability of what is being done.

II. THE CASE OF JOSEPH BRODSKY

The Story. In May 1972, noted Russian poet Joseph (Iosip) Brodsky was told by the authorities that he should leave the USSR within 10 days. The alternative would be "to have a hard time".[4] The "hard time" would have been either psychiatric assessment; or a trial followed by imprisonment or despatch to a labour camp. Brodsky, encouraged by his (genuine) friends, decided that it was best to leave, and later that month found himself in Vienna. Before long, he had been appointed to a poet-in-residence position at the University of Michigan, where he stayed for nine years. In 1981, he was appointed Professor of Literature at Holyoke College, a position he still holds.

How did Joseph Brodsky come to be exiled from the Soviet Union to the United States at the relatively young age of 32? Brodsky was born in Leningrad (which he prefers to call St Petersburg and which now again rejoices in that name) in May 1940, the son of Jewish parents. His father was away from home for his early years, serving with the Soviet Navy, first in Finland and ultimately in China. His mother was trained as a secretary and accountant. During the many times after the war when her husband could not get a job, largely because he was Jewish, her income was all the family had to live on. At the age of 15, young Joseph decided to leave school: "my parents would have preferred that I finish school. I knew that, and yet I told myself that I had to help my family."[5] This was the start for him of a series of jobs, the first in "The Arsenal". "The Arsenal" was a

---

4   Quoted in Polukhina V, *Joseph Brodsky*, referred to in Further Reading, at p 29.

5   From Brodsky J, *Less Than One: Selected Essays*, noted in Further Reading, p 12.

metal milling factory that was designed to produce arms, but was also used to produce agricultural machinery. After a spell there, young Brodsky was employed in several other places, including a morgue, and then as a geologist's assistant. In this latter capacity, he travelled over a good deal of the country, something he particularly enjoyed.

Despite his early departure from school, Joseph had the idea that he would like to be a doctor or a pilot. However, partly stimulated by reading the work of the poet Baratynsky, he gradually became aware that what he really wanted was to write poetry. At the age of 22, on one of his visits away from Leningrad, he met the poet Akhmatova, who remained a powerful influence during the formative years of his writing. Increasingly, he associated with other poets and writers, but he did not become a member of the Writers' Union because his views were not sufficiently orthodox. His work began to be published in the illegal *samidzat* papers that circulated in the Soviet Union during this period.[6] In 1963, one of these *samidzat* volumes included some 2000 lines of his original poetry written during the year, and it is said he wrote some 10,000 lines in 1961-62.[7] He was also concentrating on his work of translation[8] from which he made a little money; and was active in reading and in writing poetry. But his irregular ways, including his failure to "work" between geological expeditions, had begun to be used as the means of preventing him from publishing further. He was arrested on several occasions – in 1959, 1961 and 1962 – though on each occasion he was released because no sufficient grounds for imprisonment were found.

His name first appeared publicly in print in the January 1963 issue of *Novy Mir*, in an unusual tribute from Akhmatova by way of quotation in an epigraph to her poem "The last Rose". His name was to appear again later in the year, in a less complimentary way, on 29 November 1963 in *Vecherney Leningrad*. There he was referred to by three of the literary

---

6   There is a reference to this literature in Chapter 2, in the story about the Lithuanian struggle for independence.

7   See Polukhina, quoted above, p 21.

8   He was an expert and sensitive translator into Russian from both English and Polish.

establishment as "an ignoramus, a layabout and a parasite, who does his best to avoid socially useful activity".[9]

The consequence of his nonconforming way of life, of his poetry, and particularly of the trumped up article in *Vecherney Leningrad*, was his arrest late in November 1963 –

> I was walking along a street and three of them [sic] surrounded me. They asked for my name, and like an idiot I replied that I was "their man". They suggested that I should go somewhere with them, as they needed to talk to me. I refused – I was going to see a friend. There was a scuffle. ... They brought up a car and twisted my arms behind my back.[10]

Brodsky was held in prison during December, and in February 1964 was brought to trial in the Administrative Court in Leningrad. This involved civil rather than criminal proceedings, but could still result in severe administrative forms of punishment such as resettlement and compulsory labour. The charge was that he had offended against the labour law by being a "parasite". A Supreme Soviet decree of May 1961 had been issued to deal with the increasing problem of people not working in recognised jobs. The title of the decree is in itself informative –

> Concerning the intensification of the struggle against individuals who evade socially useful work and lead an anti-social and parasitic life.[11]

Brodsky's defence was that he was working. He spent long hours in translating, and in writing poetry. But, as Etkind points out, the law against parasites had an ulterior motive. It made it possible for a court to deprive a person of his job and, on the pretext of not working, send him away to the "tundra" to work on a farm or in a factory.

We only have illegally taken notes of Brodsky's "trial". They show the court to have been highly unsympathetic –

Judge:	... Why didn't you work?
Brodsky:	I did work. I wrote poetry.
Judge:	That doesn't interest us. We are interested in knowing what institution you were connected with.
Brodsky:	I had contracts with publishers.

---

9   Etkind, *Notes of a Non-Conspirator*, referred to in Further Reading, pp 87-8.
10   Ibid, p 91.
11   Ibid, p 89.

Judge:	Did you have enough contracts to live on? What were they, when are they dated, how much are they for?
Brodsky:	I can't remember exactly. All the contracts are with my lawyer.
Judge:	It's you I am asking. ...
	...
Judge:	How long did you work in a factory?
Brodsky:	One year. ...
Judge:	But what is your specialist qualification?
Brodsky:	Poet. Poet-translator.
Judge:	And who declared you to be a poet? Who put you on the list of poets?
Brodsky:	No one. (Spontaneously.) Who put me on the list of human beings?
Judge:	And did you study for this? ... You didn't try to take a course in higher education ... ?
Brodsky:	I didn't think it came from education.
Judge:	Where does it come from then?
Brodsky:	I think it comes ... (embarrassed) ... from God.

The court did not sentence Brodsky. It called for psychiatric evidence as to whether he was suffering from a mental illness and whether this would prevent him "being sent to forced labour in remote parts". His counsel had asked for the psychiatric examination but, according to Etkind, in ignorance of the "painful ordeal" lasting three weeks that would result. Brodsky survived the ordeal, but was almost immediately put on trial again. This time he was sentenced –

> Brodsky systematically fails to fulfil the obligations of a Soviet man in respect of material values and personal well-being, as is evident from his frequent changes of jobs. ... Brodsky to be exiled to distant places for a period of five years with the application of obligatory labour.[12]

Brodsky was released after serving less than two years of the sentence – in November 1965. He was freed at the request of Soviet and foreign writers, and returned to Leningrad with a world-wide reputation, aged only 25. The next years were filled with writing and translating. But gradually the ropes were tightening. Solzhenitsyn was expelled from the Union of Soviet Writers in 1968 and in 1969 the poet Natalya Gorbanevskaya was imprisoned. Brodsky was not given permission to travel to the

---

12   Polukhina, quoted above, p 23.

International Festival of Poetry in London at the invitation of Robert Lowell. But he refused to take advantage of the opportunities being given to Soviet Jews to emigrate. He preferred to remain in his native land. However, he was not to have a choice. In May 1972, as mentioned at the beginning of this story, he was given 10 days to leave the country.

Discussion. A first objection might be made to including the story of Joseph Brodsky in the chapter because the system in which he worked and suffered is now at least heavily modified, if not altogether destroyed. The story has been included for two reasons. First, it is not yet clear to just what extent the large enterprises necessary in the modern world will be separated off from the successor states to the Soviet Union, and thus to what extent some of the advantages (as well as disadvantages) of the old system will remain. Second, the communist countries have made unprecedented efforts to guarantee work for all who want it. Admittedly, the scheme as it evolved had grave shortcomings, but equally it did have some significant successes. Both need to be examined to reach a balanced view of the significance of the right to work.

The Brodsky story shows the Soviet system grappling with the problem of a person who was capable of working in an acceptable way, but chose instead to be a poet and translator and to maintain himself at least in part by those means. We see the Judge asking in an administrative way what particular job qualification Brodsky had, and what his training. His activities simply did not fit the accepted definitions of work. Yet the Soviet Constitution in Article 40 provides –

> Citizens of the USSR have the right to work (that is, to guaranteed employment and pay in accordance with the quantity and quality of their work, and not below the state-established minimum), including the right to choose their trade or profession, type of job and work in accordance with their inclinations, abilities, training and education, *with due account of the needs of society*. (Emphasis added)

At the same time, Article 40 is offset by Article 60, which seems to have provided much of the basis for socialist management of the labour force. Article 60 states –

> It is the duty of, and a matter of honour for, every able-bodied citizen of the USSR to work conscientiously in his chosen, socially useful occupation, and strictly to observe labour discipline. Evasion of socially useful work is incompatible with the principles of socialist society.

The story of Joseph Brodsky shows how hard the Soviet system tried to provide work for all, but equally highlights the deprivation of freedom and rights associated with the effort. If you were a person who wanted to do the kind of jobs the system believed was necessary (including writing "good" poetry), you would not have much difficulty – provided only you were not a Jew, did not have and practise a religious faith or were not a political dissenter. If you were any one of these, or in some other way got across the system, you were in difficulty –

> Those who publicly practise their religion thereby forego any possibility of becoming other than a hewer of wood and drawer of water. Positions of authority and influence are, of course, reserved to party members, and the party also vets appointments to a very wide range of professional, semi-professional, administrative and technical positions; persons engaging in religious worship are regarded *ipso facto* as unsuitable for such positions.[13]

As a "parasite" (or a member of an unacceptable religious or political group) you might well be compelled to fill the labour gaps left in the middle and smaller cities and towns, often by doing the most menial job or being paid at reduced rates. Women, despite the claim to non-discrimination in the work force, tended to be left at home in those smaller urban areas and to be unable to cope with all the jobs. The men were often away in the army or in the cities or in training.

On the whole, it must be said that the Soviet Union – and other Eastern European countries – succeeded in providing work for most people. In addition, there were many protections for women, particularly those with small children. There were reduced production quotas, time out for nursing mothers and paid maternity leave. In Hungary, where thinking about the basic problems of implementing the right to work had been

---

13 Rigby TH, "Regime and Religion in the USSR" in Miller RF and Rigby TH (eds), *Religion and Politics in Communist States*, Occasional Paper 19, Department of Political Science, Research School of Social Sciences, Australian National University, Canberra, 1986.

developed further than in the Soviet Union, there was recognition of the substantial "second economy" wedged between the primary (normal workaday) economy and the "household" (an example is the work an agricultural worker might do on his own fields).[14] Thought was, for example, being given in the 1980s to the need to make "manifold and complicated" adjustments to policy to deal with the fact that men work an average of only two hours a day in the home, compared to five hours for women. Thus feminist-style thinking had its hold even in some fairly straight-laced communist states.

But equally, there were many rigidities. The state enterprises tended to hold onto labour and, as we saw in Brodsky's case, quick movement from one job to another was often seen as undesirable.[15] There was also no income relief for unemployment. Indeed, no unemployment was admitted to exist in the socialist countries. The result was elaborate, and often ineffective and costly, systems to deal with "frictional" or "structural" situations.[16] People were guaranteed their wage for a reasonable period – three months was usual. In the last resort, the system was made to work, not through the operation of free markets but through the compulsory moving of people about the country.

The rights to freedom to hold one's own opinions and to practise one's religion (ICCPR Article 18), as well as to freedom of movement (ICCPR Article 12) were not infrequently heavily curtailed in the interests of ensuring full employment. One might also be tempted to comment that the right to be free of forced labour was also infringed. So it was, but not in terms of the International Covenant. Article 8 of the Covenant provides that "No one shall be required to perform forced or compulsory labour", but then goes on to state some exceptions to that principle. One is that "in countries where imprisonment with hard labour may be imposed as a punishment for a crime, the

---

14 There is an interesting discussion by J Timar in Adam J (ed), *Employment Policies in the Soviet Union and Eastern Europe*, at pp 110-13 and 118-21: see Further Reading at the end of the chapter.

15 This, and the associated problem of "structural " or "frictional" unemployment were problems being addressed in Czechoslovakia, as noted in Altmann F-J, "Employment Policies in Czechoslovakia" in Adam, cited in previous footnote, at pp 92-4.

16 Ibid.

performance of hard labour in pursuance of a sentence to such punishment by a competent court" will be allowed. If that exception, severe enough in itself, did not cover the situation of people like Joseph Brodsky, paragraph 3(c)(i) seems to do so –

> For the purpose of this paragraph the term "forced or compulsory labour" shall not include:
> (i) Any work or service, not referred to [in the quotation above] normally required of a person who is under detention in consequence of a lawful order of a court, or of a person during conditional release from such detention.

How profoundly unsatisfactory that set of exceptions is!

What must be concluded from the Eastern European venture into the provision of work for all is that it failed in many – though not all – respects. It failed in that it did not succeed in producing an economically efficient system, and in that it resulted in severe curtailment of important civil and political rights. On the other hand, it provided some sense of job and financial security to the large bulk of the people, avoided some of the graver forms of exploitation of workers and succeeded in giving access to work to a substantial proportion of women. But in the form it had reached by the 1960s, the "right" had begun to look more like a "duty", and one that was unpleasantly enforced by the state.

III. Overview

What the two stories have shown is the very different approach the "capitalist" and the "socialist" systems have taken to the right of the individual to work. They have also highlighted the different deprivations that ensue.

The capitalist system, epitomised by Karen Green's case, has in effect left it to the individual to find work in a "free" market. In response to the need felt since the depression of the early 1930s, all Western societies have now provided some form of income relief (or unemployment benefit) for those who cannot find work. As the economic pressures of the late 1980s and early 1990s have been felt with increasing severity, in the aftermath of the Keynesian era,[17] the "benefit" as distinct from the "right" element in the payment has been emphasised. Individuals (derogatorily called "dole bludgers") have increasingly been required to undergo training or demonstrate active search for jobs if they are to retain the benefit.

The Eastern European societies, on the other hand, always had as a prime aim the provision of jobs, even if they could not be justified on narrow economic grounds. However, as shown in the Brodsky story, they had increasingly tried to ensure that all people (the "parasites" – not the "dole bludgers") were made to work by instituting legal proceedings against non-performers. The system was designed so that individuals had to work to live. They could not legitimately obtain income independently of work.

Nonetheless, in both systems, there are those who manage to survive without on the one hand drawing unemployment benefit or on the other engaging in approved work. Some of these "outsiders" will make money through activities such as Joseph Brodsky, others will be employed by non-government agencies such as churches, or even engage in forms of assistance to friends such as cleaning or baby-minding. So at the margin the choice is not much different, although the consequences are vastly different. In the capitalist system, there is said to be a right to work, but there is no mechanism to enforce it. Indeed, the extreme right-wing forces are currently perverting the whole thrust of the right to work by using it as a means to undercut wages and to break the power of unions (by saying the right means the right of an individual to seek and obtain "any job at any wage" and that the place of bargaining is only with individual employers). On the other hand, in the socialist system, some kind of work is provided, and the individual is in the end compelled to take it; to suffer very unpleasant consequences in the "tundra", possibly in a "mental institution"; or to leave the system.

17　The Keynesian approach had been to create employment by increased public (governmental) spending, but this led to greater public sector activity. More recent thinking (not necessarily correct) has tended to emphasise "freeing up the market" so that free private competitive enterprises, rather than governments, create the employment.

In the mainstream of work, the capitalist system is clearly freer, and provides more opportunity for individuals to advance themselves and their families through talent or hard work or both. On the other hand, the individual works at greater risk of income collapse, and under greater strain. The socialist system offers less pressure, and greater guarantee of continuing employment without too much pressure. The capitalist system seems in the wealthier Western European style countries to have worked reasonably well, though it leaves people like Karen Green very much at the mercy of the state and having to look to their families for support. But it does not work so well in the poorer economies, where there is much poverty, starvation and ill-health, and little by way of publicly provided welfare and health services. These excesses of the capitalist system have been by and large avoided in the socialist systems, but at the expense of individual freedom, a frightening degree of state power and control and again, the need for family support. Which is to be preferred seems to be very much related to the economic situation of each country, and obviously the excesses of either system need to be avoided.

More broadly, it is important to ask just what is really involved in a right to work. As suggested in the discussion of Karen Green's case, the right to work is a real and important concept, but it cannot be translated as such into a set of laws. The law can appropriately regulate the incidents of a right to work. For example, it can prevent discrimination in selection and promotion on unacceptable grounds such as race or sex; ensure reasonable rates of pay; regulate hours and conditions of work; and allow workers to organise. But it is not easy for the law to give a right to work itself without becoming highly and perhaps dangerously coercive, as illustrated by the Brodsky story.[18] It may be that it is best for the law itself to confer specific rights in work, eg to fair conditions of work, and a right to income support if no suitable work is available. The core right would remain recognised as a standard by which to assess particular measures, and the task would be to ensure that at the political level a right to work is accepted and that continuing efforts are

---

18   As well, the courts hesitate to enforce rights that have substantial financial
       implications. An example of this is found in the story of the French speakers
       in Belgium – see Chapter 2, section II.

made to enhance it as conditions change and to protect those who miss out.

The socialist experience suggests that a desirable refinement of the criteria for a right to work would be to insulate the field of employment from other areas of community life by, for example, establishing independent regulators or enforcers in the employment area. Otherwise, the risks to individual liberty of mixing political and social objectives with work-related objectives are just too great. On the other hand, the need in the capitalist system is to prevent too great a separation of the different areas, of simply leaving the individual to perish with no support, or grossly inadequate services. The separation has led to injustice in the work area itself – for example through resistance to implementation of basic human rights principles, such as requiring equal pay for comparable (as well as equal) work; and failing to ensure fair and equal access to work by women, racial minorities and other disadvantaged groups. Whereas the socialist battle must be to separate the work area to some extent from political and social manipulation, the capitalist battle must be to bring general human rights fully into operation in the work area.

It is important to a full enjoyment of rights, and indeed of life generally, that the right mix of legal regulation and of free play of market forces be found. Work is a central part of a person's life –

> Work involves the assumption of one's place in the community whether in the home, the fields, the factory, or the office. One's self-respect as well as the respect of others is closely linked with what one does, how a person expresses himself through his actions, and the extent to which one assumes the full burdens of and responsibility for one's life and one's part in the social whole. A person who is not allowed to work, is not allowed to take a rightful place in society as a contributing, mature, responsible adult.[19]

If one adds to this assessment by Rosenwein of the value of work, the fact that many see in the work they do a "vocation", a way of expressing what they consider the best in themselves in the service of society, then it is clear that a right to work is very

---

19 Rosenwein S, "The Right to Earn a Living", (1987) 44 *National Lawyer's Guild Practitioner* 36.

much central in the list of human rights. As yet, too little attention has been paid to exploring the meaning of the right to work, and of putting it into practice. The two stories illustrate two different systems, with different values and approaches, coming to grips with the problems of the workplace. But the systems have mostly not focused as they did so on the central issue – giving a person a right to work. The capitalist focus has been on freedom, and then on doing the minimum acceptable by way of income benefits to assist those who cannot work. Its focus is on taking steps to deal with "dole bludgers", with highly questionable effects on basic rights. The socialist system was so concerned to make sure everyone had work that it turned the process into a means of enforcing the prevailing ideology, and adjusted the system to allow for transitional lack of work and the particular difficulties experienced by women. Its focus was on the "parasites", who for some reason were evading their "duty" to work, by forcing them to it, again with clear violation of basic rights.

Finally, the contribution beginning to be made by feminist legal theory needs to be noted. It has been pointed out that much of the work of women is unrecognised in capitalist economies though, as noted above, the problem was recognised and receiving attention in Hungary. There is a need in both systems for much more research on the implications for employment policy, and also for national economic and social accounting policy, of recognising the contribution made by activities in the "second" and "household" economies. This could, for example, be done by assessing the value of the work done by family members, and especially women, and bringing it into the national accounts in an appropriate way – a process which admittedly would be complicated, but is not impossible. Only when this is done will there be a fair recognition of the work people do, and the beginnings of an adjustment of the male-oriented and advantaging concepts of what is and is not work.[20]

Slowly, perhaps, the two systems are beginning to recognise the importance of meaningful work to all members of the community. It is to be hoped that there will be a growing recognition of the centrality of work to a person's well-being, both economic and as an individual-in-society. Further, is it too

---

20   See Graycar and Morgan, noted in Further Reading, esp Ch 5.

much to expect that those with power to affect the work world will recognise the importance of ensuring that particular steps taken to regulate the employment area will be guided and co-ordinated by the overall concept of a right to meaningful work? Then the continuing oppression of those trapped in the capitalist world in the cycle of poverty will at least be alleviated; and the cruel stunting of people and waste of the free talent of able individuals will begin to be avoided in socialist systems.

For Further Reading

The story of Karen Green is told in the law reports and the Hansard pages referred to in footnotes to her story.

There is not a great deal available on the right to work as such. Most of what is written concerns a particular right, eg to strike, or to fair treatment on dismissal, or to decent conditions of work. There is a thoughtful book by Ferdinand von Prondzynski, *Freedom of Association and Industrial Relations*, Mansell, London, 1987 on the broad-ranging relevance of the right to freedom of association that focuses on British law, but uses the law in other Western European countries as background. There is a useful paper by KD Ewing, "The Right to Strike in Britain", in *Lectures on the Common Law*, Kluwer, Deventer, 1989 and there is a discussion of the question of conscientious objection in Bailey, *Human Rights: Australia in an International Context*, Butterworths, Australia, 1990.

One good general book is White RD, *Law, Capitalism and the Right to Work*, Garamond, Toronto, 1986, which is a spirited critique of the situation in Canada and raises the question of social rights. A good brief analysis of labour law in the United Kingdom is in Elias P, *Trade Disputes*, in the Law and Work series, Sweet & Maxwell, London, 1980. It illustrates how much has been achieved to protect workers' rights without an overall concept of a right to work.

The moving story of Joseph Brodsky is briefly told in Polukhina V, *Joseph Brodsky: A Poet for our Time*, Cambridge, 1989. It is valuably supplemented by Etkind E, *Notes of a Non-Conspirator*, Oxford, 1978 which is a kind of reflective commentary on the activities of poets in and related to the Soviet Union over the past four decades. Chapter 5 deals with Brodsky's arrest and trials. One should not avoid reading Brodsky himself. His essay "*Less Than One*", in a book of selected essays by the same title, Farrar Straus Giroux, New York, 1986, is moving, evocative, humorous and beautifully written.

For an analysis of the right to work in socialist systems, perhaps the best general work is Adam J (ed), *Employment Policies in the Soviet Union and Eastern Europe*, Macmillan, London, 1982. It contains fascinating, if sometimes a little rose-coloured, accounts of policies in the USSR, Poland, Hungary, Czechoslovakia and the GDR. A good comparison of capitalist and socialist systems is contained in Butler WE, Hepple BA and Neal AC (eds), *Comparative Labour Law: Anglo Soviet Perspectives*, Gower, Aldershot, 1987.

A good introductory account of a feminist approach to work, which is basic to one's analysis of what the right should mean, is contained in Graycar R and Morgan J, *The Hidden Gender of Law*, Federation Press, Sydney, 1990. Chapter 5 deals specifically with work.

Chapter 13

Tiananmen Square and the Case of the Austrian Doctors

The Right to Peaceful Protest

I. TIANANMEN SQUARE

The Story. The world was stunned on Sunday June 4 1989 to hear that Chinese military forces had moved into Tiananmen Square in the centre of Beijing during the previous night. In the early hours of the morning tanks and troops had begun dispersing the two-month-old peaceful protest by students and others. The protesters wanted more effective recognition of the rights of freedom of speech and press already contained in the Chinese Constitution. They were also seeking an end to bans that had been imposed on demonstrations, and more money for education.

The Chinese authorities gave every appearance, during the early stages of the protest, of handling it without resort to violence. They did not make it easy for the demonstrators however, because they refused to deal with the elected leaders of the protesting group, insisting instead on dealing with the leaders of the formally recognised students' union. Nonetheless many, both inside and outside China, hoped the disagreements would be resolved without violence, thereby giving an example to the rest of the world of how to handle protests peacefully.

There probably never will be agreement about the number of people killed and injured in and around the Square itself, or about the numbers later arrested and detained throughout China. What is clear is that the patience of the authorities ran out. Fearful that China's precarious stability would be lost at a time of enormous economic problems and rapid social change, they took punitive measures, both in Beijing and elsewhere. The measures followed earlier patterns. They were like those adopted in earlier years to suppress, for example, the "hundred flowers" initiative of President Mao in 1957; the Cultural Revolution which began in 1966; and the gathering in Tiananmen Square itself in 1976 to mourn the death of Chou En Lai.

Discussion. Our focus here is on the protesters. They claimed that they had a right to protest in a peaceful way in support of what they believed. However, unlike the situations described in some earlier chapters, eg Chapter 5 on euthanasia and the right to life, there is no single right to peaceful protest. It is in fact made up of at least four basic rights, each of which is recognised in the ICCPR – the rights to freedom of expression, to freedom of opinion, to freedom of assembly and to freedom of association.

The first claim of the protesters, based on the right to freedom of expression, is recognised in Article 19 of the ICCPR. The protest does not necessarily have to be verbal. Often, as with the tents erected by representatives of the Aboriginal people in front of the Australian Parliament House in Canberra in 1972, or with those who pour petrol over themselves and then set a match to their clothing, the protest can be extremely powerful even if non-verbal. However, if the tent is pulled down, or even prevented from being erected, or if any person standing in a public place is quickly removed before the petrol can be poured or a match set, then the authorities have in effect prevented any form of protest.

The second claim of the protesters would be to the right to freedom of opinion or belief. It is closely related to the right to freedom of expression. Almost always protesters are, either together or individually, committed to belief in a particular issue or cause. The students and others in Tiananmen Square were looking for greater freedom of speech and press and better education. The Aborigines were looking for land rights. All had a belief that there would be improvements in society if what they stood for were to be recognised by governments and embodied in law or practice. It is, indeed, the pressure of a conviction, whether religious, political or moral, that drives individuals to protest against authority, even if they get hurt. The expression and acceptance of differences is a precious asset of the human species, but requires much hard work, patience and determination to achieve.

The two other basic claims of the protesters would be based on the rights to freedom of assembly and freedom of association. Each of these rights is recognised in the ICCPR. Article 21 states unequivocally that "The right of peaceful assembly shall be recognised". Article 22 continues with the proposition that "Everyone shall have the right to freedom of association with others".

For their part, the Chinese authorities would have asserted that none of these four rights are unqualified. They would note that the ICCPR, even if they were bound by it, provides specifically that some limitations may be imposed on the enjoyment of each of these rights. They would have emphasised that the limitations may be imposed when necessary, in a democratic society, "to protect the interests of national security or public safety, public order, public health or morals, or the protection of the rights and freedoms of others". They would certainly have used the "floodgates" argument.

The main question is whether the authorities could have terminated the protest in a less violent manner. It is the opinion of the author that, even allowing for reasonable restrictions in the interests of preserving order and permitting others to use the square, the mode of terminating the protest (by military force) was unreasonable. The rights of the protesters to peaceful protest were clearly violated.

It has to be faced that the fact that an assembly is peaceful may sometimes have the consequence that governments will choose to ignore it. Some of the tragic moments in history have occurred because protesters have felt they had to resort to force, simply because the relevant government would not yield to any form of peaceful persuasion. Thus the French people celebrate as their national day the date (14 July 1789) on which the hated Bastille central prison was stormed and taken by representatives of the revolutionary group. On the other hand, the British people recently celebrated the tricentenary of the bloodless revolution of 1688 when, although the army of William III had assembled in Kent, across the Thames from London, no force was used and the unpopular James II fled to France.

More hopefully, the consequence of the strong reactions from round the world is likely to be that the Chinese authorities will hesitate, and perhaps refrain, from again taking action as stringent as was involved in the 3-4 June suppression and its aftermath. Indeed, although stern action was taken against many of those involved in the protest, and particularly the leaders, there were signs of some softening late in 1991, with the release of one of the most wanted student leaders, Wang Youcai.

However, another leader, Wang Dan, was sentenced in January 1991 to 4 years in prison for "pro-democracy" activities, and there have been reports of other detentions and prison terms. A visit of an Australian human rights delegation to China was nevertheless permitted in July 1991, and a further visit has been announced to take place late in 1992. The Chinese Government also issued, late in 1991, a lengthy White Paper defending China's protection of basic rights. History has shown that the cause of human rights tends to win out in the longer term, provided there are people with beliefs strong enough to stand up to the actual or threatened violent responses of the authorities. Regrettably, in the Tiananmen case, the cost to the Chinese people in terms of personal suffering was large. All of us must be grateful that convinced and courageous individuals have been willing to stand up for what they believe and to make in some cases the ultimate sacrifice.

II. The Case of the Austrian Doctors

The Story. The Tiananmen Square incident is an illustration of a peaceful protest made against the state for essentially political reasons. But peaceful protests can be made for many other purposes. The case of the Austrian Doctors, which was heard by the European Court of Human Rights in 1987, is a fascinating illustration of the handling of a protest involving two groups in the community. Here, the government was not so much the target as the regulator or guarantor of the protest.

The case arose because the Association of Pro-life Doctors (APD) decided to demonstrate publicly against doctors who were willing to perform abortions. One protest occurred in December 1980 at a small upper Austrian town named Stadel-

Paura. The local authorities were informed of the ADP intention to demonstrate. They approved that it take place, beginning with prayer at a church. The procession was then to go, via the house of a medical practitioner who was known to perform abortions, to a field altar at the top of a nearby hill. The ADP organisers heard that there might be a counter-protest. They decided to continue with the procession but to go direct to the field. There were counter-demonstrations at the top of the hill which involved the throwing of eggs and grass tufts. The police stood by and allowed both protests to be made, but did not intervene except to separate the demonstrators and counter-demonstrators at the field altar.

A second demonstration by ADP occurred on 1 May 1982, near Salzburg Cathedral. Because of the May Day celebrations, the protest was not allowed to take place in the Cathedral Square. It was disturbed, nevertheless, and the counter-demonstrators were dispersed by the police at the end of the demonstration.

The APD brought an action in the Constitutional Court of Austria after the first demonstration. They claimed that their rights to freedom of assembly and worship had been interfered with. However, the court refused to hear the claim because it regarded it as inadmissible under the provisions of the Austrian Constitution.

After the second protest, the ADP, considering further resort to the Austrian Court pointless, brought a complaint covering both incidents to the European Commission of Human Rights. The claim was in part that, under Article 11 of the European Convention on Human Rights, the APD had not enjoyed its right to freedom of peaceful assembly, and in part that the Austrian authorities had not provided a suitable remedy under Article 13 of the Convention. The commission concluded, after trying to negotiate a friendly settlement between the APD and the Austrian Government, that the actions of the authorities had been reasonable because they had respected the right to peaceful protest and had prevented matters from getting out of hand. There was, therefore, no violation of Article 11.

The European Court of Human Rights, to which there was an appeal from the commission, said that Article 11 requires participants to be able to hold a demonstration without fear of physical violence from any opponents. But from the very fact that there is a right to freedom of assembly, it follows that counter-demonstrations can also be mounted. Otherwise, there would only be a right for single groups to make their own protests, and for no others to express contrary views. In these circumstances, the court said, the state has an obligation not only to allow the original protest, but also to ensure that any counter-protests are made within the bounds of peaceful protest. The court held that states have a wide range of discretion about the means they should use in deciding how to regulate the activities of demonstrators. In the case of the Austrian Doctors, it concluded that the authorities had not failed to take the necessary measures.

Discussion. The Austrian Doctors case illustrates the breadth of the right to assemble and to demonstrate. It extends not only to original demonstrators, but also to people who may want to protest against those original demonstrators. It is, for the community at large, a mirror of the rights of the Opposition as recognised in British style parliaments. That is, provided they operate within the framework of law, those with opposing views have a right to express them. Indeed, unless they are able to express them, important aspects of an effectively working democracy are denied.

III. Overview

Reverting to the Tiananmen Square incident, a further issue emerges. It is that, if a state is not yet fully democratic, the right to peaceful protest may itself be in jeopardy simply because the state, not yet fully responsive through democratic elections to the will of the people, cannot cope with the stresses generated by active dissent. This neatly illustrates how important it is, for the achievement of a full enjoyment of rights, to ensure that a wide range of civil and political rights including, in China's case, the right of popular participation in government, are not only incorporated in basic laws, but also observed.

A feature of the Austrian case is that the complainants, having exhausted their domestic law remedies, were able to complain to the European Commission of Human Rights, under the European Convention on Human Rights. That option was not open to the Chinese students. Nor is it open to anyone unless their country belongs to one of the regional conventions on human rights (separate conventions cover Europe, America and Africa) or has ratified the First Optional Protocol to the ICCPR! The Optional Protocol gives an individual a right of complaint to the Human Rights Committee established under the ICCPR, but there is no legal mode of redress. What is available is only a mediating role by the Committee.

The complex right to peaceful protest illustrates further the nature of civil and political rights. Civil and political rights have on the whole been developed in protest against the otherwise absolute power of the state to regulate the lives of its citizens. They formed the core of the rights expressed in the 1688 Declaration of Rights by the disaffected leaders of the British community of the day. A century later, they were central among the rights contained in the United States Independence Constitution of 1789 and the subsequent Bill of Rights amendments of 1791. It is often said that they are rights *against* the state – against its power of interfering in an oppressive or arbitrary way with the civil and political activities of its citizens.

At a seminar organised by the Australian Human Rights Commission in 1986 as part of the International Year of Peace, Senator Susan Ryan said –

> ... For any Government, ... responses to peaceful protest are a good test of the value they really place on the commitment to human rights they profess. Our response to protest tests our tolerance, our openness to divergent opinion and disparate groups, our patience and most of all our judgement.

Senator Ryan's careful but penetrating comment, made while she was Minister for Education in the Hawke Government of 1986, stands as an important statement by the member of a government in office of the basic position governments in a democratic state should adopt.

There are, of course, difficulties for governments. They have the responsibility not only to allow peaceful protest, but also to maintain order and to prevent divisive and sometimes

---

1   Australia ratified the Optional Protocol on 25 September 1991.

disruptive tactics by small single-issue groups. The difficulty is that some of the tactics these groups adopt are often barely peaceful. Sometimes the objectives they seek will have the effect of diminishing in an unacceptable way the rights of other members of the community. In the Tiananmen Square case, the Chinese authorities no doubt believed that the threat the protesters represented to order and the existing system of government was sufficient to justify major violations of the human rights of the protesters. On the other hand, in the case of the Austrian Doctors, the authorities allowed the two protests to proceed and simply regulated the interaction between the groups. Particularly when feelings run high, governments have a difficult role to play in ensuring that groups such as the right to life movement have full freedom to express their views, while not at the same time unduly harassing those who, in the exercise of their own rights, may for example be entering a hospital to have an abortion, or be standing for parliament.

Further, protests are not always in support of causes consistent with justice and human rights, and the best interests of democracy are not necessarily well served if governments give in. To quote Senator Ryan again –

> I should, of course, acknowledge that Governments do not always respond to peaceful protests, nor should they. Judgements must be made about the content as well as the form, of protest. Where the cause is just, Governments should act. Where, however, the cause is greed ... then the Government is right to resist. Whenever a cause is fundamentally aimed at restricting the rights of others, for example the protests against our Government's Sex Discrimination Act, or more recently, the protest of certain religious groups against the rights of other Australians to see a particular foreign movie, then the appropriate response is for Governments to tolerate the expression of those views, but to remain unmoved by them.

Clearly expressed law is desirable to define and protect the right to peaceful protest. Two approaches are possible. The first is for the law to allow freedom for marches, assemblies, demonstrations and so on to take place. Its role is to be available if they result in breaches of relevant laws, such as those relating to assault or obstruction of freedom of movement, or interference with the activities of police. The second is for the law to prohibit protests unless they have prior approval (often from the police). The approval will usually cover such matters as date, time and place.

In both alternatives, the courts may be called on to hear charges about offences which occurred during the protest. In the second alternative, it is sometimes provided that appeals against a decision may be made to a court, which then in effect has to decide whether the original decision was made in accordance with the legal requirements (usually appeals are only made when the decision has been to refuse the protest). In Australia, most jurisdictions have adopted arrangements on the lines of the second, more restrictive, alternative.

Whatever the means chosen to regulate protests, it is vital in the interests not only of individual citizens but of the community as a whole that the authorities genuinely attempt to implement the right. They must also be lenient with those who in good faith and according to the law approved the protest, in the event that one occasionally gets out of control. Freedom to exercise the right to protest is, as both the Tiananmen and Austrian Doctors examples show, of vital importance to a healthy democracy and the enjoyment of human rights by both individuals and groups within the community.

For Further Reading

On the subject of peaceful protest, the papers assembled in Human Rights Commission, Occasional Paper No 14, *The Right of Peaceful Protest Seminar, Canberra, 3-4 July 1986*, AGPS, Canberra, 1986 are a good introduction. They come from a wide range of practising political figures and experts in the field of protest. The references they contain are also useful.

For further reading on the right as a whole, see Bailey P H, *Human Rights: Australia in an International Context*, Butterworths, Australia, 1990, particularly Chapter 11.2. There are many books on the four specific rights making up the right to peaceful protest. One of the most interesting is that of Paul White, *Freedom and the Court*, which discusses these rights in the context of the United States Constitution and Bill of Rights. For a detailed account of the public assembly laws in Queensland, which almost certainly violated the relevant rights at that time, Hiller A, *Public Order and the Law*, Law Book Co, 1983, is a useful reference. Also relevant is the paper prepared by Robin Handley, in Human Rights Commission, Occasional Paper No 8, *The Right of Peaceful Assembly in the ACT*, AGPS, Canberra, 1985.

For an account of human rights in China there is an informative monograph by Ann Kent, *Human Rights in the People's Republic of China: National and International Dimensions*, Australian National University, Peace Research Centre, Monograph No 9, Canberra, 1990. There is also the report of the Australian Human Rights delegation to China of July 1991 (published by the Department of Foreign Affairs) and the Human Rights Watch – Asia Watch Report, *Two Years after Tiananmen: Political Prisoners in China*, 1991, which takes a fairly critical view, based on an impressive amount of detailed evidence.

The Austrian Doctors case is somewhat inaccessible, but there is an account of the main parts of it in the *Human Rights Information Sheets* Nos 21 and 23 issued by the Council of Europe. There is an interesting, but somewhat technical, discussion of the case and related issues in *Theory and Practice of the European Convention on Human Rights*, by P van Dijk and GJH van Hoof, Kluwer, 1990 (2nd ed), at pp 482-90.

Chapter 14

The Cases of the IRA Suspects and of Jeffrey Cosans

The Right not to be Subjected to Torture or Inhuman or Degrading Forms of Treatment

I. THE IRA SUSPECTS

The Story. Starting around 4am on Monday 9 August 1971, some 350 persons suspected of being IRA terrorists or of being involved or associated with the IRA were arrested throughout the Province of Northern Ireland. They were taken immediately to three specially prepared regional holding centres in the Province – in the central east in Belfast (Girdwood Park Army Centre); in the northwest in County Londonderry (Magilligan Training Centre); and in the southeast in County Down (Ballykinler Army Centre). At the centres they were all interrogated by police officers of the Royal Ulster Constabulary (RUC).

Within 48 hours, over 100 of the detainees had been released. Others were detained a little longer for further questioning, and 12 were moved to unidentified locations for "interrogation in depth". This story relates to two of the 12 selected for special processing. They are described in the records later made public only as T6 and T13 in order to protect them from possible reprisals. T6 and T13 were taken initially to the Londonderry (Magilligan) camp and were held there for two days. Then they were transferred to an unknown interrogation centre. There they were given a medical examination that was later to be used in their claims of torture and damage. They were then taken by helicopter to a place where they were served with (handed) a detention order that in effect made the detention legal. Finally, they were taken back to the unknown centre and the interrogation process began.

As the interrogation proceeded, T6 and T13 were subjected to what have become known as "the five techniques", and T6 to further physical assault. Speaking in the House of Commons in March 1972, the then Prime Minister Mr Heath said that –

> ... the techniques will not be used in future as an aid to interrogation. ... I must make it plain that interrogation in depth will continue, but that these techniques will not be used. If a Government did decide – on whatever grounds I would not like to foresee – that additional techniques were required for interrogation, then ... they would probably have to come to the House and ask for the powers to do it.[1]

The interrogation processes went on, with indeterminate breaks, from Wednesday 11 August until the following Tuesday. On that day, the two were again medically examined and transferred to the Crumlin Road Prison in Belfast. They were detained at Crumlin Prison for a further six months before being released on 3 May 1972.[2]

T6 was a teacher. He was an intelligent man and had been active for two decades in the political life of Northern Ireland. He was experienced in dealing with the Royal Ulster Constabulary (RUC) and he knew about internment procedures. In the 1950s he had been connected with the Fianna Uladh, an Ulster Republic movement, and he had been interned between 1956 and 1960. From 1968 he had also been actively involved in the Civil Rights Movement, which was not a political organisation but was concerned with promoting the development of a political arm to the independence movement. His views were definitely pro-Republican, anti-British and anti-Royalist. He had objected to swearing the oath of allegiance when enrolled as a teacher, and had written letters and poems that were not supportive of a separate Northern Ireland. All these no doubt combined to cause his detention in the broad sweep of Operation Demetrius on 9 August, when the purpose was to gather quickly as much information as possible about the sources of the growing unrest.

---

1   House of Commons, Hansard, 2 March 1972, pp 744-9.
2   Strictly, the record relates only to T6, but it seems almost certain that it is also accurate in relation to T13.

In the wake of the 9 August detentions, and of the continuing program of detentions and arrests, the Irish Government (the Republican Government of Eire) on 16 December 1971 complained to the European Commission of Human Rights. It sought findings by the commission that the operations in 1971 infringed the rights and freedoms guaranteed by the European Convention on Human Rights and an assurance from the British Government, and the Government of Northern Ireland on its behalf, that they would in future observe the provisions of the convention.

The European Commission accepted the complaint as within its charter, and considered two main issues. The first was whether the deprivation of personal liberty involved in the internments, which on its face violated Article 5 of the convention, was nevertheless justified (under Article 15) by the need to deal with the emergency situation that had developed. The second was whether the five techniques amounted to torture or inhuman treatment, which is forbidden by Article 3 of the convention. Article 3 is not subject to derogation (under Article 15) in times of emergency and so always applies, though naturally its precise content would be affected by the circumstances at the time of the incident complained of. What might be torture in quiet peaceful circumstances might not be regarded quite so seriously in the middle of a riot.

The five techniques were described by the commission in its report in January 1976 as involving –

a) *Wall-standing* – the witnesses demonstrated how they were spreadeagled against the wall, with their fingers put high above the head against the wall, the legs spread apart and the feet back, causing them to stand on their toes with the weight of the body mainly on the fingers. ... The Compton Committee, while describing the position as being a different one, found that T13 had been against the wall during periods totalling 23 hours, and T6 29 hours.

b) *Hooding* – a black or navy coloured bag was put over the witnesses' heads. Initially it was kept there all the time, except during interrogation, but later on T13 was allowed to take it off when he was alone in the room, provided that he turned his face to the wall.

c) *Noise* – pending interrogations the witnesses were held in a room where there was a continuous loud and hissing noise.

d) *Sleep* – pending interrogations the witnesses were deprived of sleep, but it was not possible to establish for what periods each witness had been without sleep.

e) *Food and drink* – the witnesses were subjected to a reduced diet during their stay at the centre and pending interrogations. It was not possible to establish to what extent they were deprived of nourishment and whether or not they were offered food and drink but refused to take it.[3]

The commission found that the two men suffered physical pain during the treatment, especially the wall-standing, where one of the practices was to beat the prisoners on the insides of their legs. It also found that they had suffered loss of weight, and feelings of anxiety, fear, disorientation and isolation. As a result of differences in their personalities, T13 had suffered more in this way than T6. There was disagreement among psychiatric witnesses about the long-term effects of the treatment, both in relation to the two men and to others subjected to similar treatment. The commission concluded cautiously that "some after-effects ... cannot be excluded".

On the question of the right to personal liberty, the commission concluded that the deprivation resulting from the detention was not, given the state of emergency that existed, excessive and could be justified by the derogation provisions in Article 15 of the convention. But in relation to the five techniques it reached the unanimous opinion that their systematic application, involving severe physical stress as well as sensory deprivation and mental and volitional disorientation,[4] amounted not only to inhuman treatment, but also to torture within the meaning of Article 3 of the convention. Article 3 reads –

> No one shall be subjected to torture or to inhuman or degrading treatment or punishment.

---

3   Report of the commission, p 406, contained in *Publications of the European Court of Human Rights, Series B*, Vol 23-1. See Further Reading for more detail.

4   The hooding would have deprived the men of sight and some sense of smell and hearing, and the other practices would have reduced their capacities to think clearly and to make even simple decisions because of the confusion generated by the practices.

In reaching this conclusion, the commission relied on findings made in earlier cases that there can be both physical and non-physical torture.[5]

The Irish Government decided to obtain the decision of the European Court of Human Rights and two years later, in January 1978, the court delivered its judgment.[6] It broadly endorsed the finding of the commission that, although there had been a deprivation of personal liberty that violated Article 5, it was justifiable in view of the state of emergency (Article 15).

However, the court disagreed with the commission on the question of torture. In relation to the actions of the Northern Ireland authorities, it noted that following the repressive actions involving T6, T13 and others, the United Kingdom had at the end of March 1972 assumed direct rule over Northern Ireland by a special Act of Parliament.[7] Under these arrangements, the Belfast Parliament was prorogued and the British Government was empowered to legislate for Northern Ireland by Order in Council. It also noted that, as mentioned above, the British Prime Minister had announced that the five techniques would not be further used, and that in April 1972 the newly appointed Secretary of State for Northern Ireland had announced the release of over 70 persons (rising to 250 by mid-May) and the phasing out of internment.

The court found that the five techniques had never been authorised in writing, but that they had been used on 14 persons in Northern Ireland in 1971.[8] Although they were "applied in combination, with premeditation and for hours at a stretch" and caused "at least intense physical and mental suffering", the court considered they did not qualify as torture for the purposes of Article 3 of the convention, although they were clearly inhuman and degrading treatment. It said that –

> ... it was the intention [of the drafters of Article 3] that the convention, with its distinction between "torture" and "inhuman or degrading" treatment, should by the first of these terms attach a special stigma to deliberate inhuman treatment causing very

---

5   Commission Report, referred to in fn 3, p 388, where the commission discusses the meaning of torture. There is discussion of other relevant cases at pp 373-5, 377-80, 400-4 and 273-6.
6   *The Republic of Ireland v The United Kingdom* (1978) 2 EHRR 25.
7   The Northern Ireland (Temporary Provisions) Act 1972.
8   Series B, op cit fn 3, p 79.

serious and cruel suffering. ... "Torture constitutes an *aggravated* and deliberate form of cruel, inhuman or degrading treatment or punishment." ... [T]he five techniques ... did not occasion suffering of the particular intensity and cruelty implied by the word torture so understood.[9]

Discussion. Three issues in the stories of T6 and T13 present themselves for discussion. First, there is the interesting disagreement between the European Court and Commission on the meaning of torture. Second, and associated with this, is the very strong international concern about torture. Third, there is the question why torture was used in the first place, which involves the long history of the struggle between the Irish and the English settlers and the way a country such as the United Kingdom, with a long tradition of respect for rights, deals with dissent.

The divergence between court and Commission on the meaning of torture goes to a central issue in the worldwide struggle to eliminate this scourge. International non-government agencies such as Amnesty International and the International Red Cross have brought individuals together all over the world in resistance to various forms of torture and cruel and inhuman treatment. Often, as in our story, and as noted in the story about Monica Mignone in Chapter 11, detention and torture go together. The detention may be simply unlawful, in which case it represents the arbitrary use of power. Or it may be the product of an emergency situation, when the government authorities suspend normal protections for personal liberty. Or it may be a combination of both – the authorities under pressure and also facing threats to their power or to the stability of government. Torture is, too, the typical form of civil right that sees the state as its chief violator. Much of the struggle for human rights is against the organised power of the state used for personal and unjust purposes. In our story, the explanation lies deep in the past, as will be shown later.[10]

The commission's conclusion, that the five techniques constituted torture, is the product of a view that what happened

---

9   Ibid, 80.

10   For a further discussion of torture by the state, see the story of Monica Mignone, in Chapter 11.

to T6 and T13 is simply unacceptable, particularly when perpetrated in what would claim to be a civilised society. The commission considered there should be no compromise with this kind of treatment and that, whatever the circumstances, it deserved to be given the strongest censure. The commission, whose chairman in the complaint was a distinguished British lawyer, was unanimous in its view that the RUC had tortured T6, T13 and others.

The court, however, took the view that seems to have been behind the drawing up of the International Convention Against Torture and Other Cruel, Inhuman or Degrading Treatment or Punishment of 1984. It is that the category of torture should be reserved for only the most atrocious acts in order to put maximum international pressure on countries to eliminate at least that group of practices.[11] It is encouraging that the international community has taken this firm stand and that State Parties to the convention not only undertake to outlaw these forms of treatment in their own jurisdictions but to take into custody and charge, or to return to the relevant country, any non-national reasonably suspected of committing torture or other inhuman treatment.[12] The outcome is that the five techniques, horrible as they were, are regarded not as torture but as inhuman treatment.

The third issue is why states – and even those normally regarded as among the most civilised – seem so often to resort to torture. In many of the stories in this book, torture or other forms of grossly inhuman treatment have been an aspect of the unfair treatment experienced by individuals. Such treatment has been meted out to members of indigenous peoples (Chapter 1) and to people striving for self-determination (Chapter 2). Members of minorities (Chapter 3) have often been tortured or treated with gross inhumanity, as have children (Chapter 10), protesters

---

11 In the 1984 Convention, torture is defined to mean any intentional act done or instigated by a public official that causes severe pain or suffering, either physical or mental. See Article 1 of the Convention Against Torture and Other Cruel, Inhuman or Degrading Treatment or Punishment, adopted by the General Assembly of the United Nations on 10 December 1984. The full text of Article 1 is contained in Chapter 11.1.

12 Australia has ratified the convention, and enacted supporting legislation: the Crimes (Torture) Act 1988.

(Chapters 11, 12 and 13) and individuals on account of their race (Chapter 8) or sex (Chapter 9).

The reasons are many, but ultimately they go back to the misuse of power. By "misuse" in this context is meant the stubborn refusal of those having the authority of the state ("public officials" in the language of the Torture Convention) to allow persons within their jurisdiction the freedom not to conform with what the state wants or requires. As the denial of free expression of dissent continues, so does the determination of those who do not want to conform increase. Ironically, the vicious circle continues, because as the pressure on the core dissenters tightens, so does their attachment to whatever it is that has caused the initial disagreement. That is illustrated from the stories in this book about the determination of peoples under bondage to gain their freedom (Chapter 1) or about the Chinese students and others in Tiananmen Square who wanted certain freedoms in education (Chapter 13).

In our story, the Catholic people of Northern Ireland wanted, at the very least, fair representation in the political life of Northern Ireland, and relief from discrimination in employment and housing. Some also wanted union with the Irish Republic (Eire), although support for this may have been declining. The origins of the hostility between the Irish and the English lie in centuries long past. Even the Norman Kings of England had located English settlers in the East of Ireland. Throughout the successive centuries after that there was always an English presence, often achieved by displacement of Irish people, and this became more marked in the early part of the 17th century when large numbers of English and Scottish settlers went to the "plantations".

The tensions resulting from English and Scottish settlement were exacerbated by religious differences. In the northern part of Ireland, the six counties with predominantly English and Protestant population gradually became isolated from the southern Irish and Catholic counties. On 1 January 1801, the United Kingdom formally annexed the whole of Ireland. But the situation through the 19th century was always volatile, and was made worse by recurrent famines which hit the southern parts particularly acutely.

After violent uprisings in support of independence, and pursuant to a treaty in 1921, Britain granted independence to the whole of Ireland in 1922. However, while the new Irish Free State was given international standing, six of the nine counties of Ulster (which formed the north of Ireland) opted out and remained within the United Kingdom. The IRA (Irish Republican Army), which was formed before the granting of independence, continued to mount campaigns of terrorism throughout Ireland. Its members supported neither the association with Britain nor the Republican Government of what is now Eire.

During the 1960s there was a period of relative quiet. However, as attempts were made to introduce fair arrangements in Northern Ireland, and thus to bring about a reasonably united community, the Protestant group began to organise more effectively, and demonstrations, disturbances and rioting became more prevalent. In 1970 the situation deteriorated significantly – the police recorded 155 explosions compared with 8 in 1969, although the number of deaths and injuries fell. In 1971 matters grew worse, and the (Northern Ireland) Prime Minister resigned. After the new Prime Minister took office, the government decided to use the 1922 legislation, still on the statute books, to round up and detain a large number of people in Operation Demetrius.

That is the historical background to the decision to mount Operation Demetrius in August 1971. However, accepting that the response of the RUC to the increasing violence was justifiable, the question remains why its members went further by using the five techniques. It will never be possible to identify the reasons. It is not just that a few of the Constabulary decided to push too hard. It is that they, and their government, were locked into an unjust situation that generated violent opposition. Were they, faced with the opposition, justified in resorting to the internment and the five techniques?

The European Court and Commission said "no". But there is a dilemma here. If strong measures are not taken, the state itself may lose internal loyalty and cohesion, and may disintegrate. In this lies part of the reason for the European Court's decision that the five techniques, though unacceptable, did not amount to *torture*. It is also the reason for accepting the applicability of the right to reduce the observance of some – though not all – human rights during emergencies that, as Article 15 has it, are "threatening the life of the nation".[13] It, in a sense, parallels the action of the Chinese authorities in Tiananmen Square and afterwards – see Chapter 13.

There is one consolation. It is that the round-ups and interrogations in Ireland occurred within a framework in which there was basic respect for the law. Thus, as mentioned earlier, the actions were authorised by the 1922 legislation, and were not simply arbitrary, though one might be critical of leaving legislation of that kind on the statute books. Further, medical and other records were kept and actually produced when inquiries began to be made. It would have been easy to destroy them. Their preservation made it possible later to retrace the steps and to reach some reasonably informed conclusions as to what actually happened. Finally, T6, T13 and others were able to seek compensation through the courts for the injury they had suffered, and the courts had jurisdiction to entertain the claims. In the end, the British Government itself instituted major enquiries, both internal and by public commissions appointed for the purpose. By 1975, it had paid £302,043 in 473 claims for wrongful arrest, assault and battery (some 1200 claims remained outstanding at that date). The claims of both T6 and T13 were settled, T6 receiving £14,000 in 1975 and T13 £15,000 in 1973.

II. The Case of Jeffrey Cosans

The Story. In the late afternoon of 23 September 1976 Jeffrey Cosans, then aged 15, was about to get over the wall dividing the school grounds of the Beath High School from the Cowdenbeath cemetery. Cowdenbeath is in Fife, Scotland, about 50km north of Edinburgh and on the other side of the Firth of Forth. If Jeffrey cut across the cemetery, he saved a good deal of time on his way

---

13   The Articles from which *no* derogation (suspension in emrgency) is
       allowed are –
       2   Right to life
       3   Right not to be tortured
       4   Right not to be held in servitude or slavery
       7   Right not to be subjected to a retrospective offence.

home, and he had fairly regularly gone that way. It was particularly useful if it was raining. He had used this route since he started at the school, and after his mother had raised with the school authorities the desirability of his using it. However, on this particular afternoon he was seen by the Assistant Headmaster. He was told that walking through the cemetery was not allowed, and that he would have to report on the following morning to receive punishment.

When he got home, Jeffrey told his parents what had happened, and that the consequence was almost certainly going to be "six of the best" (the school later said it would only have been three). His parents were strongly opposed to corporal punishment in schools, believing it was morally wrong and offensive. His father said he should go to school in the morning, but should tell the Assistant Headmaster that he refused to accept strapping with the tawse.[14] This he did, whereupon he was suspended until he was prepared to abide by the rules of the school.

This state of affairs continued, despite talks between Mr and Mrs Cosans and the Fife County education authorities in mid-October, until mid-January, when there were further talks. In January, the Senior Assistant Director of Education for the Fife Regional Council saw Mr and Mrs Cosans. He said he felt Jeffrey's long absence from school was sufficient punishment, and that Jeffrey could resume immediately. He asked them to agree, as a condition of his return, that the Rector of the school had the right to designate the entries and exits to be used, and that Jeffrey would abide by the school's rules and disciplinary requirements. However, Mr and Mrs Cosans repeated their objection to corporal punishment in schools, and stipulated that Jeffrey, if readmitted, should not receive punishment in corporal form for any other breach of rules he might commit.

Mr and Mrs Cosans' response was not acceptable to the authorities, so Jeffrey never returned to school. He ceased to be

---

14 The "Tawse" was a leather strap that was applied to the palm of the hand. If the offence was in the classroom, the tawse was applied there. Otherwise, it was administered in the room of the Headmaster or Deputy Headmaster.

of compulsory school age on 31 May 1977, upon reaching the age of 16.[15]

Mrs Cosans made an application concerning corporal punishment to the European Commission of Human Rights in October 1976, and the complaint was registered as appropriate for inquiry in December. In February 1977 the commission decided to advise the United Kingdom of the complaint and, after receiving the government's written observations in May, declared the complaint admissible in December 1977. A hearing was arranged at the headquarters of the commission in Strasbourg for a date in October 1978. On the same date, there was also a hearing of a rather similar complaint from Mrs Campbell, of Glasgow. She had complained in March 1976 of the fact that her son Gordon, then aged seven and attending St Matthew's Roman Catholic Primary School in Bishopriggs, could be subjected to corporal punishment (he never was).[16]

The commission published its report on the complaints of Mrs Campbell and Mrs Cosans in May 1980. It identified three main questions for decision. First, did Mrs Campbell and Mrs Cosans have a "philosophical conviction" about corporal punishment for the purposes of the convention. Second, did the government deny Jeffrey Cosans the right to education. Third, had he been subjected to inhuman or degrading treatment by being threatened with what the authorities said would probably have been three strokes of the tawse.

Article 2 of the first Protocol[17] of the European Convention on Human Rights provides that –

> No person shall be denied the right to education. In the exercise of any functions which it assumes in relation to education and to teaching, the State shall respect the right of parents to ensure such

---

15 The facts of the case are set out in *Publications of the European Court of Human Rights, Series B*, Vol 42, at 14-7.

16 The two applications were formally joined in October 1979 and became known as the case of *Campbell and Cosans v The United Kingdom*.

17 A Protocol to an international treaty is an additional part of it that usually is only open to signature by the parties to the main treaty. It is normally optional whether a party to the main treaty ratifies the Protocol, but as the Protocols are drawn up mainly by those who are parties to the main treaty, there is usually an expectation that the Protocols will be signed, even if after some delay.

education and teaching in conformity with their own religious and philosophical convictions.

In presenting her argument, Mrs Cosans referred to a partly dissenting opinion of Judge Maridakis in the Belgian Linguistic case (discussed in Chapter 3) in which he said –

> By religious and philosophical convictions are meant those ideas of the world in general and human society in particular that each man considers the most true in the light of the religion he professes and the philosophical theories he adopts.

The commission followed (and the court later endorsed) that line. It commented that the right to have one's opinions respected is also associated with other articles in the convention, particularly Articles 8, 9 and 10 –

> ... which proclaim the right of everyone, including parents and children, "to respect for his private and family life", to "freedom of thought, conscience and religion", and to "freedom ... to receive and impart information and ideas".[18]

The commission found that the views of Mrs Cosans (and also of Mrs Campbell) amounted to "philosophical convictions" within the second sentence of Article 2 of the Protocol. Accordingly, not respecting their desire that corporal punishment be not administered amounted to a breach of the guarantee in the first sentence of Protocol Article 2.

But did the refusal to make special arrangements for Jeffrey Cosans mean that he was in effect denied the right to education under the first sentence of the Article 2? He had been excluded from school, and in fact never went back. To the government's argument that in a fairly recent survey a substantial majority of people in Scotland had indicated support for corporal punishment, the commission responded by observing that Article 2 applied to each parent, and not just to parents as a whole. It was the responsibility of the government to make sure that parents' religious and philosophical convictions were respected and that they did not result in exclusion from schools.

The British Government argued that such a view was impracticable. The commission noted that there were three ways

18 This is a quotation, at para 92 of the commission's report (Series B Vol 42), of para 52 of the European Court's decision in *Kjeldsen, Busk Madsen and Pedersen v Denmark* (1976) 1 EHRR 711

in which the Article could be respected. The education system as a whole could allow the views to be met through children being sent to private schools. These, however, were expensive, distant and often allowed corporal punishment, and so did not provide an acceptable way of complying with the Protocol. Alternatively, the state could either provide its own schools where corporal punishment was not practised, or allow parents to protect their children from such punishment in schools where corporal punishment was administered. It had done neither, although its policy was in the long run to phase out corporal punishment, but by consensus rather than law or regulation.[19] Accordingly, the commission found that Jeffery Cosans' right to education had been denied and the Article breached.

Finally, on the question whether Jeffery Cosans had been subjected to inhuman or degrading treatment or punishment for the purposes of Article 3 of the convention, the commission found against the complainants. However, it said that, had it regarded the punishment as degrading, it would have been prepared to make a ruling against the government even though Jeffery had not in fact been punished, in order to prevent a violation of rights occurring. But it found no evidence that the mere fact of being within an education system that provided for the use of physical chastisement would constitute degrading treatment for the purposes of Article 3. It drew a distinction between Jeffery Cosans' case and that of Mr Anthony Tyrer.

In the Tyrer case,[20] the court found that birching (three strokes) by the judicial authorities of Mr Tyrer while a schoolboy for beating up another schoolboy who had reported seeing him

---

19 In 1968 the Liaison Committee on Educational Matters, which had subsequently become defunct, had issued a Code of Practice for teachers which stated that "Until corporal punishment is eliminated its use should be subject to the following rules". Section 6 of the Code went on to list eight limitations, eg that it should not be administered for failure or poor performance in a task, in infant classes, or to girls (except in exceptional circumstances), and only as a last resort and by striking the palm of the hand with a strap. Judge Sir Vincent Evans of the United Kingdom, when the case came to the court, was the sole dissentient. He took the view that only separate treatment of dissenting students was possible, and that it was wrong to make arrangements along those lines, and would be so regarded by other pupils and by teachers.

20 *Tyrer v United Kingdom* (1978) 2 EHRR 1.

taking alcohol into the school amounted to degrading treatment. This was because the punishment was seen as exceeding the usual level; as being generally unacceptable in the member countries of Europe; as being degrading for one so young; and as amounting to institutionalised violence and an assault on Mr Tyrer's dignity and physical integrity. The court and Commission distinguished Tyrer's case from that of Jeffery Cosans by reference to the fact that no corporal punishment had actually taken place and that there was not the same degree of humiliation involved.

Discussion. It is interesting to compare the outcome of the Cosans case with that in the Belgian Linguistic case, discussed in Chapter 3. There, the court refused to order a continuing subsidy for French-speaking schools because of the expense involved and of the legitimate state interest in having a largely monolingual community. In Jeffery Cosans' case, despite some argument along the same lines by the British Government, the court held that arrangements should be made by the education system to exempt children from corporal punishment.

The court probably reached the seemingly different conclusion in the Cosans case for three main reasons. First, it attached greater weight to "philosophical opinions" than to language. This ground does seem questionable to the author. Language is a very special characteristic of the total personality. Effectively preventing its use as a medium of education does seem to be at least as prejudicial to the whole culture and belief structure of families as would refusing to prevent corporal punishment. Second, the court probably considered the cost of insisting on provision for exemption from corporal punishment to be less than insisting on further subsidisation of schools. Finally, the court probably took note of the slow move of the United Kingdom authorities towards abolition of capital punishment, whereas the Belgian policy was clearly and consistently towards monolingualism. Whether this is appropriate is a question that needs careful examination.

In terms of the right to education, the decision in Cosans' case seems to be more sympathetic to the freedom of minorities to have their opinions and life styles respected than does the Belgian Linguistic decision. In part, the reasons mentioned in the previous paragraph are relevant. May it also be that the court is gradually asserting more complete observance of rights? The Belgian Linguistic case was admittedly in 1968, only a few years before the Tyrer case (1972) and the Cosans case (1976), but it may be possible to detect some move in that direction. At least the movement is not backwards.

It may be, too, that one can see a progressive refinement of the perception of what is degrading treatment. The majority decision in the Tyrer case was strongly criticised by Sir Vincent Evans in dissent. In particular, he considered that corporal punishment might in at least some circumstances be preferable to either meaningless tasks such as writing lines or (though he did not say it) to severe psychological punishment of offending pupils. This is an issue worth considering. Is it better to eliminate wholly what many have regarded as a reasonable form of punishment, or to regulate it carefully to ensure acceptable bounds are not transgressed? If it is better to eliminate it totally to avoid the kind of abuse suffered by T6 and T13 in the first story, then will the consequence be "acceptable" forms of control through psychological pressure, or the beginning of potential complaints of degrading "psychological" methods of discipline? The author would strongly support opting out as desired by Mrs Campbell and Mrs Cosans but, hesitantly, continued allowance of carefully supervised and strictly moderate corporal punishment where, in all the circumstances, that was judged the best means of maintaining order and administering a rebuke.

It remains to note that, spurred on by the decision of the European Commission and Court, and by a number of other complaints made to the commission, the British authorities have legislated to change the law. Under the common law of assault, a person may be subjected to civil or criminal proceedings for a wide range of actions, which can be of quite minor nature and not necessarily involve touching. However, because of their special position, parents and teachers have been allowed, by the common law, to apply corporal punishment in moderation in order to maintain discipline or to encourage good behaviour. In most European countries, corporal punishment is no longer permitted in school, and the British Parliament moved in two stages toward this. The first step was enactment of the Education (No 2) Act 1986. It removed the defence to a charge of assault, arising from corporal punishment, of the plea that "moderate and reasonable" punishment only was administered. But it did not make the punishment a criminal offence. In the next year, abolition of corporal punishment in all government schools was achieved by the implementation of sections 47 and 48 of the Education (No 2) Act 1986, until then not in operation, following a narrow affirming vote in the House of Commons (231-230)[21]

III. OVERVIEW

The two stories have illustrated just how widely in the community corporate punishment of one kind or another is practised. It occurs when groups and whole peoples are at odds with one another, but it also occurs within the family and at schools. On one of the arguments put forward by the European Court in the Tyrer case, it does seem that the dissent of Sir Gerald Fitzmaurice is more cogent. The majority said that the birching of Mr Tyrer (while still a juvenile) was "institutionalised violence".[22] It saw the birching as "constituting an assault on that which it is one of the main purposes of Article 3 to protect, namely a person's dignity", and its effect as compounded by "the whole aura of official procedure" and the fact that those inflicting the punishment were total strangers to the offender.

Sir Gerald Fitzmaurice, on the other hand, regarded as tautologous the characterisation of the punishment as institutionalised violence and as an assault on the offender's dignity.[23] He noted that the whole purpose of state-administered punishment is to avoid, as far as practicable, "personalised" retribution, and that all punishment (including imprisonment, parole reporting etc) tends to affect a person's self-concept. He saw the proper question as being whether, *in the circumstances*, and having these factors in mind, it was "inhuman or degrading". He did not consider corporal punishment as in itself always and necessarily worse than other forms, or "institutional" forms as necessarily worse than other forms. What he saw as

---

21 For a fuller discussion, see Peter Newell's book *Children Are People Too*, referred to at more length in Further Reading, esp Ch 6.

22 2 EHRR, 11.

23 Ibid, 19.

necessary was careful consideration of the appropriate form – and degree – of punishment in the particular circumstances of the case. At least for youthful offenders in the circumstances of Mr Tyrer, he felt carefully regulated corporal punishment was justifiable (though not, it appears, necessarily in the form of "birching").

The two stories also illustrate different ways in which questions of torture and inhuman treatment can arise. In the story of T6 and T13, much history regulated the way the Northern Ireland authorities reacted to the suspected terrorists. It showed the force of past ideas and experience at the law enforcement (RUC) level prejudicing efforts at political level to change the approach to inter-communal strife. And it showed how those opinions set back for at least a decade the slow, painful progress towards some form of reconciliation or at least mutual tolerance.

In the story of Jeffery Cosans, we see the force of new perceptions of how people should treat each other, and particularly young persons, impinging on powerful systems, in this case those of the education authorities. We see the unwillingness of those authorities, supposedly teaching people to live at peace in the community, to accommodate their practices to new perceptions of how children can best learn to live with others. The unfortunate student is ultimately expelled because of a refusal by his parents, and perhaps himself, to accept corporal punishment as a legitimate way of maintaining discipline. Whichever way the issues come to light – through the legacy of past history or the rigidity of institutions, in itself perhaps part of that legacy – we see the situation changing only because of the courage of the victims and the intervention of international institutions.

We come here to the final dilemma. It is how the human rights of oppressed individuals or groups are to be respected when they resort to terrorism, or other uncivilised actions. Is it then legitimate to apply the five techniques, or otherwise unacceptable practices, in the interests of obtaining information on other possible activists and thus of forestalling further acts of terrorism? A lead is given by Article 15 of the European Convention which, as mentioned earlier, declares that there may be no derogation from some of the key rights, including the right not to be subjected to torture or inhuman or degrading treatment or punishment. It is more than arguable that the long history of dispossession, of arrogance, and of cruelty that accompanied successive British occupations of particularly the northeastern portion of Ireland have led to a depth of hopelessness and frustration that have too often spilled into terrorist type actions. But to torture the terrorists, or those suspected of even knowing something about them, as in the cases of T6 and T13 and the other ten detainees, is hardly likely to build up the trust that is at the heart of civilised relationships. Nor is the knowledge that the authorities are likely to use measures of this kind likely to inspire loyalty and affection in citizens whose main links are with the minority or oppressed group. The "floodgates" argument simply does not work.

The same is often said of the use by school authorities of physical methods of punishment. Such methods may lead to conformity, but not necessarily to the kind of eager pursuit of learning that must be a primary objective of education. The author's only criticism of the focus on corporal punishment is that psychological or social methods can be just as cruel, alienating and destructive of a sense of dignity and self-worth, and of motivation, as physical punishment. What is really needed is to ensure that, whatever means are used, they are used in a way that will not prove counter-productive. If, following the view of the majority in the Scottish poll on corporal punishment, physical means continue to be used, then they must be used with restraint and in a way not calculated to degrade, oppress or stultify. The same must be said of any other means of punishment – none should be used in a way that simply degrades or oppresses, or asserts or confirms the inferior status of the object of the punishment.

We have now reached the centre of the problem. It is not so much about the *means* used to punish a person, but whether punishment should be used at all. However much effort is put into educating people, restraining them in the interests of peaceful living and guiding them as to proper conduct, the bottom line is that on occasions punishment, including restraint, will have to be resorted to. The message of the stories in this chapter is that punishment or harsh treatment inappropriately administered, as in the cases of T6 and T13, is unlikely to yield positive results, or good in the long term. Similarly, to administer punishment in one form when that is against the beliefs of a person, cannot be expected to lead to good results. What seems to be necessary is more carefully thought out means of administering a rebuke or achieving a change in conduct, as in the case of Jeffrey Cosans; and avoidance of "punishing" one person or group in order to trace or inhibit others, as in the case of T6 and T13.

For Further Reading

The cases of T6 and T13 are very fully recorded in the publications of the European Court of Human Rights. The hearings and report of the commission, and some useful documentation, are to be found in the thousand pages contained in *Publications of the European Court of Human Rights, Series B: Pleadings, Oral Arguments and Documents*, Vol 23, Parts I and II, Heymanns Verlag KG, 197. The commission's report is reproduced in Part I and the papers submitted by Ireland, Britain and the commission staff in Part II. The judgment of the court is in Vol 1 (1978-80) of the European Human Rights Reports (EHRR), at p 25. It is about 120 pages in length. There is a discussion of the case and of several related cases in the comprehensive and scholarly book by P van Dijk and GJH van Hoof, *Theory and Practice of the European Convention on Human Rights*, Kluwer, 1990 (2nd ed), pp 226-41. A useful account of the history of Northern Ireland is contained in *Encyclopedia Brittanica*.

The handling by the European Commission of Human Rights of the case of *Campbell and Cosans v The United Kingdom* is fully set out in *Publications of the European Court of Human Rights – Series B*, Vol 42, 1985, a volume of 250 pages. The 20 page judgment of the European Court is set out at (1982) 4 EHRR 293. There has been some discussion of the case, as well as a major focus throughout the book on corporal punishment, in Peter Newell's lively *Children Are People Too – The Case Against Corporal Punishment*, Bedford Square, England, 1989. See also van Dijk and van Hoof, quoted in the previous paragraph, at pp 467-76, esp 472-4. A more general discussion of the rights of children at schools, that considers also the problems created by compulsory attendance particularly beyond the age of 14, is in Jeffs T, "Children's Rights at School" in Franklin B (ed), *The Rights of Children*, Blackwell, 1986.

PART V

Ways of Advancing Rights

Whereas recognition of the inherent dignity and of the equal and inalienable right of all members of the human family is the foundation of freedom, justice and peace in the world,

Whereas disregard and contempt for human rights have resulted in barbarous acts which have outraged the conscience of mankind, and the advent of a world in which human beings shall enjoy freedom of speech and belief and freedom from fear and want has been proclaimed as the highest aspiration of the common people,

Whereas it is essential, if man is not to be compelled to have recourse, as a last resort, to rebellion against tyranny and oppression, that human rights should be protected by the rule of law, ...

Now, therefore, the General Assembly proclaims

This Universal Declaration of Human Rights as a common standard of achievement for all peoples and all nations ... .

First three preambular statements in, and concluding proclamation of, the Universal Declaration of Human Rights, 1948

In the following chapter, thought is given to how human rights can actually be obtained and protected. The importance of individuals and community organisations in this endeavour is underlined. Their goal is that the organised legal force of the state should be kept in check and used for the increasing protection and enforcement of human rights rather than for the neglect or oppression of its citizens.

Chapter 15

Ways of Advancing Rights

The 31 stories told in the earlier chapters of this book show that people can advance their rights in many ways. Courts, dedicated individuals, community organisations, political movements and the law can all advance the cause of rights. Equally, however, those same individuals, institutions and groups can deprive people of rights and cancel advances painfully won in earlier years. Constant watchfulness and action are needed if the move is to be towards greater rather than less enjoyment of rights. The tides do not stop, but are always ebbing and flowing. So it is with rights. If a community becomes complacent because of the high standards it has achieved, it is almost certain that under the surface the movement is away from that desirable state: before long, serious deficiencies will begin to emerge.

This chapter views the stories in the earlier chapters from a new vantage point. Instead of concentrating on the person or group claiming rights, the focus is on the means people have used to protect and improve their rights. Five main means are identified, with the action taking place sometimes at local, sometimes at national, and sometimes at regional or worldwide international levels. The first, and probably the most important, means of protecting and advancing rights is the courts. Their most potent activity is at the national level, but regional and general international level courts have also been important. Second in importance to the courts is probably political action – again involving national and international forums, but with the international arena becoming of increasing importance. The third means for promoting rights is the group, sometimes taking the form of a minority or people, and sometimes of a community or non-government organisation. Here again, the action can be at national or international level. The fourth means is education, by which is meant not just the formal education provided in schools and other educational institutions, but also what people learn from leaders and real-life cases such as those discussed in this book. Finally, and in a sense underpinning all the other means, is the law. The most important protection comes from domestic law, but much of the setting of standards and of advancing the enjoyment of human rights comes from regional and general international law. They in their turn, of course, are designed to influence domestic law.

I. THE COURTS

The role of the courts is to hear and fairly determine, according to law, cases brought before them. The cases may be criminal, as with the prosecution against Norma McCorvey (Jane Roe) for breaching the Texas laws about abortion (Chapter 6); or they may be civil, as in the proceedings by the Maori under the Treaty of Waitangi (Chapter 1). In either event, the court is required to reach its decision according to law and without bias or regard for the status of the parties.

The fact that the courts have to decide according to law can be a problem if the law is not good. The courts face special problems when human rights are not flourishing, as evidenced by the way they tried to handle the criminal cases brought against Nelson Mandela and his Congress colleagues in South Africa (Chapter 8). Courts also face problems when the climate of opinion changes, or is antipathetic. Examples are the hesitancy of the United States Supreme Court in its later decision in *Webster v Reproductive Services* (Chapter 8); and of the European Court of Human Rights in the Belgian Linguistic case (Chapter 3). The courts may also be overborne, as they were in the request on behalf of Monica Mignone for a writ of *habeas corpus* to be returned (Chapter 11). On the other hand, the courts can be seen at their best when defending the rights of individuals, as when the British House of Lords decided to protect the rights of the children of Mrs Gillick (Chapter 10) and the US Supreme Court those of minorities in *Wisconsin v Yoder* (Chapter 3).

The primary task of the courts is to determine how the law should apply to the cases before them. Most countries now have in their constitutions a Bill of Rights, or other statement of basic principles to guide the actions of governments and the courts. Such statements of principle make it much easier for the courts to base their decisions on grounds of principle, when the law is silent or perhaps uncertain in its application, than if there is no Bill of Rights available. That is how the United States Supreme Court developed the right to privacy (Chapter 6). Even with a Bill of Rights or an instrument such as the European Convention on Human Rights, the courts still may avoid substantive decisions. The Austrian Constitutional Court, for example, avoided a substantive decision in the case of the Austrian Doctors (Chapter 13).

The tendency to avoid basing decisions on principle is much greater in the so-called "common law" countries such as Britain, New Zealand and Australia: the courts take a much more literal approach in their application of the law and avoid drawing, at least overtly, on principles. Nonetheless, the courts in common law countries can and do draw on principles from time to time, as illustrated by the Gillick case (Chapter 10). Sometimes, however, as in the case of James Malone (Chapter 6), they can find themselves limited – even frustrated. Sir Robert Megarry was frustrated in that case by the absence of any general protection of privacy. Courts mostly feel bound to apply the law as it is, without being able to go beyond it to basic principles.

At the regional international level, the most active court is the European Court of Human Rights, although the Inter-American Court of Human Rights is gradually growing in strength[1]. The work of the European Court is discussed in the accounts of the Belgian Linguistic case (Chapter 3) and of the cases involving James Malone (Chapter 6) and Jeremy Cosans (Chapter 13). These cases show how the European Convention on Human Rights constitutes a common standard for the countries of Western Europe, and how countries are one by one being brought into line on human rights issues by decisions of the court. This kind of action at the regional international level has been developed only in the last half of the 20th century (the European Convention only began to operate in 1954). It is to be hoped the other regions of the world will follow. So far only the Organisation of American States has established a regional court, though the Organisation of African Unity now has a

---

[1] The Inter-American Court of Human Rights was provided for in the American Convention on Human Rights, signed at San Jose, Costa Rica in November 1969, but was only appointed in 1979 after 13 states had ratified the convention.

Commission on Human and Peoples' Rights.[2] There is no human rights convention for the Asian and Pacific area.

None of the cases discussed in this book refer to the International Court of Justice (ICJ), though the opinion of Judge Tanaka in the South-West Africa case was referred to in Chapter 8. So far, that court has no jurisdiction to handle cases brought by individuals. Its jurisdiction is limited to cases between states, though sometimes these do have important effects for individuals and groups, as in the Western Sahara[3] case. At issue there were the rights of the nomadic tribes of the Sahara desert to claim some territory as a result of long usage. The court upheld their claim against the main parties in the case, who were Spain and Morocco. It may be hoped that before too long the ICJ may acquire a jurisdiction to handle the human rights, and perhaps other problems, of individuals. In this, it could act much as the European and American regional courts of human rights do. It might, for example, be given power to receive and adjudicate upon cases from the committees appointed under several of the important international conventions such as the two Covenants, and the Conventions against Racial Discrimination and Discrimination against Women and on the Rights of the Child.

The courts, then, stand as important bulwarks to protect the individual. They are of course limited by the content of the law they have to apply, and by the often very considerable cost of proceedings, which limits their availability, particularly to less-advantaged persons. They are also less independent in countries based on communist theory, because they are regarded as "People's Courts". People's Courts reflect the ideology of the government rather than, as in Western liberal theory, standing to some degree over and against those who exercise the legislative, executive and administrative power of the state. An indication of what can happen in a communist system is given in Joseph Brodsky's story (Chapter 12). The evasion of the right in a Western legal system is described in the same Chapter, when telling the story of Karen Green.

---

2   The African Charter on Human and Peoples' Rights was adopted in 1981 and came into force in 1986, but it contains no provision for the appointment of a court, as do the European and American Conventions.

3   Advisory Opinion of the International Court of Justice, 1975 ICJ Reports.

The courts are often criticised for delays. To some extent, that criticism is justified, but it has to be remembered that when major issues are at stake, time is necessary to clarify facts and argument and to ensure that a genuinely fair trial is held. Despite some shortcomings, courts are, and can and should be, seen and cherished as perhaps the most important single protectors of human rights, particularly where the legal system itself embodies those rights.

II. POLITICAL ACTION

Political action takes many forms. It may result from the efforts made by a single individual, such as Martin Luther King, in combating racial discrimination in the United States (Chapter 8); it may be generated by a group, such as the Maori of Orakei, when seeking restoration of their marae (Chapter 1); or it may arise from the search by a people, like the Lithuanians or the Bengalis, for separate nationhood (Chapter 2). In all cases, what distinguishes this kind of action from the community action mentioned in the next section is that its primary target is the sources of political power – the governments, the parliaments and the political parties, rather than the courts or the community at large. Although the objectives of political action can be very varied, one of the underlying reasons for it is to achieve changes in the law – changes in for example the racially discriminatory laws in the United States, or in the homicide laws in the Netherlands (Chapter 5), or in the mental health laws in the Australian Capital Territory (Chapter 11). Sometimes, the change is more radical and involves the institution of a whole new regime, such as in Lithuania and Bangladesh.

Political action can be potent whether or not the target groups are heading a democratic or an authoritarian regime. The Chinese authorities, faced with the protest in Tiananmen Square, and with the international consequences, have taken some action to meet the demands of the students (Chapter 13). So did the Soviet authorities, when faced with the problems created by their handling of the case of Joseph Brodsky (Chapter 11), or of the environmental destruction following the Chernobyl disaster (Chapter 7). But the Brazilian authorities seem not to have responded very positively to the pressures on them from the forest people, or even the European Parliament (Chapter 7). It has taken the Indonesian Government many years to begin to respond to the continuing international criticism of, and internal resistance to, the situation in East Timor. Even after the Dili killings in late 1991, the Indonesian Government has resisted all the way the holding of an international inquiry and even the conferring of a significant measure of self-government on the East Timorese (see Chapter 2). Perhaps the most spectacular of the results of political action has been in the move towards change in South Africa (Chapter 8). That involved political action at both domestic and international level. Internally, and with immediate support from neighbouring countries, the ANC developed a formidable opposition to the regime. By all accounts, the continuing international pressure has also been a major factor in the remarkable move towards power-sharing that culminated in 1992 in the prospect of appointing some African members to a national Cabinet.

The examples mentioned in the previous paragraph show that combined political action at international and local levels can be highly effective. International action alone is sometimes less effective, examples being the continuing destruction in Brazil of the rain forests and the failure to deal adequately with the Chernobyl disaster (both in Chapter 7) and the continuing tragedy in Eritrea (Chapter 10). Action at domestic level can be effective, particularly when there is a good legal system backed by effective courts, as the story of the Mennonites of Wisconsin shows (Chapter 3). But if either the local law, or the local political system, is deficient in its protection of rights, the individual can be left unsupported, as were Karen Green and Joseph Brodsky (Chapter 12) and little Awet Joseph of Eritrea (Chapter 10).

A final note: minorities are often not well served by political action. The reason is itself political. If the minority is reasonably numerous or prominent, active political interventions will tend to generate fear and even repressive activity by the majority. This has been the experience of Jewish minorities, and is part of the problem of the Mennonites and even of the Francophones of Belgium (Chapter 3). If it is a very small minority, political action is simply not feasible, and the only resort is to the courts, as it was for the Mennonites. The only exceptions to this seem to be where the minority group is very strong, as in the case of the fight against racial discrimination (Chapter 8); where a strong and convinced liberal group exists within the ruling parties, as when race and sex discrimination legislation, and other reforming measures, have been introduced in Western countries (Chapter 9); or where there is strong international pressure. Otherwise, if the law is reasonably satisfactory and well administered, minorities' best protection is probably through the courts.

3. ACTION BY COMMUNITY (NON-GOVERNMENT) AGENCIES

Action by community organisations – most often referred to by the somewhat uncomplimentary and negative title "non-government agencies", as if government agencies were the primary mode – is by its nature immensely varied. It may range from child care to religious activities; from clearing up waste in a neighbourhood to support groups for people who are mentally ill; from providing first aid to organising support for overseas famine relief. Community action is usually less focused than political action, and works more through gradual changes in public sentiment than by producing immediate responses from government agencies. It will often be the precursor to political action, as in the case of the Aborigines of Noonkanbah (Chapter 1) and the movement led by Martin Luther King in its earlier stages. It may lead to court action, as in the case of the Amish of Wisconsin (Chapter 2). In the broader sense, community action, often expressed through non-government agencies, has been behind the major movements for reform – the Pan African Congress in South Africa and the Black movements in the United States. Action by non-government agencies has also led to public demonstrations of one kind or another, as in the case of the Mothers of the Plaza del Mayo (Chapter 11); and even to court proceedings – as with the Right to Life protest against the doctors practising abortion in Austria (Chapter 12) and the privacy cases in the United States (Chapter 6).

Non-government organisations are now a recognised part of the fabric of Western societies, and there is often legislation to allow them to have the powers and protections available through incorporation. This makes it easier for them to raise money, to make contracts, to employ people, and to protect their members and office bearers from unlimited liability if the agency commits some offence. But being an incorporated association is not necessary, and in the case of religious bodies may often be thought to be inappropriate. The fact is that voluntary organisations exist all over the world, and make large contributions to the welfare and quality of life of individuals and groups. It is of vital importance that their existence be protected. Even when they are in receipt of funding assistance from government sources, for example to run schools, to provide health or hospital care, or to organise relief for the poor, the elderly or the unemployed, their activities should be subjected to light rather than heavy scrutiny and to the minimum of case by case investigation and control.

Nonetheless, a balance has to be struck. Some non-government organisations, for example the Pan African Congress (Chapter 8), have promoted illegal activity, as did many of the vigilante organisations in Brazil (Chapter 11). Some have conducted activities that lead to the detention or brain-washing of particular individuals. Others have conducted terrorist activities, as in the case of the IRA (Chapter 14). A fine balance needs to be struck between interference and control on the one hand, and the perpetration of human rights infringements on the other. Simply that these organisations are breaking the law is, in the author's view, not an adequate reason for state control. State intervention is only justifiable if the both the law against which the protest is made, and the law under which it wishes to intervene, are themselves consistent with human rights standards.

At the international level, non-government organisations have played an enormously valuable role in identifying and following up violations of human rights. Amnesty International, with its focus on detention and torture, is one such organisation. It had a significant role in Argentina (Chapter 11). The International Red Cross or Red Crescent, with its emphasis on the victims of war, is another. There are major aid organisations at work, such as Freedom from Hunger, Pax Romana of the Roman Catholic Church and World Vision of the World Council of Churches. Much educational, aid and relief work is also done by churches through their missionary outreach. All these activities contribute to the development of a climate at international, national and local level that makes people aware of others, and of their needs and rights, and that stimulates and encourages people to help others.[4]

The stories in the book have mostly not focused on the activities of these bodies. However, their influence is hard to underestimate and runs like a golden thread through all the stories. They have, for example, been of great importance in the achievements of all the groups discussed in Chapters 1-3. They have been leaders in thought, and encouragers of more enlightened practice, in dealing with the problems of euthanasia discussed in Chapters 4-5. They have developed public awareness of the importance of the environment, including of the problems discussed in Chapter 7. They have been important in supporting moves to end racial discrimination (Chapter 8) and sex discrimination (Chapter 9). It is impossible to overestimate the contribution of the many organisations involved in the feminist movement in making people aware of the rights of women and in getting some first steps taken to right the wrongs they have suffered (Chapter 9). Likewise, voluntary organisations have been involved in promoting the rights of children (Chapters 10 and 14); in supporting the unemployed (Chapter 11); and in attempting to heal the divisions in Northern Ireland (Chapter 14).

Without the awareness of the community, and the activities of voluntary agencies all over the world, little of the significant events that have resulted in *on the ground* progress in human rights would have occurred. Voluntary agencies are the primary examples of people banding together in the cause of human rights. They are a valuable expression of the important rights to freedom of association (Chapter 13) and to free expression of belief (Chapters 3, 6, 8, 13, 14).

---

4   Mention should perhaps be made of the criticisms being expressed of the amount of resources given for overseas aid that are not reaching the victims. However, it is not clear that government-sponsored aid does better, and indeed the effectiveness and practice of supporting self-help projects is increasingly being recognised.

4. EDUCATION

Education is, as Ivan Illich pointed out, much broader than the processes conducted in formal educational institutions. Education for human rights can in part be carried forward through teaching, and importantly through practice, in schools, colleges, universities and institutions of technical training. A growing body of material is available for educational agencies. It comes from the United Nations itself, and specifically from the Center for Human Rights located in Geneva. It is noteworthy that the Center has in part, in producing its educational material on human rights, drawn on teaching materials prepared by the Australian Human Rights Commission during the early 1980s. Community-based agencies such as Amnesty, the Red Cross, Councils of Civil Liberties, churches, Rotary and Lions Clubs and United Nations Associations – to mention but a few – are all ready to use material generated by the primary institutions in the interests of better informed and more aware communities. All of them are working to meet the growing appetite for information about human rights.

Perhaps of even more importance is the indirect education that takes place in the workplace, and through the ever expanding coverage of television. Scenes of human rights violations are beamed across the world day by day, and people everywhere are becoming more aware of rights and of who are perpetrating the violations. Moreover, as illustrated by the story of Tiananmen Square in Chapter 12, the story of the struggle in South Africa in Chapter 8, and the story of the disappearances in Chapter 11, people everywhere are influencing the course of events in favour of the recognition and observance of human rights. Each day's experiences are educative. The conclusion most people draw from what they see, hear and experience is that human rights are an important new venture of humankind, and that action actually can improve the lot of many of the less fortunate.

The kind of education mentioned in the previous paragraph is probably most important of all in assuring continued support for the cause of human rights. Even the most conservative countries and leaders are progressively recognising this. Indeed, whether the leaders of the community – be it in government, in politics, in employment or in other positions of power – respect and observe human rights is not, in the educative sense, of critical importance. Given the greater awareness of rights, the actions of leaders are promoting rights whether their actions violate or protect them. In the end, human rights will best be properly observed, and be safe from attack, where there is an educated and aware community which is free to discuss problems as they arise and to act in support of remedial action. The message of this book is that even if there are impediments to the flow of information or to action, heroic individuals and groups emerge who will rally to resist, and in the long term to overcome, the violators.

5. THE LAW

Much of the work of human rights activists is directed towards building human rights principles into law. This may be by way of amendment of particular provisions, such as the pass laws and other apartheid laws in South Africa (Chapter 8) or the laws about abortion (Chapter 9) or mental health (Chapter 11). It may be by way of seeking a new legal order, as in the case of Lithuania and Bangladesh (Chapter 2). The objective may be to build new recognition or protection into law, as in the case of recognising the claims of indigenous peoples to land (Chapter 1). Or it may be to ensure that religious minorities can worship and practise their religion according to their beliefs (Chapter 3). Sometimes, what is needed is a sensitive review of law and practice in order to refine the law and develop guidelines for practice within it. This is what is required to respond adequately to the problems associated with euthanasia for either competent or incompetent persons (Chapters 5 and 4 respectively) or to achieve an effective educational process (Chapter 14).

Every country has means for changing the law. In human rights terms, the best countries are those in which the law is accessible to all, and can be changed when community sentiment requires. The results of inadequate access to the law-making process are illustrated by the way the Tiananmen Square incident was handled (Chapter 12) and by the handling of dissent in Argentina (Chapter 11). There was no readily available democratic process to pick up the issues and effect changes in law and practice. On the other hand, even democratically elected legislatures may at times come under the control of powerful minority groups, or act insensitively against individuals or groups in the interests of a majority. That is what is happening in the case of the widening legislative prohibition of abortion in the United States (Chapter 9). In such cases, the courts can sometimes act as defenders of the rights of the individual and the minority group. They can stand as interpreters of the law in ways that protect rights rather than allowing them to be swept away by legislatures, particularly if they have Bills of Rights to enforce. As noted in Chapter 9, the question of reasonable access to abortion in the United States is still in the balance, though more secure than it was in 1990.

The law itself is, in Marxist theory, the most powerful engine of oppression available to the propertied class. Accordingly, Marxist thinkers expect the law to oppress workers and members of the community generally. Much of the effort of achieving democratically elected legislatures is directed at avoiding this kind of criticism and at ensuring that all important interests are represented in the Parliament. Unfortunately, notwithstanding the efforts of democratically minded people all over the world, there is still truth in the Marxist view. The law can be a terrible instrument of oppression. Many of the stories in the book illustrate that: the story of the almost all the groups – indigenous, national and minority – mentioned in Part I illustrate that only too graphically. But so do the stories in Parts III and IV. In Part III, where equality is the theme, the stories are about the way the law has imposed excessive and unreasonable limitations on people simply because of their race, because they are women, or because they are children. In Part IV, the stories are about how the law can allow, if not actually lead to the practice of, torture and unlicensed detention in gross violation of human rights. So the law is both the greatest instrument for good – protective, stabilising and right-conferring – and also, in the wrong hands, and when the practice of democracy and the observance of rights falters, the most powerful instrument of tyranny. It is then much to be feared. Escape from a tyrannical state is one of the most difficult tasks the human race has to undertake and inevitably is costly in terms of effort and sacrifice.

Observance of a just rule of law is one of the greatest marks of a civilised and rights-respecting community. As has been well said: "eternal vigilance is the price of liberty"[5]

It is to the maintenance of that vigilance, and the awareness of issues associated with it, that this book is dedicated.

For Further Reading

A brief account of local and international remedies is contained in Chapters 9 and 10 of Paul Sieghart's book *The Lawful Rights of Mankind*, Oxford, 1985. A more thorough study of international remedies is in Hannum H (ed), *Guide to International Human Rights Practice*, Philadelphia, 1984. A book with a broader coverage of international relations and human rights, and which deals with the issues in a more political context, is Vincent RJ, *Human Rights and International Relations*, Cambridge, 1986.

An excellent survey of the way the European Convention on Human Rights works is contained in van Dijk P and van Hoof GJH, *Theory and Practice of the European Convention on Human Rights*, Kluwer, 1990. The best available work on the African Convention is in Welch CE and Meltzer RI (eds), *Human Rights and Development in Africa*, State University of New York, Albany, 1984. There is unfortunately no readily accessible general book on the Inter-American Commission and Court of Human Rights. There is a fairly technical collection of documents in *Protecting Human Rights in the Americas: Selected Problems*, 1986 (2nd ed), compiled by the well-known American human rights lawyer Thomas Buergenthal, and an informative article by him "The Revised OAS Charter and the Protection of Human Rights" in (1975) 69 *American Journal of International Law*, 828.

At the domestic level, there are few books yet that compare human rights standards against domestic law and practice, and set them in an international framework. One such is Bailey PH, *Human Rights: Australia in an International Context*, Butterworths, Australia, 1990.

For other reading, the best course may be to consult the reading suggestions contained in each of the chapters referred to in this chapter, depending on what particular subject focus the reader has, eg if there is concern about children's rights, Chapter 10 would be relevant; for indigenous people, Chapter 1; and for euthanasia, Chapters 4 and 5.

---

5   A version of the quotation from Curran in the introductory page to Part IV.

PART VI

Concluding Comment

Power tends to corrupt, and absolute power corrupts absolutely.

Lord Acton, in a letter
to Bishop Mandell Creighton,
3 April 1887.

This concluding chapter is about the ultimate issue in human rights, the use of power. It reflects on the struggle between power and rights, on the value of power well used, and on its dangers when not so used.

Chapter 16

The Human Rights Enterprise

If the stories in the earlier chapters of the book have shown anything, it is that rights are not easy to establish. Individuals pursuing their rights have ended up in prison (Chapter 14), or being shot (Chapter 8) or tortured (Chapter 11). Groups have found the going hard: it costs to maintain one's group identity (Chapter 3). Peoples have often had to struggle for centuries, and even then have not found recognition as indigenous people (Chapter 1) or as separate nations (Chapter 2).

Why is it that there is always a struggle of some kind associated with the human rights enterprise?

Probably the main reason is that rights are about how power is exercised. The relevant kind of power is the power some people have over others. Since the beginning of history, men have exercised power over women, basically because they have been physically stronger. Wealthy people have tended to use their money to employ others and to manage their lives as they wanted, even if others suffered because of it. It is being increasingly realised that this happens not only at the individual level, but at the national level – witness the current arguments about how far the "developed" countries will assist the poorer and less developed countries to preserve the environment (Chapter 7). Parents exercise power over their children (Chapter 10). Landlords exercise power over tenants. Demagogues and minority groups often exercise more power than their numbers warrant (Chapters 4-6, 13). Rulers exercise power over the citizens of their country, imprison them for wrongdoing and even condemn them to random suffering and death in war (virtually all chapters).

The powerholders mentioned in the previous paragraph are greatly outnumbered by those who are powerless, or considerably less powerful. These "poor" people, if they wish to claim their rights, find the powerful will resist. So if women seek equal treatment, the poor some share in a country's wealth, children a degree of autonomy, tenants a fair deal, the "silent majority" freedom from religious or other extremist direction, citizens respect for their rights – they will encounter resistance from the powerful. The only way they can claim their rights is to struggle against oppression by imposing conditions on the way the powerful use their power, possibly using one of the means of asserting their rights described in the previous chapter.

Human rights are an assertion about how power is to be used: that all people must be treated fairly by those who have power. So far, the primary human rights focus has been on regulating the actions of the state, because it has so much power and is the only group allowed to use force on citizens. If it is brought to respect human rights, all citizens will benefit. Naturally, all substantial groups in the community want to be able to control the state in their own interests. That is why building strong democratic processes into state constitutions and laws is so important. They make hijacking by minority power groups, whether based on wealth, political dominance, military power, extremist views, or social status, much more difficult.

As the examples in the previous paragraphs indicate, there are many powerholders apart from the state. They too must be brought under a human rights regime. To some extent the state that accepts an obligation to implement human rights will use its power to control those other centres of power – the employers, the landlords, parents and so on. But one must not ask the state to do too much. As Bishop Challen said (Chapter 10), rights talk must start with, and be practised in, the home and every other situation in which individual people are dealing with each other. All of us must learn to stand up for the rights of those who are being hurt by the exercise of power by another, whether it be parent, husband or wife, teacher, shopkeeper, tram conductor, priest, employer or any of the huge number of people who in some circumstances exercise power over others.

The human rights standards set by the international community provide a basis for reasonable and respectful action in an increasingly interconnected and multicultural world. It is the author's belief that, although human rights are not themselves a religion, they are a vehicle which can draw on the best in human experience and provide a neutral ground on which people with different religious and life views can identify, discuss and peaceably resolve problems. Human rights allow no preference for male or female, black or white, rich or poor, powerful or weak. They assume that all people are fundamentally equal. They call for non-violent resolution of disagreements on the basis of agreed standards and the maximisation of the rights of all those involved in the particular situation. The human rights cause does not call for the destruction of powerholders – of whites in South Africa, of parents, of wealthy people. Rather, it calls for a more equal sharing of the relevant resources and power, and a more collective way of controlling the use of power, and points to ways of achieving these through internationally agreed standards.

Human rights envisage, and provide a vehicle for, the full development of every person's capacities and the use of those capacities in the service of all. They envisage the flourishing of groups and of the members of those groups. And they contain important messages for the life of each of us. Each one of us can bring human rights to life for others as well as ourselves.

Index

This index, or finding aid, is designed to help the reader check whether the book discusses a general topic, such as "indigenous peoples" or "abortion", or a particular person, such as "Mandela", at some length. Where it discusses a topic, it indicates first that there is a "main theme", and then the relevant pages, eg for indigenous peoples the main theme is shown as pages 1-12, for abortion pages 78-85, and for Mandela pages 107-12. Any points of particular interest either within those pages or elsewhere are then mentioned. Where there is a sub-theme, eg "floodgates argument" or "rule of law", it simply lists the pages containing references.

Thembu people, 107
Three Mile Island nuclear reactor
(USA), 98
Tiananmen Square (China)
main theme, 214-7, 233, 248
Tibet, 29
Timor, 20-1
Torture and inhuman or degrading
treatment
main theme, 167-78, 224-43
Declaration on, 186
definition, 177, 228-9
quoted, 177
degrading treatment, 237-8
ESMA, 169-70
punishment, as, 242-3
superior orders defence, 176
Transkei people, 107
Treaty, significance of, 99*n*
See also International Covenants
and Conventions
Treaty of Waitangi, 8
not law, 9, 245
Trial, 86
defects in, 5
dissidents, of, 67-8, 202-3
fair t, right to, 112, 198-200
minority group members, of, 32
Rivonia, 109, 110
South Africa Treason, 109
Truman, Pat, 194
Tutu, Archbishop, 122
Tyrer v United Kingdom 1978
(ECHR), 237-8, 239, 240-1

UDT party, 21-2
UNCED (UN Conference on
Environment and Develop-
ment, 1992), 99-100, 104-5
Unemployment benefit, 193-4
non-existent in USSR, 206
not a right, 195, 196
United Kingdom, 88, 121, 228, 233,
236-8, 246
United Nations, 151
See Commission on Human
Rights, International Cov-
enants and Conventions,
International Children's
Emergency Fund, Inter-
national Law Commission,
Sub-Commission on Minor-
ities, UNCED
Charter
art 1 *quoted*, 23
General Assembly, ix, 10, 19, 21
human rights work, 174, 253
Secretary-General, 17, 22
Security Council, 22, 26*n*
United States of America (USA), 28,
46, 121, 123, 153, 164, 247

Constitution, 178, 220
Bill of Rights (Amendments 1-
10, 14) 32, 80, 220
1st Am, 80-4
quoted, 32
4th, 5th, 9th 14th Ams, 80-4
Interstate Commission, 115
USAID, 172
See also Supreme Court of USA
Universal Declaration of Human
Rights 1948, ix, 93
art 12 *quoted*, 93
Universal Declaration on the Rights
of Indigenous Peoples,
proposed, 10, 12
USSR
See Soviet Union
U Thant, 17, 22-3, 27

van Boven, Theo, 173*n*
Vegetative state, *see* Chronic
vegetative state
Vera, Patient
See Patient Vera
Vervoerd, Prime Minister, 110
Victoria, Aust, 64
Videla, General, 169
Vietnam war, 119

Waitangi, Treaty of
See Treaty of W
Waitangi Tribunal, 7
Wales, UK, 97
Wang Dan, 217
Wang Youcai, 217
Ward of court, 52
Washington, USA, 119
Webster v Reproductive Services 1989
(USSC), 82-4, 141, 245
Weddington, Sarah, 78
Western Sahara Opinion 1975 (ICJ),
23, 247
West Norfolk and Wisbech Area
Health Authority, 156-7
West Germany, 91
Whitlam, Hon E Gough, 21, 196
William III of England, 216
Wi Parata v Bishop of Wellington
1877 (NZSC), 8
Windscale nuclear power station
(UK), 97-8
Wisconsin
See Mennonites of
Wisconsin v Yoder 1972 (USSC), 32,
35, 245
Wollongong, Aust, 127-8
Women, Convention on Elimination
of Discrimination against
See International Covenants and
Conventions